CRUDE NATION

CRUDE

Caribbean
Sea

ATLANTIC
OCEAN

Punto
Fijo

Coro

Maracaibo

Cabimas

Caracas

Cumana

Port-of-
Spain

TRINIDAD &
TOBAGO

Valencia

Maracay

Lake
Maracaibo

Barquisimeto

Maturin

Merida

ORINOCO OIL BELT

Ciudad
Guayana

San
Cristobal

Apure

San Fernando
de Apure

Orinoco

Ciudad
Bolivar

Georgetown

VENEZUELA

El Dorado

COLOMBIA

Meta

Puerto
Ayacucho

Orinoco

Caroní

GUYANA

SOUTH
AMERICA

La
Esmeralda

Boa
Vista

BRAZIL

0   50   100 mi

NATION

HOW OIL RICHES
RUINED VENEZUELA

RAÚL GALLEGOS

POTOMAC BOOKS | *An imprint of the University of Nebraska Press*

Library of Congress Cataloging-in-Publication Data
Names: Gallegos, Raúl, 1973– author.
Title: Crude nation: how oil riches
ruined Venezuela / Raúl Gallegos.
Description: Lincoln: Potomac Books, an
imprint of the University of Nebraska Press, 2016.
| Includes bibliographical references and index.
Identifiers: LCCN 2016010857
ISBN 9781612347707 (hardback: alk. paper)
ISBN 9781612348575 (epub)
ISBN 9781612348582 (mobi)
ISBN 9781612348599 (pdf)
Subjects: LCSH: Petroleum industry and
trade—Venezuela—History—21st century.
| Financial crises—Venezuela—History—21st
century. | Venezuela—Economic conditions—
21st century. | BISAC: POLITICAL SCIENCE
/ Economic Conditions. | BUSINESS &
ECONOMICS / International / Economics.
Classification: LCC HD9574.V42 G35 2016
| DDC 330.987—dc23 LC record available
at https://lccn.loc.gov/2016010857

Set in Garamond Premier by Rachel Gould.
Designed by N. Putens.

To Emma

Be skeptical. Be pragmatic.

Understand money.

You should have fear'd false times when you did feast.

—WILLIAM SHAKESPEARE, *Timon of Athens*

If you want to sustain a reputation for generosity, therefore, you have to be ostentatiously lavish; and a prince acting in that fashion will soon squander all his resources, only to be forced in the end, if he wants to maintain his reputation, to lay excessive burdens on the people.

—NICCOLÒ MACHIAVELLI, *The Prince*

CONTENTS

ILLUSTRATIONS

Following page 106

ACKNOWLEDGMENTS

Writing a book about Venezuela's economy was a challenge. Most government officials refused to return calls, canceled appointments, and ignored questions. Sometimes top politicians whom I knew well from my years in Venezuela felt they could not risk speaking openly or privately about how they ran the country. Most business leaders refused to talk about their operations for fear of incurring the wrath of the government, losing their livelihoods, or getting thrown in jail. And street vendors would immediately clam up once they knew I was writing a book. Sometimes it seemed as though I would find more openness if I were writing an exposé of the sexual lives of Venezuelans. Talking about money and economics in Venezuela has become taboo. It is for this reason that those who helped my research and spoke to me on or off the record deserve my gratitude.

I am indebted to the gracious help of Oscar García Mendoza, who generously shared his Rolodex for my research and gave me a breathtaking insight into banking. Luis Vicente León, from Datanalisis, proved invaluable with data and insight into the tastes, desires, and political inclinations of Venezuelan consumers. Datanalisis polls are the gold standard of polling in a nation where honest, reliable data is hard to come by. Robert Bottome, from VenEconomía, has always been there to dispel doubts and share his vast insight into the economy of a country he knows well. Antonieta de López and Melquíades Pulido were generous with their time and contacts to help me get a better view of private sector companies. Alexandra Belandia opened the world of the Caracas barrios.

Economists such as Asdrúbal Oliveros, at Ecoanalítica, and Alejandro Grisanti, at Barclays, were always ready to share insights and economic estimates. Ruth de Krivoy shared her experience as a former central banker in Venezuela. Francisco Monaldi shared contacts and suggested research as an expert oil economist. Carlos Mendoza Potellá was generous with his time and research, providing me his take on the government's oil ideology. Luis Xavier Grisanti offered his vast knowledge of the oil business from both an academic perspective and the point of view of foreign oil companies. And the late Juan Socías López gave unique insight into the workings of Venezuela's arcane exchange rate rules. His vast experience will be missed.

In the world of business, Alberto Vollmer, the CEO of Ron Santa Teresa, did not hesitate to discuss his experience as a rum maker, a rich and valuable testimony for future Venezuelans. Manuel Larrazábal minced no words in laying out the experience of food company Polar. Many other company executives and legal experts in various industries shared their time, but for safety reasons I cannot mention them here. I am particularly indebted to many working in the oil industry who took a risk by giving me far more information about the business than they were obligated to do. You know who you are.

Elio Ohep, a gracious counselor and friend, proved invaluable in my look into oil and was a loyal hiking partner up the Ávila during my visits. Many thanks for that. My friends in the media, especially Pietro Pitts were invaluable in their willingness to speak openly about life in Venezuela and to share tidbits that helped shape this book. Above all, I owe an immense debt to Mayela Armas, a friend and colleague whose deep experience covering economics was a wealth of information. In my humble opinion, Mayela is and has been for years the most dogged, well connected, and knowledgeable economics journalist in Venezuela.

Thanks go to my many other friends in Caracas, too many to name here, for their time, hospitality, and help, particularly Marvin and Adriana. My friend 1-800-LEO made my life possible for years in Venezuela, and his resourcefulness was always impressive, even inspiring. He exemplifies the warmth and welcome I have come to expect from Venezuelans and that I truly admire.

On the writing stage, I am especially grateful to Oscar Melhado, whose long friendship provided encouragement and whose deep economic knowledge and experience in oil-rich African nations informed key stages in the writing and editing of this book. Matthew Walter, a friend and longtime colleague, provided valuable editing. Vladimir Marcano was a top-notch companion in the reporting stage, and his photographic work enhances this book.

I am very grateful of course to my agent, Jill Marsal, who understood the book from the start and whose guidance in the publishing business was precious. My thanks to the team at Potomac Books, particularly Alicia Christensen, who took a chance on this project. And last but very far from least, I owe absolute gratitude to my loving wife, Beatriz. She patiently fed and changed the diapers of our baby while I spent weeks in Venezuela making this book a reality. She supported my Venezuela obsession as I spent hours writing and editing on weekdays and weekends. She was and still is my first and most demanding editor and reader. Thanks to her this book exists.

AUTHOR'S NOTE

Some names and details of people who spoke for this book have been changed to protect their identities. In Venezuela, speaking about the economy can get people into legal trouble. And many Venezuelans are forced to engage in illegal activities to survive or get ahead.

CRUDE NATION

PROLOGUE

The World's Craziest Economy

On my first flight to Venezuela, in June 2004, I smuggled in more than US$9,000 hidden in a money belt. It was a risky thing to do, but I believed I had no choice. I had just taken a post as a Caracas-based correspondent for Dow Jones Newswires and the *Wall Street Journal*, and several colleagues warned me that Venezuela's strict foreign currency rules made it difficult to bring dollars legally into the country. My job paid me in dollars in a U.S. account, and I was assured that my salary would be more than enough to live comfortably in this oil-rich nation. I had heard stories of foreigners enjoying a five-star lifestyle in Caracas: living in luxury apartments in the ritziest neighborhoods, being catered to by cooks and cleaning ladies, and frequenting the best restaurants, bars, and clubs. Some kept weekend apartments by the beach, drove around in SUVs, and saved plenty of money as well.

But there was a catch. Converting a dollar salary into bolivars, the local currency, could be tricky. Dealing in greenbacks was an illegal, obscure business. Foreigners exchanged their money by wiring dollars to people they hardly knew. Everyone had some unnamed contact that secretly converted dollars into bolivars. People had two options: deal with black market dollar traders or exchange their money at the official rate with local banks, which made life very expensive. Selling dollars legally meant an expat could no longer afford a life of luxury. Legality didn't stand a chance.

I had no contacts in this dollar underworld—in fact I didn't know anyone in this country—and I was not ready to wire my money to a complete stranger. But I reckoned someone would be willing to take greenbacks in cash, face to face, with no obscure banking transactions. Packing my bags, I decided to smuggle just enough money shy of the US$10,000 limit that usually requires you to report cash to the authorities. I was a nervous wreck but tried not to show it.

Smuggling too much cash into Venezuela could get you into trouble, and not just with customs inspectors. Thieves were known to prey on wide-eyed foreigners newly arrived at the airport. I was advised to take the right cab to avoid getting mugged. Only the fleet of black Ford Explorer SUVs parked outside the airport was considered safe. All other cabs could end up driving you to a slum, where a group of thugs would take your luggage and your money. Thankfully, I managed to get through customs with no issues. I jumped in a black SUV that took me up the winding freeway that links the coast to Caracas. As my driver made small talk, I eyed the poor barrios perched high in the mountains surrounding the city, all the while holding on tightly to the money belt tied around my waist. I felt relieved only when my cabdriver finally dropped me off at my hotel.

I soon found plenty of trustworthy locals eager to get their hands on hard currency. It seemed almost anyone was willing to give me plenty of bolivars for my dollars. They found it funny that I had smuggled cash when I could just as easily have wired money to their dollar accounts overseas. Nearly all moderately well off Venezuelans kept accounts abroad. Still, my stuffed money belt helped me rent an apartment and float financially for a while in my new home. Since I had no place to put my money—local banks were banned from taking dollar deposits—I kept my night table drawer filled with cash, like some small-time drug dealer. It was a rather odd way to live.

Venezuela was going through a unique moment in its history. The country was run by Hugo Chávez, a leftist paratrooper and former coup plotter who had become president in 1999 after promising to scrub clean decades of corruption and to redistribute the country's oil wealth among the poor. The charismatic leader wanted to transform Venezuela, and to do so he had passed scores of new laws and revamped the constitution. He even changed the country's name to Bolivarian Republic of Venezuela, to honor his personal hero, South American liberator Simón Bolívar. The man seemed indestructible, too. He survived a 2002 coup that unseated him for forty-seven hours and overcame a two-month national strike, both organized by his political foes.

The economy was not immune to the president's sweeping changes. Chávez fixed the rate of exchange and regulated the flow of dollars in and out of Venezuela. He fixed prices for basic consumer goods, which made them very cheap, and he made it illegal for companies to downsize staff. The president had clear leftist sympathies, but no one could really pin down at the time what this meant for one of the most important oil economies in the world. Chávez had famously said that he was "not a Marxist, but not an anti-Marxist." He was a close friend and ally of Cuba's Fidel Castro, but he also courted bankers on Wall Street eager to do business with his government. Shortly after getting elected, Chávez rang the closing bell of the New York Stock Exchange, a bastion of capitalism, but he demonized Venezuelan business leaders as "savage capitalists." More important, Venezuela under Chávez wanted world prices for oil to go as high as they could possibly go, at the expense of U.S. gasoline consumers and pretty much anyone else, and Chávez lobbied fellow members of the Organization of the Petroleum Exporting Countries (OPEC)—the world's oil cartel—to cut oil output to keep prices high. Chávez even befriended Iraq's Saddam Hussein in his campaign to prop up oil prices. The president wanted more money to spend at home, but he didn't like to talk in detail about his future economic plans. He was a savvy political operator, not a technocrat or an economic policy wonk.

My job was to report on how this man ran a nation that was a key player in the world of oil. Here is a country just twenty-seven hundred miles south of the U.S. border that few Americans know about, yet every time they fill their gas tanks, a few cents go to Venezuela. The asphalt that originally paved many U.S. highways came from Venezuelan crude. Venezuela's government owns the Citgo Petroleum Corporation, an important oil refiner in the United States and a name familiar to Boston baseball fans accustomed to seeing the iconic Citgo sign from the bleachers of Fenway Park. Venezuela's main export has global importance. Oil is the source of the plastic and rubber used for car tires, computers, shoes, television sets, ballpoint pens, furniture, clothes, cellular phones, shampoo, trash bags, even the baseball mats used in America's most beloved pastime. Venezuela controls the largest reserves of oil in the world, a vast ocean of a commodity without which we would all years old was too young, she said. She made it a point to lend money only for the surgeries of girls who were at least eighteen. Setting aside the custom of giving breast implants to young girls, it defied logic for struggling Venezuelans to go into debt for plastic surgery. It seemed equally risky for banks to eagerly finance consumption by people with a questionable ability to repay. Yet, during the oil boom in the first decade of the twenty-first century, this kind of thing happened every day in Venezuela.

Visiting a Venezuelan slum with makeshift shacks, I was struck by the sight of scores of DirecTV antennas jutting from hot tin roofs. For the struggling poor, choosing to spend money on cable television seemed like an odd priority. Venezuelans spent their money as quickly as they could on pretty much any consumer good—a television, an air-conditioning unit, brand-name clothes—saving nothing. In fact, Venezuelans never saved money and consistently went into debt instead. They eagerly took on any loan a bank was willing to extend, almost regardless of the interest rate charged. For decades Venezuelans have been brought up to think that saving money in a bank is the fastest way to lose it, because oil riches are unpredictable and, with time, money becomes worthless.

A century of topsy-turvy oil riches has shaped the tastes, spending habits, and political beliefs of generations of Venezuelans. They have learned to prize fleeting things such as physical beauty, cars, and flashy consumer goods today, because they may not have them tomorrow. History is littered with examples of strange economic happenings, but they occur mostly in places suffering bouts of high inflation, usually in countries at war. In a Venezuela that has been at peace for decades, something turned the country's economy on its head and kept it there. The odd became commonplace. Venezuelans constantly make unusual economic decisions as part of leading normal, everyday lives. I lived in Venezuela for five years, and by the time I left I had become dangerously accustomed to this unreal way of life as well. The longer I stayed, the more money I managed to save. Expats and diplomats posted in Venezuela were known to save enough to pay cash for nice houses back in their home countries. Why ever leave?

People grow accustomed to living in a world where oil money flows freely. Those who earn dollars want the bolivar to become worthless, because that makes them richer. Venezuelans expect to have the value of their old vehicles rise over time, to pay nothing for gas, to consume things with abandon, and to become indebted with no negative consequence. And business owners expect to quickly become rich by satisfying the unstoppable demand of Venezuelan consumers. Most of them want the highest returns for doing as little as possible, without innovating or creating new things. Why feed and raise a cow when one can import the best meat cuts from Argentina or Brazil? Why manufacture chairs when one can buy them from Europe? Why launch a clothing brand when one can bring the latest fashions from the United States? For years Venezuelans have equated entrepreneurship with importing goods they can resell at home with a generous markup.

Venezuelans believe they live in a rich country and have come to expect the leaders who control the oil spigot to flood the economy with easy money. Voters elect politicians who promise economic miracles and hand out as much money as possible. This is the people's money, after all. Volatile oil riches have distorted the spending priorities of politicians too. Under Chávez's movement the government has lavished billions of dollars on fighter jets, helicopters, and advanced military technology for armed forces that have never fought a war. Politicians spend untold sums on social programs but fail to invest enough to keep pumping oil, the original source of the country's fantastic riches. Chávez, convinced the state could run companies better than they were already being managed, nationalized dozens of them in every industry but turned them into corporate zombies instead. The companies operate, employ thousands of workers, and are seemingly alive. But they produce little, lose gobs of money, and survive because the government props them up.

Politicians, like regular Venezuelans, spend oil money generously while they still have it, because oil prices will fall eventually. And when that happens, Venezuela is usually left with little to show for it, with no savings to speak of. It soon dawned on me that Chávez and his leftist movement were really just a blip in a long history of larger-than-life leaders who promised to use oil to quickly turn Venezuela into a modern, powerful nation, only to disappoint voters in the end. For the better part of the twentieth century, Venezuela served as a cautionary tale for other nations and regions rich in natural resources, an example of the fate they must avoid.

Venezuela's troubles go beyond left and right political ideas: the world's largest oil patch hasn't learned how to properly manage its wealth. Venezuela is a country that has played and will play an important role in the global energy industry, as long as cars still run on gasoline and not on electricity, water, or cow manure. Three centuries from now, when most of the world's oil is gone, Venezuela could still be pumping crude, if no other energy source has rendered oil obsolete. Venezuela's reality is a tale of how hubris, oil dependence, spendthrift ways, and economic ignorance can drive a country to ruin. Venezuela can teach us all an important lesson: too much money poorly managed can be worse than not having any money at all.

1 1-800-LEO

Staying on the twentieth floor of the Renaissance Caracas La Castellana, a Marriott hotel, can be a bizarre experience. Rooms have the usual upscale hotel amenities: expansive city views, a king-size bed, a forty-two-inch flat-screen television, high-speed Internet, and twenty-four-hour room service. Guests can swim laps in the hotel's infinity pool, work out at the gym, and have a daily buffet breakfast. In January 2015 one night in a standard single room cost 9,469 bolivars, or US$1,503 calculated at Venezuela's top official exchange rate.[1] At that price the Renaissance was one of the most expensive hotels in the world. But reality here is not that simple. At the oil-rich country's second exchange rate, the hotel room went for US$789 a night.[2] That was still pricey, and enough money to buy a round-trip economy flight from New York City to Barcelona. At a third exchange rate the room went for US$190 a night.[3] That should have been the real price of the hotel room, but it wasn't.

Having dinner was equally mystifying. One could ride the elevator down to the hotel restaurant, Mijao, and enjoy a tandoori chicken for 520 bolivars. What was the price of that plate in U.S. dollars? Depending on which of the three legal exchange rates was used: US$83, US$43, or the more realistic US$10. It is hard to wrap one's head around various prices for the same plate of spicy chicken. The puzzle doesn't end there. I stayed at the Renaissance for three weeks in late January to do research on my book, but I exchanged my dollars in the black market, a fourth and illegal exchange rate that I negotiated in secret.[4] I ended up paying US$53 a night for my room, and my occasional two-course meals at Mijao never cost me more than US$5—a fraction of what I would have paid for a hotel room and dinner of the same quality nearly anywhere else in the world.

This is Venezuela, a country where a dollar can have four different prices and where the cost of living can be both the cheapest and one of the most expensive in the world at the same time. The U.S. dollar affects everything in this country, from the price of a box of matches to a car or a home. How much did satellite service provider DirecTV make in bolivar sales in 2014? Was it the US$900 million the company reported on its books, or was it US$216 million or US$60 million? DirecTV's profitability in Venezuela depends on which exchange rate is most realistic to value its sales.

The various dollar rates affect the size of the Venezuelan economy too. How does one value the size of Venezuela's nominal gross domestic product (GDP) in dollars?[5] Was it US$658 billion, larger than the economy of Sweden and twice the size of Denmark's GDP, or US$346 billion, slightly larger than Malaysia's economy, or US$83 billion, less than what global oil giant ExxonMobil averaged in quarterly sales in 2014? It could have been less still, if the economy were valued at the black market rate. That would put the value of all goods and services produced in Venezuela that year at just US$23 billion—equivalent to the net worth of Chinese magnate Jack Ma, founder of e-commerce company the Alibaba Group.[6]

For many years Venezuelans have lived in different economic dimensions. A small percentage of people who earn dollars inhabit one of them. In that world, a Big Mac was worth 270 bolivars in early 2015, or US$1.50, a fraction of the price one paid for the same burger nearly anywhere else in the world, according to the *Economist* magazine's Big Mac Index.[7] How much for a twelve-ounce can of Coca-Cola? That was 52 bolivars, or 29 U.S. cents. Try finding a coke that cheap in the United States. People living in this economic stratosphere could—and often did—hire a car and driver to chauffeur them around the city for less than US$50 per day.

The reality most Venezuelans faced was very different. For them, a no-frills forty-two-inch LG flat-screen television could cost 80,000 bolivars, or US$6,667, at the second strongest exchange rate.[8] This amounted to more than a year's salary for a minimum-wage worker.[9] A bolivar-earning Venezuelan may aspire to buy Apple's sixteen-gigabyte iPhone 6, a luxury item in Venezuela. But the smartphone sold for as much as 208,000 bolivars, or US$17,333, at Mercadolibre.com, Venezuela's version of eBay while selling for a few hundred dollars with a phone service contract elsewhere. A Venezuelan worker earning minimum wage would have to save every penny earned for three years to afford that phone.[10]

In Venezuela the price people pay for a dollar depends on who they are and what they do for a living. Venezuela's leftist government sold dollars for 6.3 bolivars to an elite few. These people included business owners in a handful of industries like food processing, pharmaceuticals, and personal care products. The reasoning behind this arrangement is that these firms require access to foreign currency at the most favorable rate to acquire the raw materials they need to produce everyday necessities in Venezuela. Those who import paper products and clothing could sometimes get the 6.3 rate as well. A number of well-connected government cronies—and there are too many of them in Venezuela—can buy dollars at the cheapest rate too.

The 12-bolivar-per-dollar rate was the cheapest that regular people could get if they were lucky. Venezuelans were allowed by law to charge US$3,000 on their credit cards at that rate, but they could use those dollars only overseas. And Venezuelans could acquire dollars only after spending hours filling out forms and waiting for days, weeks, even months for a government bureaucrat to approve their dollar quota. Theoretically, foreign companies based in Venezuela could also buy dollars at the 12-bolivar rate to repatriate their gains, but the government stopped making dollars available for that purpose in 2012.

The third, 50-bolivar-per dollar exchange rate was reserved for everyone else who couldn't access the first two. The central bank auctioned dollars at that price to industries that lobbied and cajoled the government hard enough to get a few dollars so they could stay in business. Dollar auctions have been held for auto part companies that are running out of inventory, glassmakers who need to import soda ash, footwear makers who need leather or grommets or want to import finished shoes, dentists who need anesthesia and the material used to fill cavities, even eye doctors who are running out of imported contact lenses and lens fluid. Occasionally regular Venezuelans got to bid for dollars at that rate too. Foreigners who used credits cards in Venezuela were charged one dollar for every 50 bolivars they spent in the country. Everyone else desperate to buy greenbacks had to go to the black market, where a dollar in early 2015 cost 180 bolivars—but that was temporary, because the black market dollar rises daily, weekly, monthly. As I edit this text in March 2016, the black market dollar stands at nearly 1,200 bolivars per dollar, a 5,600 percent increase in roughly a year. The truth is, I cannot write fast enough to keep up with the bolivar's loss of value. In this country, those who earn dollars can live like royalty, and those who don't do whatever they can to get their hands on them.

I arrived at the Renaissance on a Saturday at 10 a.m. carrying no credit cards and no cash, but my room was ready because someone had arranged my stay. Fifteen minutes after my arrival that someone called my room. The man on the line asked me to meet him at the café next door so we could do business. Minutes later I sat across from my contact in a crowded café in the heart of La Castellana neighborhood, an area of the city known for glittering office buildings, chic hotels, and top restaurants. We exchanged some pleasantries, and the man nonchalantly slid a fat brown paper bag across the table. It had 40,000 bolivars in cash. I didn't count it, not for fear of offending him, but because discretion is important and holding a five-inch-thick brick of money tied together by rubber bands in a public place is an invitation to get mugged or arrested in Caracas.

What my moneyman and I were doing made us enemies of the Venezuelan government. As far as the state was concerned, a dollar was legally worth 6.3, 12, or 50 bolivars. Any other price negotiated outside the banking system was the kind of thing that could get you into trouble. In the black market, where my friendly dealer does business, a greenback fetched twenty-nine times more than the cheapest official rate. At those prices, anyone with basic mathematic literacy and a handful of dollars had an incentive to sell U.S. currency in a back alley. This explains why I flew into Venezuela with no cash. Someone was willing to provide me with as much cash as I needed. No informed foreigner ever charges purchases in Venezuela using an international credit card. If I had done that, my hotel bill would have added up to more than US$4,000 for a twenty-one-day stay. Thanks to my dollar dealer I paid far less—$1,105 in total.

The name of my contact is not relevant here. All I will say is that he is known by some of his customers as 1-800-LEO. That's not an actual working phone number but a playful pun that says a lot about his line of work. Need to pay for furniture in Venezuela? Call 1-800-LEO. Want someone to pay your phone or cable bill, even the monthly rent of your Caracas apartment? Call 1-800-LEO. You get the picture. He's a six-foot-plus-tall economist who abandoned his career to become a professional black market dollar dealer— and he is impeccably professional for someone doing something illegal.

He punctually paid my hotel bill every week, he gave me cash on demand, he secured transportation to and from the airport, he took care of airfare reservations and provided me with a cell phone ready for use. When his services were done, he promptly e-mailed me an account summary in a PDF or an Excel file. I never paid him in cash, not in Venezuela anyway. I wired money to his dollar account overseas. In most cases I didn't even pay him at all. I sent money to someone else's account, someone to whom he owed money. This is preferred. If his name rarely appears in a check or wire transfer he becomes invisible—that is exactly how he likes it.

He is a human credit card for me and for scores of diplomats, oil executives, journalists, and any person living in Venezuela who needs to convert a dollar paycheck into bolivars. He buys dollars from those who have them and sells dollars to Venezuelans and companies who desperately need them. He operates in secret. As far as the government is concerned his business doesn't exist. He naturally gets a commission for his services and has done quite well in this line of work for more than ten years. His two-hundred-plus-square-meter apartment has enviable views of the city, and he takes his family on overseas vacations almost every year—when he's not too busy doing business with people like me.

Some consider this line of work shady or, worse, a plague. The late Venezuelan president Hugo Chávez referred to people like my dealer and me as currency speculators. The political movement he built, known as *chavista*, blames those who openly buy and sell dollars for feeding what they call an economic war against their socialist revolution.

In 2003, four years after Chávez came to power, the president banned the buying and selling of dollars. It was a time of political upheaval. Chávez's enemies in the oil industry, fed up with what they saw as the leader's heavy-handed intrusions into their business, organized a nationwide strike they hoped would unseat the president. Oil engineers and industry executives abandoned their posts in the fields and offices. Wells stopped pumping crude. For weeks oil tankers floated near Venezuelan ports, unable to load their precious cargo. The resulting collapse of the country's fuel supply caused long lines of cars to snake out of gasoline stations across the country. Crude exports, the country's main source of income, trickled down to almost nothing. Nervous about the economic implosion to come, Venezuelans did what they have learned to do over and over again in times of crisis—they began to buy any hard currency, especially U.S. dollars, to protect themselves from a devaluation of the bolivar.

Under normal circumstances a weaker currency shouldn't hurt people too much, but in Venezuela where almost everything people consume comes from abroad, especially from the United States, a weaker bolivar means virtually everything a family might need or want, from food to clothes, television sets, fridges, washers, and cellular phones, can become more expensive in just days. The more dollars people demanded, however, the more the value of the bolivar fell, making it increasingly expensive for Venezuela to import the food, medicines, and machinery the country needed. Nearly seven of ten goods people buy in Venezuelan stores, supermarkets, and shopping malls are imported.[11] Clothing and footwear are shipped in from the United States, frozen chicken sometimes comes in from Jamaica, and beef cuts arrive from Brazil. If the Andean country suddenly stopped all imports, most Venezuelans would be left naked and hungry. This is because Venezuelans produce very little apart from oil, but they want to consume everything.

The government stopped making dollars freely available in 2003 and fixed the price of the exchange rate by law, hoping to stop the dollar frenzy. It didn't work. People bought and sold dollars illegally, and a black market price for dollars emerged in the streets, hotel rooms, homes, and cafés of Venezuela. Regulation of the flow of dollars, known as capital controls, was meant to last just six months until the country's economic troubles passed, but as of 2016 capital controls were still in place. Chavistas believe the country needs these restrictions to survive. The open dollar market, leftist politicians claim, sabotages the entire economy, making everyday products impossibly expensive. This is why people like 1-800-LEO and myself are considered dangerous.

In truth, nearly everyone in Venezuela who is in a position to do so becomes a speculator. Companies, politicians, doctors, lawyers, chefs, cabdrivers, and quite a few prostitutes[12] engage in the illegal U.S. currency trade in some way or another. In an ideal world, companies would stick to their business. Doctors would tend to patients, and lawyers would defend clients. But Venezuelans have a perverse incentive to buy and sell dollars on the side, even abandon their careers altogether to trade dollars illegally.

Put a price limit on any good, and chances are that increased demand will eventually make it scarce—dollars are no exception. The government's dollar auctions are met with insatiable demand. Think of the free-for-all one sees on television when aid workers deliver food to a starved African community. People run over themselves for a share of what's being given. The fast-rising price of the dollar in the black market is an indication of this madness. By late May 2015, the black market price had reached 400 bolivars per dollar, a 120 percent increase in four months. At that rate Venezuela's 100-bolivar note—the country's largest bill—which was worth 55 U.S. cents in January, was worth only half in May 2015. By the time my editors and I got around to reviewing this text in March 2016, with the black market price at almost 1,200 bolivars per dollar, that same bill was worth 8 U.S. cents, and when you read this book the 100 bolivar bill will be virtually worthless against the world's major currencies.

There should be no shortage of dollars in Venezuela. In recent years, the country's government earned roughly US$100 billion annually from oil sales. That is the equivalent in today's dollars of what the United States spent on the Marshall Plan to help Europe recover from World War II.[13] From the day Chávez took office all the way through 2014, Petróleos de Venezuela (PDVSA), the country's state-run oil company, earned US$1.36 trillion in oil sales—more than thirteen times the Marshall Plan expenditures.[14]

The annual flow of money was so large it amounted to nearly 60 percent of Venezuela's GDP, which the British bank Barclays estimated at US$181 billion in 2014.[15] The country can get more greenbacks too. Venezuela has more than 299 billion barrels in proved oil reserves trapped underground, the biggest known cache of crude on the planet. That is more oil than can be found under the sands of Saudi Arabia. Yet in 2016 Venezuela doesn't have enough dollars to invest in its depleted oil sector. It doesn't have enough so that it can finance the imports of milk, chicken, beef, cell phones, and even the polyester and cotton fiber local paper companies need to produce toilet paper. The central bank's dollar reserves, a widely watched indicator of how many dollars Venezuela has handy to cover imports and pay debts, stood at US$13.5 billion in mid March 2016, its lowest level in seventeen years.

Having multiple prices for dollars creates multiple opportunities for corruption. For years, unscrupulous business people bought dollars at the cheapest exchange rates and sold them in the black market for fabulous gains. Back in early 2015, buying dollars at the 6.3-bolivar rate and selling them in the black market for 180 bolivars netted a 2,800 percent profit. No legal business generates those returns, except maybe cocaine trafficking. Scores of fly-by-night companies that produce nothing or overcharge the government for what they do produce have emerged and disappeared over the past thirteen years since capital controls were imposed for the single purpose of tricking the government into selling them cheap dollars they resell in Venezuela's black market for astronomical gains. Some used the bolivars obtained from selling foreign currency to once again buy cheap dollars to resell at home, again and again, in a never-ending cycle that has produced overnight fortunes. To curb the practice the government stopped handing dollars to companies and took on the job of paying the foreign suppliers and lenders of local producers directly.

The government has also become a leading importer of food, medicines, and personal hygiene goods in a bid to retain control over how the country spends its precious foreign currency. Venezuelans found a way around this too, setting up sham companies abroad to directly do business with Venezuela's government. In 2014 Venezuelan authorities gave $125 million to three recently created companies in payment for imports of personal care goods. Nearly US$64 million went to a company known only as Sunflower Extra that was registered as a new company in Delaware the year before.[16] This was no Procter and Gamble or Colgate-Palmolive. Sunflower had no track record as a manufacturer or supplier in the personal care space. A Venezuelan government investigation later showed that Sunflower and the others had inflated the price of every shampoo, deodorant, shaver, and roll of toilet paper shipped to Venezuela by more than 30 percent, a common way of defrauding Venezuela's dollar rules.

Jorge Giordani, a seventy-six-year-old electronics engineer and the main architect of Venezuela's economic policies under Chávez—known as "the

Monk" for his ascetic ways and almost religious devotion to orthodox leftist ideas—famously admitted that US$20 billion, or one-third of the country's total import bill, was lost to obscure enterprises in 2012 alone.[17] Seen another way, corrupt foreign currency dealings took US$658 from the pocket of every Venezuelan that year.[18] That is twenty times the amount of money Saddam Hussein and his son Qusay reportedly stole from Iraq's central bank just before U.S. troops began to demolish their oil-rich regime.[19] Under different circumstances, that much money lost would count as one of the largest heists in history.

Regular Venezuelans cheat too. In November 2014 authorities detained Zuely José Rodríguez at Venezuela's airport shortly before he was to board a plane to Madrid while carrying 165 credit cards owned by different people.[20] He was not a credit card thief; he was part of an organized scheme commonly known in Venezuela as the *raspao*, or "scraping," named after the motion of sliding a credit card through a card reader. Rodríguez was allegedly in cahoots with a group of Venezuelans that included airport officials who had presumably tried to make it easier for him to avoid detection.

The raspao racket works in two ways. A Venezuelan who can't travel secures his annual US$3,000 credit card quota, paying the government 12 bolivars for every dollar in that card, and sells the credit card to someone traveling who can use it overseas. With the black market price at 150 bolivars per dollar when Rodríguez was caught, selling a US$3,000 credit card quota would have left a cardholder a 1,150 percent profit for doing nothing.[21] To put things into perspective, at the going minimum wage in December 2014, that amounted to almost seven years of work for a Venezuelan.[22]

A second approach to the raspao involves a Venezuelan getting a dollar quota, then traveling and converting the card's credit into cash. Scores of Internet and brick-and-mortar companies that charge Venezuelan credit cards for bogus services and give cash to the cardholder for a fee mushroomed in such cities as Bogotá, Panama City, Miami, and Quito. The traveler returns home, sells the dollars in the black market, and makes enough money to cover the cost of the plane ticket, hotel stay, and shopping, with plenty left over to spend afterward. At one point, Venezuelans could simply cross to the Colombian border town of Cucuta, scrape themselves some cash in a shady outfit, and return home richer just hours later. The country's exchange rate rules have become a huge subsidy that has allowed thousands of Venezuelans to travel for free and to profit at the same time for several years.

Cencoex, the government body in charge of approving dollar sales to companies and individuals, has tried to curb this practice to no avail. Engaging in the raspao racket not only lands people in jail but, if they're found guilty, also gets them blacklisted by Cencoex officials, which means they lose their dollar-buying privileges. Yet scores of Venezuelans have done it because the chances of getting caught are slim.

To discourage the raspao racket, Venezuela's attorney general, Luisa Ortega Díaz, regularly took to her personal Twitter account to publish the names and ID numbers of people condemned for engaging in foreign exchange crimes. In mid-May 2015, Ortega tweeted a list of 277 people, boasting of the government's "fight against corruption."[23] But the temptation to engage in the dollar-trading business has proved too great even for government officials to resist. Just a few weeks before Ortega's tweet, military counterintelligence officers rounded up six Cencoex officials who were allegedly caught manipulating the institution's computer system to erase the names of people banned for engaging in foreign currency irregularities so they could once again purchase cheap dollars from the government.[24] Clearly, someone was paying these officials off to do so.

The black market dollar has become such a headache for Chávez's successor and disciple, President Nicolás Maduro, that in 2013 he launched a war against websites that published the price of the black market dollar. He ordered the closing of seven sites, including a popular one known only as lechugaverde.com, or "green lettuce dot com," calling them a "perverse mechanism" orchestrated by the Venezuelan "bourgeoisie."[25] Local newspapers used to publish the Green Lettuce rate, but they are now banned from printing any reference to the black market dollar. The whole thing became a joke when, just days after the president's decision, at least six new websites, including lechugaverde.net, published the same black market price. Since then, the term *Green Lettuce* has become a euphemism for the black market dollar rate in Venezuela. In October 2015, Maduro's government blamed another popular site, dolartoday.com—a website based in the United States—for the currency decline and sued its owners. The suit was unsuccessful and dolartoday.com continues to report on the black market dollar rate.

The government has tried to make it tougher for regular Venezuelans to obtain cheap dollars in the first place. In early 2014 the government passed a law that limited the amount of dollars Venezuelans could obtain for travel, depending on their destination and length of stay. Only those traveling to a country outside the Americas for more than eight days could get the usual US$3,000 spending limit on their credit cards. Traveling to Paris for seven days? You would get only US$2,000, no more. Those hoping to make a quick hop to Miami or Bogotá to turn their credit into cash in some obscure storefront could get only US$300.

The idea was to make it economically unattractive for Venezuelans to travel for the sole purpose of getting quick cash. That explains why Rodríguez was caught with 165 credit cards. Having a single person travel to Europe carrying several credit cards was still a profitable business back then. In April 2015 Cencoex authorities tightened restrictions further but still allowed a US$1,500 credit card quota for Venezuelans traveling to Cuba for eight days or more. Since then, the Communist island has become a favored destination for dollar-crazed Venezuelans.

And the restrictions have gotten tighter. In April 2015 the government reduced the credit card spending limit to US$2,000 and banned private banks from processing dollar credit card quotas, hoping to further cut down on how many dollars Venezuelans use for travel. Now only state banks can process the transactions, and delays in obtaining increasingly scarce dollars can stretch on for six months or more. The paperwork demands are onerous, and banks have been held up by shortages of the imported plastic and security bands needed to manufacture new cards.

There is no sign, however, that the government's effort to crack down on currency speculation works. The byzantine network of rules governing the foreign exchange market has only further whetted the appetite for dollars in Venezuela. People will sell their homes, their cars, and their furniture, even the clothes they wear, if they can use all that money to buy dollars at Venezuela's unrealistically low official exchange rates.

This system of currency controls and corruption can wreak havoc on Venezuela's real economy. Ford, Fiat Chrysler Automobiles, and General Motors idled their Venezuelan assembly plants for a combined eight months in 2015, because the government would not sell them enough foreign currency to import needed car parts. Carmakers owe billions in outstanding debts to overseas suppliers and in huge dividends to their parent companies.

General Motors' local assembly plant was down for four months in 2015, which means GM's roughly three thousand employees in Venezuela had nothing to do for almost half a year in a factory with a capacity to assemble as many as six hundred cars a day. GM has been forced to send most of its workers home on paid vacation because a law passed under Chávez forbids companies from downsizing the workforce without an express government authorization, even if the layoffs themselves result from the government's own currency policy. In April 2015 GM announced it had let go 446 workers, with a special government approval, but soon the labor ministry recanted that decision and ordered the automaker to hire the workers back.

Combined, the three automotive companies produced little less than eleven thousand cars for the entire year in 2015. Eight years earlier, Venezuela's car industry produced more than that every month. In the five-year period through 2015, the auto industry ran up US$3 billion in dollar purchase orders with Cencoex but has managed to obtain very little of that accumulated amount, because the government doesn't have enough dollars to sell.

When Ford threatened to close its plant in early 2015, the government allowed Ford to sell its pickup trucks and other vehicles in Venezuela for U.S. dollars. The government also pondered allowing Ford to export cars to neighboring countries so the carmaker could get some of the needed hard currency that Venezuela's government was unable to provide. Reuters reported in May 2015 that under dollar pricing, a Ford Explorer Limited would sell for US$69,000 in Venezuela. The price—that would include a luxury tax—would amount to roughly 170 years of work for a Venezuelan earning minimum wage. Faced with the prospect of being paid worthless bolivars for assembling cars that their employers would sell for hard currency, worker unions asked Ford to pay their salaries in U.S. dollars as well. By March 2016, Ford had been selling cars to Venezuelans in U.S. dollars for almost a year and still paid its workers in bolivars. But few customers in Venezuela had the ability to buy cars paying foreign currency prices.

Airlines have cut down on flights to and from Venezuela, with some, such as Air Canada and Alitalia, no longer flying there because Venezuela's government won't convert the bolivars they earn from ticket sales into hard currency. In early June 2015, Alitalia had US$250 million dollars in pending dollar purchase orders that Cencoex had yet to honor. American Airlines, Delta, and Lufthansa began selling plane tickets to only those Venezuelans willing to pay for them in U.S. currency. The dollar scarcity in the airline business is so acute that even the state-owned carrier Conviasa—created by Chávez—charges customers U.S. dollars for international plane tickets because it cannot get any foreign currency from its owner.

Travel agencies in Venezuela are no longer in the business of setting up travel plans for customers. They've become more like travel advisers, explaining all the pitfalls of trying to venture outside the country. "It has come to a point where we just tell people 'this is what's available; take it or leave it,'" says Nelly, a Venezuelan travel agent with more than ten years in the business. People like Nelly may be lucky to have a job. The Venezuelan airline trade group reported that air travel ticket sales fell 35 percent in 2015 following an 84 percent decline the year before, due to a combination of a lack of flights and expensive dollar-priced airline tickets.

Scarce plane tickets have also given rise to plane ticket resellers, an organized mafia of people known as "the cherubs" at the Maiquetía international airport. Cherubs collude with airline employees to sell a certain amount of tickets for every flight to travelers in exchange for "a fee." A flight may appear fully booked on the airline's computer system, but a traveler can still secure a seat by paying a "commission" to a well-placed cherub. By some estimates in 2013, cherubs handled as many as four tickets for every flight leaving the airport. The country's national guard now patrols the airport hoping to interrupt this practice, and they occasionally arrest a few people.

The airline industry accumulated US$3.8 billion in outstanding dollar purchase orders at Cencoex in the six years through December 2015. Maduro's government refuses to honor that bill and has even accused airlines of overcharging travelers in bolivars so they can later exchange that money for dollars at the government's cheap official rate. Uncertainty surrounding when or at what price dollars will be available for sale has prompted some airlines to increase ticket prices as often as they can as a form of insurance. In a world of unreal dollar prices and equally unreal opportunities to profit from them, eventually everyone has an incentive to abuse the system whenever possible.

Headaches for companies stemming from the dollar scarcity don't stop there. Balancing a company's books in Venezuela can be a nightmare. At what exchange rate does a company value its costs if some raw materials were imported with dollars acquired at the 6.3 bolivar exchange rate, others at 12, others at 50, and so on? How to value a company's sales is another problem. Take satellite television provider DirecTV. The company estimated it earned US$900 million from sales in Venezuela in 2014, assuming it could exchange its bolivars at the 12-bolivar-per-dollar rate. But considering that in practice it was virtually impossible for foreign companies in Venezuela to buy dollars at that rate, this almost certainly overstated the company's sales. In January 2015, a more realistic rate would have been 50 bolivars per dollar, which would cut DirecTV's sales down to less than one-third the original estimate, or US$216 million. At the black market's 180 bolivars per dollar, sales would have been even lower, US$60 million.

Many companies in Venezuela calculate the value of their assets and cash at the exchange rate that makes their financial statements look best. But that comes at a price. When Venezuela devalued the currency from 4.3 per dollar to 6.3 per dollar in early 2013, DirecTV was forced to recalculate the value of its assets downward by US$166 million. When Venezuela announced a year later that companies could only repatriate their dividends at 12 bolivars per dollar, DirecTV's assets declined in value another US$281 million. Scores of U.S. companies, from Ford to Kimberly-Clark to PepsiCo, incur millions of dollars in write-downs every time the government devalues the currency, which has happened roughly eight times during the past decade. In April 2015, Bloomberg News estimated that forty-six publicly listed companies with shares in the Standard and Poor's 500, accounting for 10 percent of the index, were regularly exposed to Venezuela's dollar uncertainty.

Companies don't know the real value of their bolivar sales and their Venezuelan assets converted into dollars; they guess and hope for the best. "No one really knows what rate they will get until the government sells them dollars," Juan Socías, Venezuela's foremost expert on the country's contorted exchange rate rules, told me. Socías made a living out of explaining exchange rate regulations to a stable of corporate clients. Over years of studying Venezuela's capital controls Socías learned an important lesson: companies can't assume they will ever get dollars from the government for their bolivar earnings. Subsidized exchange rates are akin to a perverse game of musical chairs. Things are fine as long as people have a place to sit, or get some dollars from the government. Eventually the game ends, the government no longer sells any cheap foreign currency to companies, and plenty of people are left with nothing.

* * *

The consequences of Venezuela's distorted economic system start to play out inside a secretive, fifty-six-acre industrial complex eighty-one miles west of Caracas. There lies the central bank's Casa de la Moneda, Venezuela's mint, protected by a double electrified fence, closed-circuit cameras, and plenty of guards. In a vast hangar-like structure in the west wing of the complex, technicians wearing white polo shirts manage two printing lines that include the Super Simultan IV, a German-made money press that those in the money-printing business affectionately call SUSI for short. It turns out the government with the help of SUSI can print more than 750 million bills of various denominations per year. In 2011 the mint was upgraded with the latest technology to double its capacity, so it could print nearly all the bills the country would ever need, without having to hire private companies or other central banks to print Venezuela's money.

These days the mint has a problem. It turns out SUSI can't keep up with the amount of banknotes the central bank wants to print, particularly the largest bill denomination of 100 bolivars. Venezuela has been forced to hire European money-printing companies like the United Kingdom's De la Rue and Germany's Giesecke and Devrient, as well as the central banks of other friendly nations, to produce the tons of 100-bolivar banknotes the government can't print on its own. Venezuela's central bank has farmed out the printing of most of its brand-new bills to overseas companies during the past two years.

Boeing 747 planes[26] filled with cash landed in Venezuela's airport every two weeks in 2015, carrying anywhere between 150 and 200 tons of bills (roughly 150 million bills), packed in large crates that are unloaded using a special railing system.[27] Experts in the bill-printing business estimate Venezuela will need 10 billion new bills in 2016, which amounts to one-third of the total printing capacity controlled by all money-producing private companies in the world. After unloading the cargo from planes in Venezuela, the cash is transported via heavily armored trucks guarded by military convoys late at night or at dawn to central bank vaults, the first stop before they make their way into people's pockets. Printing money is not in itself a problem—almost any nation with a money press and enough special paper with watermarks and antiforgery features prints cash. The issue in Venezuela is the amount of money printed and how it's created. In simple terms, the more an economy produces goods and services and the more foreign currency the country earns from exports, the more batches of fresh bills a central bank will eventually have to print to accommodate the amount of transactions in the economy. Venezuela's central bank does something considered economically danger-ous—it creates money out of thin air.

The bank creates more money than would normally result from the coun-try's production of goods and services and oil exports. In fact, for years the bank has lent money to the country's oil company Petroleos de Venezuela (PDVSA), so it can pay the salaries of state workers and finance the govern-ment's social spending plans. In exchange, PDVSA gives the bank pieces of paper, or IOUs. By the end of 2015, PDVSA had run up a tab with the central bank of US$145 billon, equal to far more than a year's worth of the company's annual oil sales. This has only added to Venezuela's overspend-ing problem. For almost a decade, the country grew rich as the price for oil increased fivefold, rising as high as US$147 a barrel in 2008.

The oil price boom, one of the greatest in history, was accompanied by a surge in prices of such commodities as copper, gold, and zinc, which countries with emerging economies, especially China, needed to grow. Since 2003, Venezuela has devoted a large portion of its oil riches to pay for massive social programs, including cash transfers for the poor and subsidies for food, homes, home appliances, electricity, water, and phone services. Selling dollars at preferential rates, giving cut-rate oil financing to friendly nations, providing the world's cheapest gasoline to Venezuelan car owners, financing losses at scores of state-owned companies, and paying for a ballooning state payroll that doubled in size have all blown a wide hole in the government's finances. No money was saved, and little of it was used to build productive infrastructure.

Indeed, in 2001 Chávez stopped saving oil revenues in a Venezuelan rainy-day fund meant to help the government in times of low oil prices.[28] When that was not enough he sacrificed investment in the oil business—the sector that makes Venezuela's livelihood possible—to fund more social spending plans. He later stripped the central bank of independence and began tapping its dollar reserves.

Having a central bank lend money to the administration in power is considered bad economic policy the world over. In fact, the idea of making a central bank independent from political decisions is meant to avoid the runaway inflation that almost always comes as a result. Those who raised concerns in Venezuela when Chávez decided to turn the central bank into his personal piggy bank were ignored or intimidated.

Back in August 2007, Giordani, the Monk, offered a rare press conference to answer questions about a constitutional reform Chávez had successfully persuaded Venezuelans to pass; it eliminated the bank's independence and allowed the president to spend its dollar reserves. Since every dollar held by the bank already backs bolivars in circulation at the going exchange rate, spending those dollars would lead to more bolivar printing and eventually weaken the local currency's rate of exchange vis-à-vis other major currencies.

At the time, I worked as the Caracas correspondent for Dow Jones and the *Wall Street Journal*. I attended Giordani's nationally televised conference and asked the minister whether the law change, by giving the presidency too much discretion, wouldn't lend itself to abuse by leaders in the future. Plus, spending the bank's reserves would mean the bank would print bolivars twice for the same amount of dollars.

The Monk's response was an angry forty-minute rant during which he accused me of showing a "lack of respect" for central bank board members and President Chávez. "The reserves belong to the nation, not the bank," he said. "What discretion are we talking about?" The president, as the people's elected representative, he insisted, had every right to decide how to spend that money. The cameras of state television channel V T V, the only television feed allowed at the conference, would often zoom in to film my facial expressions as the minister railed on. Other reporters in the audience seemed stunned.

Later that night a friend called to inform me that I was being called an enemy of the revolution on a well-known government propaganda television program. A nationally televised show called *La Hojilla* ("the Razorblade"), known for attacking the government's perceived enemies, replayed the incident and accused my employer, Dow Jones and Company, and me of manipulating information. The Monk and the government's media apparatus had made an example of me for the entire country, especially those who questioned the government's economic policies. Debating the idea of turning the bank into the president's petty cash fund would not be tolerated.

When tapping the central bank's reserves was not enough, Venezuela took to borrowing money from banks, bondholders, and friendly governments like China. And when the Chávez administration ran through that money, the government pressed the central bank to lend cash to PDVSA, essentially to start printing money at will. The scheme has flooded Venezuela with an ocean of paper money. There is more money circulating in Venezuela's streets than products consumers can buy with it. As a result, prices for everything from pencils and television sets to cars and homes rise rapidly. Annual inflation topped 180 percent in 2015, which means that a bolivar lost that much of its purchasing power in twelve months, the highest rate of inflation in the world today. The more money the bank lends the government, and the more bills it prints, the more worthless bolivars become.

By March 2016 it took several 100-bolivar notes to buy a cup of coffee. People have been forced to handle ever-bulkier wads of cash. In one of our last transactions in a local restaurant, 1-800-LEO handed me a box made for Johnnie Walker Black Label whisky but filled with money. It was the only container big enough to hide more than 40,000 bolivars in cash but small enough to avoid suspicion. The avalanche of newly minted bolivars, combined with the depletion of Venezuela's dollar reserves, has wreaked havoc with the bolivar-dollar exchange rate as well. The central bank's dollar shortage is so acute that in 2015 the mint fell behind on payments to the foreign companies that print Venezuelan bolivars. To put it simply, Venezuela now owes money to the companies it hires to print the country's own money.

Admitting the bolivar is increasingly worthless is a politically sensitive issue in Venezuela. Officials at the country's mint used to follow a simple rule of thumb: the lowest-denomination bill should equal roughly one day's worth of the going minimum wage, and the largest bill should amount to two weeks of minimum wage work. The central bank abandoned that standard long ago. If Venezuela were to follow that rule in March 2016, the smallest bill in circulation would be between 300 and 400 bolivars, and the largest would be 6,000, or sixty times larger than the current 100-bolivar bill. Central bank officials know this, but the idea of printing larger-denomination bills has become taboo in government circles. Doing so amounts to admitting that inflation is getting out of hand. Yet runaway inflation is already affecting people's everyday lives.

Castor, a Venezuelan intellectual property lawyer in his mid forties, knows firsthand what inflation means. He purchased a Caracas apartment in 2008 for 340,000 bolivars in one of the city's most prized neighborhoods. Seven years later, the apartment's original purchase price is roughly enough money to buy Apple's IPhone 6 in Venezuela. The inflationary distortion gets even worse. Castor took out a bank loan to pay for half the apartment's purchase price. When I spoke to him in May 2015 he still made payments of roughly 1,200 bolivars a month for his mortgage—about the cost of a cab ride to the airport.[29]

I asked Castor why he didn't just pay off the loan, if the outstanding balance was so low. His answer said a lot about how things work in an economy gone wild: he continued to pay ridiculously low monthly payments because the longer he takes to pay off the loan in a country where the bolivar is increasingly worthless, the less money he'll ultimately pay the bank. Castor said he would pay off his mortgage if and when he decided to sell his apartment. In an equally baffling experience, 1-800-LEO bought a brand-new Ford Escape SUV in January 2006 for 66,000 bolivars,[30] but the same amount of bolivars in March 2016 bought two bottles of twelve-year-old scotch. Aside from U.S. dollars, cars and real estate are the only other assets Venezuelans can purchase to protect their money. Prices for homes and automobiles rise steadily, closely tracking the value of the U.S. dollar in Venezuela's black market.

The old saying "time is money" has never been truer. Every minute that passes, the bolivar is worth less. In this mad reality, people have three options: spend their money quickly before things get too expensive, buy dollars and save them in overseas banks or under the mattress, or take out as much debt as possible at a fixed interest rate. Saving bolivars in a Venezuelan bank makes no sense because the interest rate paid on deposits is far below inflation.[31] For most, it's better to spend money today on food, clothes, housing, education, and everything else before the price goes up tomorrow. Every minute that cash sits in a Venezuelan savings account, it loses value.

The bolivar loses purchasing power so quickly that Venezuelans have learned to max out their credit cards and play with their card's cutoff dates to beat inflation. People like Castor and 1-800-LEO will make large purchases on the day after their credit card's monthly cutoff date. That charge will show up on the credit card statement thirty days later, and the cardholder has another thirty days to pay it—roughly sixty days in total to pay for a purchase. That is valuable time in a country where inflation rises anywhere between 9 and 10 percent every month. That same product purchased with the credit card will be worth 18 percent more in two months' time. That's not all. In Venezuela the government has decreed that banks cannot charge users an annual credit card interest rate of more than 29 percent per year, but with inflation rising at several times that rate, banks are charging cardholders negative real rates. In essence cardholders are getting free money by using their credit cards. "That's a tremendous incentive to consume," Castor said.

One can observe this phenomenon by looking at data too. The Economist Intelligence Unit, the analysis unit of the *Economist*, expects retailers in Venezuela to increase sales in bolivars by an average of 35 percent a year over the five years through 2019, but the volume of actual products sold is expected to contract or grow very little at the same time.[32] In other words, more and more cash allows people to buy less and less, but the cash bubble creates the illusion of prosperity.

Inflation is such a touchy political subject that in 2014, central bank authorities stopped making inflation figures available every month. It was not until December 2015 that the bank released partial inflation figures. Inflation in 2015 reached 180.9 percent, making it the highest in Venezuela's history. But trying to hide reality does little to solve the problem. At this rate Venezuela is well on its way to reaching hyperinflation.[33] When Germany experienced this economic phenomenon in 1923, the German mark became so worthless that people used bank notes as wallpaper.

Naturally, Venezuela's central bank authorities no longer give press conferences, and bank board members avoid public appearances that can expose them to embarrassing questions. In the eyes of the bank and the government, anyone taking a close look at the economy is suspect. After months of asking to speak with central bank president Nelson Merentes for this book, I received a call in May 2015 from Merente's office informing me that a preview meeting had been arranged for me with two bank officers.

In an office on the top floor of the central bank I sat across the table from two poker-faced officials, Cesar Maza, from the statistics department, and

Rafaela Cusati, the bank's press officer, who told me they were not allowed to answer any questions. But the meet-and-greet opportunity quickly devolved into something akin to an interrogation. Maza would not too subtly lean over to try to read my notebook whenever I took pen to paper. They peppered me with questions about whom I had interviewed for my book and whom I planned to interview in the future, and they tried to coax my views on the Venezuelan economy. I kept my answers vague and mentioned no names for a reason. A well-placed government official in Venezuela had the power not only to intimidate any business leader willing to speak openly for my book but also to have me thrown out of the country.

Venezuela developed a reputation for arresting journalists and writers and accusing them of being spies. In 2013 a *Miami Herald* reporter, Jim Wyss, was arrested and accused of espionage while he investigated product shortages and smuggling in Venezuela for an article. He was released days later but not before military officials had gone through his laptop's hard drive and his phone contacts. I explained to the central bank officers that my book focused strictly on economics and business. "The economy is a controversial issue in this country," Cusati said. The meeting ended, and my interview with the central bank president was never approved. It was a far cry from the openness I experienced during the five years I worked in Venezuela, a time when Merentes, then a finance minister, would often speak to me and other journalists.

Maybe it was paranoia, but after that odd central bank chat, I made it a point to back up all my notes in the cloud constantly while I was in Venezuela and to keep my laptop and notebooks locked up in my hotel room's safe when I was out interviewing people. Writing about economic problems that stem from the country's inflation and weak currency has landed major newspapers in trouble too. The government has used its capital controls as a tool to restrict dollars to newspapers whose coverage is not aligned with the government's ideas. The Inter American Press Association has complained that scores of news organizations have had trouble securing newsprint, and several of them have stopped their presses and publish news only online because of what they perceive as a calculated dollar stranglehold to silence dissent.

Venezuela has a dark history with exchange controls. The country first experienced a serious currency devaluation on February 18, 1983, an infamous day in Venezuelan history known as "Black Friday," when the bolivar suffered its biggest ever one-day devaluation against the dollar. The debacle occurred for a simple reason: several Venezuelan presidents had spent lavishly on agriculture and industry as well as other pet projects, and had made no effort to save for the future, thinking oil prices would stay high forever. As the price of oil declined, the state's profligate spending and the value of the bolivar became unrealistic.

In the aftermath of Black Friday, the government imposed a dual exchange rate of 4.3 and 6 bolivars per dollar managed by an institution called Recadi—an earlier version of Cencoex—and prohibited using the country's foreign currency reserves to import goods considered luxuries such as perfume and lingerie. The exchange controls lasted six years and led to large-scale corruption. When President Carlos Andrés Pérez, who took over in 1989, lifted the Recadi exchange controls he found a rotten culture of kickbacks, bribes, and commissions for allotting subsidized foreign currency to powerful buyers, and over-invoicing for imports of everything from food to auto parts.

The corruption purge that followed ensnared former presidents, top government officials and executives of U.S. companies. Politicians had misspent the country's riches, wasted the central bank's dollar and gold reserves, and left Venezuela saddled with debts. In 1989, the end of capital controls and the price increases that followed on most food items, gasoline, utilities, and transportation caused a wave of looting, riots, and protests in Caracas, known as El Caracazo, that left more than three hundred people dead.

In the mid-1990s a banking crisis prompted Venezuela to once again impose capital controls, this time managed by an office known as Office of Exchange Rate Administration (OTAC) that also became notoriously corrupt. It all came to a head with a 38 percent devaluation of the bolivar two years later. When OTAC was closed, businesses wondered what would happen with their pending dollar purchase orders under the abolished official exchange rate. The planning minister at the time informed them that only those petitions that had been approved would be honored—all others would be dismissed.

The cheap dollar party—in which politicians decided who got dollars, how many, and when—was over. All that was left were monumental losses for businesses that couldn't convert their bolivars into dollars soon enough and a hard lesson for most Venezuelans: never trust your own currency.

The bolivar's worthlessness in the eyes of Venezuelans has changed the way people live. The worthless bolivar made it possible for Girish Gupta, a journalist from the United Kingdom, to afford one of the most unusual living arrangements. When I met Gupta in January 2015, he had lived on the twenty-first floor of the Renaissance for more than a year. He paid roughly US$1,000 a month, sometimes less, for a room that included utilities and all the benefits of an upscale hotel. His monthly rent even included unlimited amounts of toilet paper and complimentary soap and shampoo. That was worth a lot, since Venezuela's nationwide shortage of dollars had decimated the local production of personal hygiene products and had cut the imports of other basic goods. Meanwhile, renting a one-bedroom apartment in one of Caracas's top neighborhoods cost between US$1,200 and US$1,500 a month. "Some people think I'm crazy or that I just like living in luxury, but if you do the numbers, it makes sense," Gupta told me.

He also got another perk from living in a top hotel: reward points. Renaissance guests got ten Marriott reward points for every dollar they spent in the hotel, which means long-term guests accumulated large amounts of points they could later redeem for free nights at any Marriott worldwide. That took care of Gupta's vacations too.

In January 2015 the Marriott system of reward points took 50 bolivars to equal one dollar, which turned reward points into another way to obtain cheap U.S. currency that could be spent on lodging abroad. Since then, some Venezuelans have taken to using hotel reward points like money. Occasionally Gupta sold the points he earned for a month's stay at the hotel for US$200 or even US$300, which made his monthly living arrangement even cheaper. Someone with dollars to spend in Venezuela could easily get used to this way of life. During my years in Caracas, Venezuelan landlords preferred to find a brand-new foreign tenant every year instead of renegotiating a lease with the same renter, because it was easier to keep up with the bolivar's plunging value by raising rents 40 or even 50 percent. I was forced to move three times during my five-year stretch in Venezuela. In 2015, however, Venezuela's currency was worth so little that foreigners could afford to forgo apartment living altogether and stay in a hotel year-round.

2 INFINITE WANTS

Venezuelans have a problem when they go to the toilet. A toilet paper short-age has forced many people to use paper napkins, paper towels, anything but a normal household roll of toilet paper, which is almost impossible to find. Fortunately for me, I had two rolls in my hotel bathroom during my visits to Caracas, but there wasn't a single one to be found in Venezuelan supermarkets, stores, or pharmacies. I made it my goal in January 2015 to buy a household roll of toilet paper somewhere, anywhere in the Caracas metropolitan area within three weeks.

In early 2015 Venezuela suffered chronic shortages of basic consumer goods. Finding food staples like rice, milk, sugar, beef, and chicken was tough. Basic personal care products like deodorant and shampoo were practically nonexistent. It had been roughly two years since store shelves were regularly stocked with toilet paper rolls in Caracas, the city in Venezuela where con-sumers were most likely to find scarce products. Other major cities and towns in this oil-rich nation were worse off: their store shelves were barren almost all the time. People traveled to Caracas from all over the country hoping to find body soap, laundry detergent, and toilet tissue somewhere in the capital.

When delivery trucks carrying toilet paper drove into stores, dozens or even hundreds of Venezuelans already stood in lines that were blocks long, waiting for hours, hoping to get four, twelve, any number of rolls they could find and however many a store would sell. Some stores sold only twelve rolls per person to make sure as many people as possible could buy the product. Owning several rolls of toilet paper in 2015 meant two things: you were both extremely lucky and paid a hefty price for them in the black market or you spent days and weeks scouring the city and standing in line for long hours outside stores hoping to get a few rolls at the government decreed price.

Odd things happen when toilet tissue disappears. At the Nugantina café, a fixture in the Los Palos Grandes neighborhood in eastern Caracas, a stack of brown paper towels normally used to dry hands sat atop the toilet in the unisex bathroom. There was no toilet tissue available for customers. An employee said the cafe had been forced to close the bathroom for long stretches because people got into the habit of stealing the few toilet tissue rolls the cafe staff could find. They tried using heavy, jumbo-sized, industrial rolls of toilet paper instead, which were slightly easier to find, but people stole those too, taking handfuls of paper before exiting the lavatory, or outright hiding the whole roll in large bags and purses. The café staff decided that the best way to keep the bathroom open for customers was to offer no toilet tissue and leave extra paper towels on hand. Some restaurants took other precautions. Catar, a trendy eatery for well-heeled Venezuelans, managed to prevent customers from stealing its industrial roll of toilet tissue by keeping the roll screwed to the wall inside a hard plastic dispenser.

Household-type toilet paper rolls are so hard to find that consumers are forced to buy industrial-size ones if they can find them. Melquíades Pulido, a former president for the Venezuelan American Chamber of Commerce, Venamcham, experienced this first hand. I met Pulido for coffee because I wanted to hear from someone with his experience about the difficulties involved in doing business in Venezuela. He headed the trade group that represents the largest multinational corporations working in the country, such as McDonald's, Coca-Cola, and American Airlines, and he ran the Andean unit of global petrochemical giant DuPont for years. But our discussion quickly gravitated to the far less lofty subject of the toilet paper shortage. Pulido managed to purchase a small hoard of industrial-size toilet tissue rolls for his home. "I haven't needed them yet, but that may soon change," he said.

By the time the traditional Holy Week holiday arrived three months after our chat, small hotels and bed-and-breakfasts in the city of Merida, a main tourist center in the Andes near the border with Colombia, began asking guests to bring their own toilet tissue.[1] Luxury hotels like the Marriott Renaissance developed a privileged relationship with suppliers that allows them to get toilet paper before everyone else does when a shipment is ready to be sold, but small hotels are not that lucky. A Renaissance manager told me the hotel took the precaution of keeping a three-month stock of toilet tissue. "It's all about having the right suppliers. And having lots of them," the manager said. The hotel devoted one whole floor of the building exclusively to storing its inventory of prized toiletries.

Shopping for toilet paper, or anything else in Venezuela, became a fraught experience. Visiting more than a dozen supermarkets and pharmacies in Caracas over several days left me with nothing. People stood in one line or another outside supermarkets at all hours of the day. And most did so to buy sugar or milk, but there was no toilet paper to be found anywhere. Visiting state-owned supermarkets could be an especially grueling experience. On a Saturday, at the state-owned Bicentenario supermarket in Plaza Venezuela, a middle-class enclave, people showed up in droves to shop. The Bicentenario is housed in a massive 151,000-square-foot structure, the size of a shopping center, where roughly sixty-five hundred people a day buy anything from chicken to flat-screen televisions at subsidized prices and pay for them at any one of fifty-two cash registers. Outside, several hundred people lined up in a dirt field under the sun, holding umbrellas and sitting on folding chairs, to wait for a chance to enter the building. Entire families of mostly low-income Venezuelans showed up with children of all ages to sit in the heat.

A handful of portable toilets were strategically placed on the edges of the field for those who needed to relieve themselves, a woefully inadequate number given the growing mass of people in line. Of course shoppers were expected to bring their own toilet tissue if they planned to use the toilets. At the main entrance, however, employees dressed in red vests—the colors of the late Hugo Chávez's leftist political party—warned shoppers not to get in line if they wanted to buy toilet paper. The Bicentenario had run out a few days earlier, and there were no more rolls for sale.

Days later, on a Wednesday at lunchtime, I caught a glimpse of a man walking down the street carrying a transparent plastic bag with a packet of four toilet paper rolls. I asked him where he bought them, and he pointed to a supermarket nearby, but he told me not to waste my time. "They're all gone now," he said. Shopping is something that Venezuelans no longer do weekly, as before, but daily, maybe even several times a day. The arrival of toilet paper or scarce products at a particular retail location is the kind of thing that goes viral in social media networks and prompts workers to leave the office at a moment's notice to shop. Employers complain of a growing absenteeism problem, but they can't do anything about it because everyone, from the cleaning lady to the company manager, has to find time to shop for scarce goods.

People walking with shopping bags draw attention in the streets, and Venezuelans keep a close eye on each other's purchases to see what they are missing. I discovered this phenomenon as I left a supermarket after buying some fruit. I quickly noticed that total strangers discretely eyed my bag as they walked by, to see if I had managed to purchase milk, chicken, detergent, or some other prized product. Finding a roll of toilet tissue has become the equivalent of a form of lottery. Getting the product is ridiculously difficult, and there is a special kind of elation and pride shoppers feel when they succeed.

Venezuelans first became angry enough to protest shortages of toilet paper in 2013. They started Twitter campaigns and marched outside ministries, but the problem worsened over time. The government has blamed the toilet paper shortage on an orchestrated campaign by those who oppose their leftist revolution. In the eyes of the government, there are three types of enemies: companies that intentionally produce less toilet paper, distributors who hoard the paper rolls hoping to sell them to desperate consumers for higher prices, and misguided Venezuelans who buy more rolls than they should. As far as the government is concerned, the mark of a revolutionary Venezuelan is to stoically wait and endure toilet tissue shortages while politicians work to erect a socialist system with the country's oil wealth. In July 2013 Elías Jaua, Venezuela's minister of foreign affairs at the time, became so aggravated with recurring demands for a solution to the toilet tissue problem that he famously asked a crowd at a political event, "Do you want the fatherland or do you want toilet paper?"[2]

Others tried to put a positive spin on the toilet paper shortage. That same month, Elías Eljuri, head of Venezuela's National Statistics Institute, said in a televised interview that the toilet tissue shortage was in fact a good sign. It shows "Venezuelans are eating more," he said, because they have more access to food, thanks to the social policies of the revolutionary government.[3] In other words, Venezuelans use more toilet paper because they are defecating more often and this is proof of their well-being. In May 2013 the government estimated that Venezuela consumed 125 million rolls of toilet paper each month, but excess demand called for another 40 million toilet paper rolls. Government officials promised to import 50 million rolls, and the president even forced a takeover of a toilet paper manufacturer hoping to force more production, but that did little to solve the problem.[4] The ministry of commerce imported 80 million rolls of toilet paper in 2014, but shortages continued.[5]

The average Venezuelan used 5.7 pounds of toilet paper in 2014, which is not much. It's more than what people in India consume, which is zero (they use their left hand), and a fraction of the twenty pounds a year used by the average consumer in the United States.[6] Toilet tissue use in Venezuela mirrors the rise and fall of the country's oil fortunes. In 2008, at the height of the oil boom, Venezuelans consumed roughly eight pounds of toilet tissue, 60 percent more than they did eight years earlier, when oil prices were at rock bottom.[7] Toilet tissue consumption in 2014 declined close to where it had been fourteen years earlier, but Venezuela's population had grown by a quarter and its economy was supposed to be far richer after a decade of hefty oil revenues.

The real problem lies with toilet paper production. Venezuelan paper company Papeles Venezolanos, PAVECA, dominates more than half of the Venezuelan toilet paper market with a brand called Rosal. The company, which can produce as many as 62 million toilet paper rolls a month, supplies more than half the market. But PAVECA has trouble keeping production going because it cannot get the U.S. currency it needs to pay for imports of polyester and cotton fiber to manufacture toilet tissue rolls. Its competitors, U.S. company Kimberly-Clark and smaller local producer MANPA, face a similar problem.

In June 2015 PAVECA notified its workers that the company could face a partial or total shutdown in coming months if it continued to have problems importing raw materials.[8] Worse yet, the government forces the three toilet tissue producers to lend each other paper pulp whenever one of them runs out. When a toilet paper manufacturer manages to import raw materials, customs officials often ask for bribes to allow the material to leave customs.[9]

PAVECA has another problem—it loses money on each roll of toilet paper it produces. Toilet paper manufacturers must sell each toilet paper roll at a price dictated by the government, but when raw materials run out, the company must still pay its workers because it is illegal in Venezuela to downsize the workforce without express government authorization. PAVECA must also pay for other costs even if it fails to produce a single roll of toilet tissue. And while the state-regulated price of a roll of toilet paper can remain the same for months, the costs of producing it, including the salaries of the workers at the factory, rise along with inflation.

Venezuela first decreed price controls on a few basic goods in 2003 to make these products affordable to poor Venezuelans in the face of a weaker bolivar and rising inflation. Any basic economic lesson teaches that price controls rarely work, especially if they stay the same for long periods. They discourage production and at the same time encourage excess demand, a dangerous combination. In 2015 the list of price-controlled products in Venezuela, however, had grown to include 1,400 pharmaceuticals, 140 food items, and more than 240 personal hygiene goods[10]—and the prices for these products are rarely updated. Toilet tissue is one of the most important items on this list. By law, the price of a roll of toilet paper depends on the number of squares of paper per roll.[11] State bureaucrats decided consumers should pay no more than 0.026 bolivars per square of toilet tissue, regardless of the quality of the roll. No one knows for sure how state number crunchers came about that arbitrary number. The price doesn't account for thickness or paper quality. There is no different price for quilted versus plain rolls, scented or unscented. And it doesn't matter anyway, because premium toilet paper has ceased to exist in Venezuelan bathrooms.

Most toilet paper available in the market has a gauzy thickness and a rough, almost cardboard-like texture. Forget about Kimberly-Clark's Scott brand with triple-layer thickness, quilted texture, and smell-clean technology. That's as rare as caviar, and just as coveted. In the black market for consumer goods, a pack of four no-frills toilet tissue rolls can fetch several times the regulated price. It is illegal for Venezuelans not only to resell toilet paper above the state-mandated price but also to smuggle it across the border. Resellers can be arrested and go to jail for one to three years, but people still do it because in the face of scarcity, a toilet paper roll has become a rare and valuable commodity.

Stores found to be hoarding toilet paper or any other price-controlled goods can be closed, fined, and seized by the government, its owners thrown in prison for eight to ten years. But there is no legal definition of "hoarding." Is it reasonable for a business to maintain a day's worth of toilet paper sales in stock, a week's worth, or a month's worth? No one really knows. In 2013 Venezuela arrested two shop owners, Limin Zheng and Marco Zingg, for allegedly hoarding toilet paper.[12] In Zingg's store officials found only eleven packets of toilet paper, each containing ninety-six rolls, and Zheng's store had 220 similar packets, yet both owners went to jail.[13] Consumers buy as much toilet paper as they can; there is no law against that. They accumulate toilet paper rolls at home, because they don't know when they will see a roll of toilet paper in a store again. The government calls this phenomenon "nervous purchases," and constantly calls on people to buy no more than what they really need.

The toilet paper craze has affected the everyday business of toilet paper companies in other ways too. In 2015 Ana María, a salesperson at one of Venezuela's top three toilet paper manufacturers, had a privileged position in the toilet paper value chain. Her job was to dispatch toilet paper shipments to the country's largest supermarkets. Early in 2015 Ana María and her colleagues discovered that trucks carrying toilet paper to supermarkets would arrive with fewer rolls than the number they loaded onto trucks at the factory's dispatch unit. After investigating further they found that truck drivers had struck secret deals with some supermarket managers to set aside a portion of each toilet paper shipment, keep it out of supermarket store shelves, and sell them to black market merchants for a profit. To prevent this practice, the government has forced companies to track every truckload of toilet paper from point A to point B, but "we don't control what our clients do with the product once they get it," Ana María said to me. She admitted she also does what she can to help her family. Her work at the toilet paper company gives her unique access to the product, and whenever possible she would set aside packs of toilet paper for her brothers and her mother.

The search for toilet paper took me to Petare, a Caracas municipality known for its shantytowns and a commercial hub that surrounds a roundabout with heavy traffic of buses, motorcycles, and stray dogs. Vendors hawk their wares on sidewalks, leaving little room for pedestrians, who are forced to squeeze past and bump against one another. Discarded food wrappers, banana peels, and small plastic coffee cups litter the streets. The stench of urine floats in the air. Locals say Petare is an epicenter of the black market, where a whole new class of informal merchants called *bachaqueros*—the people who make a living from reselling price-controlled goods—plies its trade.

Their name comes from *bachaco*, a large and industrious ant found in the Venezuelan Amazon. And it is a fitting name. After all, ants are known for the ability to carry several times their weight, just as Venezuelans haul away bags full of merchandise they later resell. I was struck, however, by how little merchandise these bachaqueros had to offer. One vendor sold a Speed Stick deodorant and a packet of Pampers. A woman with a toddler in her arms offered for sale two bottles of Head and Shoulders shampoo, five disposable Gillette razors, and a bag of detergent placed on a blanket over the sidewalk, but there was no toilet paper to be seen anywhere.

I asked the woman if she knew where I could find toilet paper. "I have some," she said cryptically, almost in a hush, but there were no rolls on her blanket. The woman signaled her teenage daughter, who started rummaging through a large black bag inside a grocery cart, guarded by the nursing mother. She instantly produced a pack of four toilet rolls, the first I had seen in weeks. The price: 80 bolivars—four times the price mandated by law.

I paid the teenager and examined the four-roll pack called Caricia, a brand I had never heard of. The plastic wrapper said the product was imported by the Venezuelan Corporation of Foreign Commerce, CORPOVEX, the government institution charged with obtaining food and consumer goods from outside the country. And the manufacturer was Sunflower Extra LLC, one of the shady U.S.-based companies accused of overbilling the Venezuelan government in U.S. dollars for personal hygiene products. Ironically, these toilet paper rolls were the result of the type of corrupt foreign exchange dealings that depleted Venezuela's dollar reserves enough to hurt domestic toilet tissue producers. As I headed out of the Renaissance days later, I handed a tip to the lady responsible for cleaning my room and offered to give her the pack of toilet paper rolls from Petare. She agreed to take the packet on the condition that I write and sign a note explaining they were a gift, so she could exit the building with the rolls. Hotels usually keep tabs on the cleaning staff to make sure they don't steal valuables from guests. In Venezuela, hotels also make sure they don't take toilet paper as well.

* * *

On a Thursday afternoon in mid-May 2015, there seemed to be a problem with the product aisles in a Farmatodo pharmacy on the east side of Caracas. The shelves labeled "Soap" were stocked full of Colgate toothpaste and bottles of mouthwash. Farmatodo (which translates into PharmaEverything) is not some obscure drugstore but Venezuela's largest pharmacy and general merchandise chain, with eight thousand employees and 167 stores across the country.

The family-run business has been around for almost a century and has grown to become the local, albeit smaller, equivalent of Walgreens or CVS in the United States. Farmatodo has even expanded to neighboring Colombia, where it has thirty-two stores and counting. When Venezuelans need an aspirin, a diet coke, even cosmetics, many walk or drive to the nearest Farmatodo. The stores are pristine and well lit, and they are easily recognizable by their emblematic blue-and-white facades. Pharmacy counter employees wear spotless white lab coats, and shelves are usually neatly tended. In the adjoining aisle, however, under "Baby Care" the shelf offered colored paper gift bags. The cosmetics section was well supplied with toothbrushes and more mouthwash, and the pet products section had starch sprays, shoe shine, Tupperware products, even tinfoil. It's as if a shelf stocker suffering from some form of dyslexia was charged with arranging the merchandise.

A hubbub of activity began to form in the picnic and plastic cutlery aisle, a strange place for a commotion. Customers were frantically grabbing six-pound bags of Ariel laundry detergent priced at 88.16 bolivars per bag, or roughly thirty U.S. cents, placed right next to the plastic plates and party cups.[14] "How many bags per person?" a young woman asked, her mother in tow. "Two," said another customer as he hurried to join the cash register line that by then snaked around various aisles. Ariel is a Procter and Gamble (P&G) product that is almost impossible to find in Venezuela.

The absence of pretty much any laundry detergent has forced Venezuelans to create a homemade mixture of a soapish liquid, using industrial-strength soap, to wash their clothes. Street vendors sell this by the liter in plastic bottles in Caracas, but its exact contents are a mystery. Buyers complain that clothes sometimes tear up after a wash or two. Ariel has the government-set price printed on the bag, and just a few inches away, another printed disclaimer with a Venezuelan flag: "Only for sale in Venezuela." The label is an example of the lengths to which companies will go to stay in the government's good graces so they can obtain the foreign currency needed to produce or import finished goods into Venezuela. The government asked P&G to print this disclaimer on the bag in hopes that it would somehow discourage the active smuggling of price-controlled goods across the border to neighboring Colombia. Goods with price controls have become speculative items, just like the U.S. dollar.

The state first imposed controls on household cleaning products like Ariel in April 2012. As the value of the bolivar eroded and the state-mandated price for Ariel stayed the same, Venezuelans began to resell the product across the border in Colombia for ten times its original price or more. Continued smuggling increased the demand for Ariel, which in turn made the detergent scarce inside Venezuela. When that happened the bachaquero resellers began selling the product at higher prices just blocks away from established retail chains for a profit. The bag of Ariel can and likely will sell for several times its price once it leaves Farmatodo; it can fetch far more across the border.

With a 69 percent share, P&G dominates Venezuela's detergent business, manufacturing Ariel and two other brands in Barquisimeto, an industrial hub 168 miles west of Caracas. Alejandro Betancourt, P&G's manager for the detergent business, told local business magazine *Producto* in January 2015 that the company's plant produced as much as possible but demand for detergent in the past year had risen as much as 20 percent, which explains why detergent quickly disappeared from store shelves.[15] In a matter of minutes the Ariel shelf in Farmatodo lay bare.

Farmatodo and its exacting standards are trapped by Venezuela's widespread product shortages. The scarcity of all kinds of products makes it almost impossible for a retailer like Farmatodo to have a diverse product offering. Leaving shelves bare is not considered a good practice for any retail business, so Farmatodo employees stock any shelf with whatever product they happen to have at any given time. In this reality, shelf labeling and concerns over customer comfort become secondary. The same or worse happens in practically every store and supermarket across the country. Demand for products subject to price controls is so high that retail outlets opt not to shelve them at all. Crates filled with milk or cooking oil are often dumped in the middle of a supermarket aisle or just steps away from the cashiers so customers can quickly grab the product and stand in line. A price-controlled good won't last long on the shelves anyway.

A Farmatodo employee suddenly made a quick announcement: It was one Ariel bag per customer only. That was all the store would sell. A crestfallen man left his spot on the line to return one of his two bags. "Bad luck for us in life," he said out loud. Others were forced to leave one bag at the counter. A mountain of Ariel soap bags sat next to one of the cashiers, and it was unclear whether it was there because people were asked to leave their extra bag at that point or to make it easier for customers to purchase the product without having to stand in line while holding six pounds of detergent.

Ariel is just one example of the grief Venezuelans face when shopping for groceries, medicine, or cleaning products. Diapers are almost nonexistent, and when they arrive in stores, shelves are filled with one size only, small, medium, or whatever the store is lucky to get. Venezuelans have grown used to swapping diaper sizes through Facebook or other social media networks. Diapers are in such high demand that childless couples, even unmarried shoppers, will buy diapers so they can later exchange them with friends, family, or total strangers for products they do need. The practice has caused such problems to the country's diaper distribution that government authorities in San Cristóbal, the capital city of the southwestern state of Táchira, forced Farmatodo employees to ask diaper shoppers to produce a copy of a baby's birth certificate as proof of legitimate need. Only visibly pregnant women were exempt from this requirement.

Feminine hygiene products like tampons and sanitary napkins have also disappeared from stores. Farmatodo carried copious amounts of P & G's Always, a daily protection liner, for the state-decreed price of 19.70 bolivars, or 7 U.S. cents, for an eight-pack. But the far more absorbent feminine pads were rarely stocked. A female Farmatodo employee told me one can almost always find Always, primarily because it doesn't do the job of a regular menstrual sanitary towel. In Venezuela the words *Always* and *Everything* have become risky names for a mass-consumed product or any company involved in the sale of consumer goods.

State television station Vive TV, a culture channel, took a stab at offering a solution to the sanitary napkin shortage in a video aired in early 2013, when scarcity of the product was just becoming a problem. Vive TV called on Venezuelan women to make their own sanitary pads at home. The channel's video tutorial features a woman dressed as a nurse practitioner, explaining how to make washable and reusable pads out of cloth, layers of cotton, and plain-woven fabric such as canvas. By making these menstrual pads at home "we avoid becoming a part of the commercial cycle of savage capitalism. We are more conscious and in harmony with the environment," the woman says in the video. "Our ancestors, our grandmothers used pads made out of cloth." The Venezuela state-sponsored video was asking people to turn back the clock almost a century to adapt to the country's worsening economic reality.

Just like Ariel, feminine hygiene products are rarely seen on store shelves because artificially low retail prices create excess demand for them. Producing these goods remained barely profitable for companies like P & G only because the government made available dollars at the 6.3-bolivar preferential exchange rate to import the raw materials companies needed to produce them in the first place. In June 2015, P & G introduced Always Postparto, feminine pads intended for women who had recently given birth, and sold the product at a price seventy times higher than the government-regulated kind, the equivalent of one-fifth of a monthly minimum-wage salary.[16]

The move earned P & G a public scolding from the minister of women, Gladys Requena, who accused P & G of committing a "criminal act against the Venezuelan people" and "playing its part in the economic war." P & G quickly responded that not only was the specialty product not subject to price regulation but the multinational had expanded its local production capacity 56 percent in the previous three years to increase output of detergent, sanitary towels, shavers, and shampoo. Investing to increase production does not guarantee that a company won't run into trouble with Venezuela's leftist government.

Companies and retailers try to find ways to sell products with no controls to compensate for the money they often lose by selling price-controlled ones. Some retailers, however, get carried away with their markups. The El Patio supermarket in the chic Los Palos Grandes neighborhood, probably the priciest supermarket in the country, sells a ninety-two-ounce bottle of

Tide detergent combined with Downy softener for 14,216.68 bolivars, or US$47.30, more than two and a half times what it would cost, including shipping and handling, to order it from Amazon in the United States.[17] The same goes for a box of Splenda with a thousand packets of sweetener. It sells for 15,570.13 bolivars, or US$52, twice what it would cost in the United States.

Needless to say, regular Venezuelans cannot afford such prices. It would take almost two and a half months of work for a minimum-wage earner to afford that box of Splenda packets.[18] Some business owners call this markup the replacement cost, or the cost to the store of replacing this product. In Venezuela retailers figure they won't soon get dollars to replace that product on the shelves. And there will always be someone desperate enough to pay such prices.

Venezuelans have come up with creative ways to endure shortages of deodorant, another product absent from Farmatodo's shelves. Solisbel, a community organizer in La Pastora, a low-income Caracas barrio, tells me of a formula for homemade deodorant that a friend shared with her. The recipe includes a tablespoon of uric acid, two tablespoons of body lotion, and a teaspoon of sodium bicarbonate, all blended into a cream-like substance. Solisbel says some people keep the deodorant cream in the type of plastic containers that labs use to store fecal or urine samples, one of the few medical supplies one can still find in Venezuela.

Indeed, scarcity of foreign exchange has affected the availability of gauzes, syringes, and other medical materials hospitals need to treat the most basic of ailments. Condoms and birth control pills, which are also not manufactured in Venezuela but have to be imported, have disappeared from pharmacies for months, a problem that has left medical authorities concerned that unwanted teen pregnancies and cases of sexually transmitted diseases will likely spike.[19] In February 2015 a box of thirty-six Trojan condoms sold at Venezuela's Internet retail site Mercadolibre.com for 4,760 bolivars, almost a month's earnings for a minimum-wage worker.[20]

Getting sick can become a problem in Venezuela. Atamel, a local brand of acetaminophen produced by U.S. pharmaceutical company Pfizer, is a much-in-demand product because the country in 2015 suffered from an epidemic of chikungunya, a virus carried by mosquitoes that causes high fever, joint pain, and in some cases death. Pfizer has tried its best to keep manufacturing the product even though the company struggles to obtain foreign currency to import the ingredients.[21] The lack of U.S. dollars has also left Pfizer struggling to locate basic parts for its machinery. As a result, finding Atamel can be tricky. The unrealistically low price for Atamel tablets also makes them a target for bachaqueros. Venezuelan law dictates that each box of twenty Atamel five-hundred-milligram tablets must be sold by Farmatodo and other retail outlets for 5 bolivars, or less than 2 U.S. cents at the time, an almost impossibly low price. In the black market, the same box sells for 120 bolivars, more than twenty times its state-mandated price.

Atamel also offers a unique example of how controls have created wild distortions in the relative value of different products in the economy. At the regulated price, fifty boxes of Atamel cost slightly less than a Big Mac hamburger at a McDonald's in Venezuela.[22] It would be unheard of anywhere else in the world for acetaminophen medication to be that cheap. It is no wonder acetaminophen tablets have disappeared. It costs almost nothing for Venezuelans to purchase large amounts, keep some at home, and sell the rest in the black market or in Colombia, where they will fetch far more money. For my January 2015 trip to Caracas, I packed a suitcase with acetaminophen, bottles of shampoo, packets of coffee, and a couple of boxes of Splenda sweetener meant for friends desperate to get them. Venezuelans from nearly every socioeconomic background get by with the help of friends or family who travel and purchase these hard-to-find goods abroad.

Farmatodo began rationing the sale of price-controlled products in April 2015 by using the last number in customers' *cedula*, their state-provided ID —a practice the government first adopted in its state-owned food distribution chains three months earlier. Under this system, consumers are assigned a day in the week to purchase products with price controls like detergent and diapers. On Monday people with IDs ending in 0 and 1 can buy these goods. On Tuesday it's 2 and 3, and so on, all the way through 8 and 9 on Friday. On weekends people have the chance to purchase products again. Farmatodo's internal network alerts cashiers when consumers try to purchase the same product again at another location in the same week, and when this happens cashiers won't process the sale. No law in Venezuela forces retail outlets to implement this mechanism, but the government has urged retailers like

Farmatodo to adopt it as a way to slow the resale of products by bachaqueros, and most retailers have had no option but to comply. Having set dates for a purchase also helps reduce the long lines that the media have circulated around the world as proof of Venezuela's economic mismanagement.

Many Venezuelans believe the government has avoided codifying the rationing scheme in a law because doing so would turn the country into an oil-rich version of communist Cuba, a country famous for forcing its citizens to use a "supply booklet" that determines how much of a product the person can buy in a week or a month. Venezuela is not far off. Right next to the cash register area, I caught a glimpse of a Farmatodo chart that laid out how much of thirty-three items a consumer could purchase per week. "Our objective is to contribute with the supply of medicines and products for all of you," the chart read and then listed the products: four kilograms of rice, two kilograms of coffee, four of pasta, two of corn flour, three units of dental cream, two bottles of shampoo, two packs of diapers, three body soaps, twelve rolls of toilet paper, and so on. Retailers like Farmatodo are no longer in the business of offering options to consumers. They have been forced into the business of managing scarcity.

Rationing began in Venezuela in June 2013 in the crude-rich state of Zulia, which sits on the northwestern border with Colombia. Zulia's governor, Francisco Arias Cárdenas, a former army officer and a Chavista loyalist, began hearing of a recurring problem. Basic goods like rice and corn flour were disappearing from stores throughout the state, especially those closest to the border, because people were smuggling goods to Colombia.

In Venezuela, prices for several of the disappearing food items had been legally frozen for years, and given that the bolivar was constantly losing value against other currencies, these goods could be sold for far more money just across the border. The governor came up with an idea for an experiment: he would impose limits on the quantity of goods a consumer could buy, focusing on twenty key products, and he chose sixty-five supermarkets in and around the city of Maracaibo to conduct the trial. The measure appeared to slow the loss of products to smuggling, but it angered Venezuelans unaccustomed to limits on how much they could buy.

Arias defended the plan as a means to curtail smuggling. "We're not in

Cuba, we're in Maracaibo," the Associated Press quoted the governor as say-ing in defense of the measure.[23] Smuggling became such a good business that soon products began to disappear from stores in states farther away from the border. A year later, on returning from a trip to visit his ailing friend, Cuba's Fidel Castro, President Maduro decided to expand rationing to the rest of Venezuela. State-owned retail chains soon adopted fingerprint technology to track how much of a product each consumer bought.

When incidents of angry shoppers fighting for products made headlines, the military became a presence in stores to maintain order. When trucks, filled with consumer goods headed to stores, were diverted to the border, the government began tracking every shipment of diapers, shampoo, flour, or detergent from its origin to its destination. And when Venezuelans tried to skirt these rules by shipping bags of sugar and flour to friends and family using UPS and other carriers, the state banned packaged delivery service companies from shipping goods with price controls from one state or region to another.[24] In May 2015, Farmatodo adopted fingerprint technology in a handful of Caracas stores as well, a system the chain used, in addition to the last digit in people's IDs, to limit product purchases.

In 2015 executives at pharmacy chains like Farmatodo had unusual everyday worries. How long should the lines of customers get in a store before they become a problem? Should Farmatodo employees ask people to wait outside or line up around product aisles? Keeping too many people inside a store can be a fire hazard and makes it easier for desperate shoppers to ransack the place or to steal products while they wait in line. On the other hand, having people line up outside can anger the authorities eager to avoid any public displays of economic trouble. Also in May 2015 Venezuela's national guard began arresting those who took photos of people lining up outside stores, an attempt to clamp down on the media's focus on product shortages.

Should Farmatodo sell scarce products like sugar and detergent that can cause angry scuffles between desperate buyers? Selling such products often involves having military officers or government inspectors supervising long lines. Is all of this trouble worth the business? Can government authorities accuse Farmatodo of sabotaging the economy if it fails to carry a particular product line? If a store only receives a handful of bags of detergent, should employees place those on shelves immediately and risk customers' anger because not enough is being sold? On the other hand, keeping the few products in storage could expose the company to being accused of hoarding if government inspectors suddenly decided to visit the store.

Enrique, a Farmatodo executive, told me that the chain's headaches come from what he called "infinite demand" for price-controlled goods. "Demand is literally infinite," he said. "Demand for any product that offers a high margin for resellers in the black market will be infinite. So everyone wants the supply of those products to be infinite as well."[25] Farmatodo does not produce or import products. Its retail business depends on the local supplies of large producers like P & G, Kimberly-Clark, and Colgate Palmolive.

Nearly nine out of ten products the chain carries is subject to state-mandated price controls. This situation gives the chain a unique view of how price regulation affects people's purchasing habits. Enrique used an example to explain the hunger for these goods: If Farmatodo suddenly received one hundred truckloads of diapers to sell, consumers would buy those diapers in a day and want more. It doesn't matter whether stores sell far more detergent or diapers than ever before. Venezuelans will continue to buy and continue to resell these goods elsewhere, and a lot of these goods will end up in neighboring countries.

Normally, one six-pound bag of detergent should be enough to cover the laundry needs of any consumer for more than a month. No human being can possibly consume two 400-gram bottles of shampoo, a couple of 4-ounce sticks of deodorant, or two 171-gram tubes of toothpaste in seven days. The restrictions are really there to deter the business of bachaqueros. Farmatodo executives chose to adopt rationing controls when they noticed that the same customers would jump on motorcycles or even board buses and visit several stores at a time to buy boxloads of products. Merchandise would disappear in hours, leaving the stores with nothing.

But rationing is not really working. People will stand in lines several kilometers long and are willing to fight each other to get their hands on products they can resell and net 1,500 or 1,000 percent returns. To fight the issue, the government has taken to blaming retailers. In late January 2015 Venezuelan intelligence officers arrested the president and operations vice president of Farmatodo and charged them with "boycott and economic destabilization" for not having enough cash registers functioning in one of the chain's pharmacies.[26] The executives were held in jail for fifty-six days and given a conditional release that forced them to show up in court every fifteen days while the case continued.

Bachaqueros have become an object of study ever since their peculiar line of work emerged. And probably few people have studied the bachaquero phenomenon and the long lines outside stores as closely as Luis Vicente León, head of Datanalisis, Venezuela's leading polling firm. León has stark data at his fingertips. For instance, he found in early 2015 that nearly two-thirds of people standing in one line or another to buy regulated products were bachaqueros making a living from reselling these goods.[27]

Venezuelans have chosen to abandon their jobs in established companies to work as bachaqueros, especially if their formal jobs pay minimum-wage salaries, which a bachaquero can outearn with minimal work, standing in line for several hours and later selling shampoo or toilet tissue in the streets with a generous markup. León has seen some of his own field-workers and pollsters leave their jobs to become bachaqueros. As León sees it, price controls and the resulting bachaquero class "have built a system of economic redistribution from richer Venezuelans to the poor."

Product scarcity has also become an unusual form of forced social integration. Standing in line to enter a supermarket in a wealthy neighborhood, one can see people from all socioeconomic backgrounds mixed together, from very poor to upper-middle-class Venezuelans. Retail outlets that usually catered to the well-off now have a more diverse clientele because poor Venezuelans will go to any retailer to buy regulated products, even if it involves traveling long distances.

Those people who do not make a living as bachaqueros accumulate as much food and other products as they can at home. For instance León found that nearly 93 percent of stores lacked cooking oil, a basic food item, in early May 2015, but less than one-third of households did without the product. That means that the inventory sold by retail outlets that doesn't end up in other countries is stocked in people's cupboards. The same has happened with coffee, a product that was absent from the shelves of nearly 88 percent of stores. But only 29 percent of homes surveyed by León's Datanalisis reported having no coffee.

The government has tried all kinds of tactics to persuade Venezuelans not to buy more than they need. Tune in to any Venezuelan television channel in January 2015, and you would see government-funded ads featuring famous singers, soap opera actors, and television personalities with one message for shoppers: "Cool it with the nervous purchases." The government insisted there was no need to buy large amounts of a product. Consumers were supposed to trust the state to ensure the supply of goods.

Some officials even dismissed the desperation of Venezuelans. In a televised interview in January 2015, Colonel Yván José Bello Rojas, the country's minister of food, the man responsible for making sure the country had enough to eat, turned to gallows humor when a reporter asked him whether he ever stood in line to buy food, like most Venezuelans. "I've stood in line a lot. This week I went to a [baseball] game. I had to wait in line to get into the parking lot. Then I stood in line to buy my stadium ticket. And once I had my ticket I stood in line to go into the stadium. And you know what, once I was inside to find my seat I also stood in line,"[28] the minister said with a wry smile. His remarks incensed many Venezuelans, but neither Bello Rojas nor any other government official ever apologized for those remarks.

Food scarcity has become such a sensitive subject that in February 2014, the central bank stopped making available a product scarcity index that tracked what percentage of basic food staples was absent from stores. The last official measure was 26 percent in January 2014, which means that a quarter of these goods could not be found in retail outlets. León's Datanálisis now does the job the government refuses to do and tracks the scarcity of basic foods like cooking oil, margarine, and coffee on store shelves. León's scarcity index touched 57 percent during the first quarter of 2015, and he warned things would get much worse. León says Venezuela is a "primitive economy," an economic reality where people are not dying of hunger but production is almost impossible and there are no real jobs for most Venezuelans. In his view Venezuela has averted a social explosion because bachaqueros can make a living in the black market and consumers have accumulated plenty of food at home. "The day people's cupboards run out and they have nothing to eat, watch out," León told me.

To witness the Venezuelan tendency to stock up on goods I met Ramón Barrios, a sixty-eight-year-old retired policeman, who lives in a spartan home on a slope in the low-income barrio La Pastora. Barrios developed the habit of leaving his home with a folded plastic bag in his back pocket to carry the products he could find in the streets. "If there are people lining up somewhere I will get in line and buy whatever is for sale," if no ID number is required, Barrios told me. Barrios is what the Chavista government would define as a "nervous buyer," a hoarder of food. He opened his old wooden cupboards and allowed me to take out whatever I could find. Several minutes later, I had managed to dig out at least twenty-two pounds of white rice bags, another twenty pounds or so of sugar, roughly ten pounds of black beans, at least a dozen packs of pasta, fifteen pounds of corn flour, bottles of cooking oil, ketchup, mayonnaise: goods that were almost impossible to find and buy in large quantities anywhere. And far more than a retired man living alone would need.

Many of these products come from state-owned retailers and prominently feature government propaganda printed on the plastic packaging. Cartoons depict political scenes that show, for instance, the heroes—dark-skinned, poor Venezuelans—kicking capitalists, portrayed as a pink-skinned Satan wearing a suit. Barrios proudly said he accumulated his stash over a period of five months, but he admitted that his hoard was less than it used to be because he often helped his sons' families and friends with a few packets of rice, flour, or a bottle of cooking oil. "Some people are lazy and don't make an effort to stand in line and buy," Barrios said.

When it comes to basic food staples, Venezuelans from all walks of life have learned to make small everyday sacrifices. Pietro Pitts, a forty-five-year-old foreign correspondent for the financial news agency Bloomberg, is one of the lucky few in this country who gets paid in U.S. dollars. He is a U.S.-educated journalist who worked as a financial analyst before becoming a reporter. In theory he is part of a privileged group of people who can live comfortably in Venezuela. But Pitts couldn't find powdered milk anywhere—forget about the liquid kind, which is so rare in Venezuela that coffee shops and restaurants run out regularly. It is common for restaurant waiters to apologize to patrons for not serving several menu items because they ran out of milk to prepare a soup or sauce.

Over coffee, Pitts confessed he decided to give up cereal in the mornings so his four-year-old daughter could have the little milk that he and his wife managed to find. "She needs it more than I do," he said, and then quickly put things into perspective. "People are not starving in the streets, but food shortages have become a serious issue." The last time he saw large quantities of powdered milk was during a trip to Aruba with his wife and daughter in August 2014. He bought several cans and stacked them in his carry-on luggage to avoid the risk of having them stolen from his checked-in luggage by bag handlers in Venezuela's airport. Theft from checked luggage has become a constant problem in Venezuela, especially now that Venezuelan travelers return home loaded with food.

The extent to which food scarcity has hurt middle-class Venezuelans became apparent to me on a Saturday in May 2015 when I attended a late lunch hosted by Marvin and Adriana, two architect friends in their late thirties. The couple lives with their twin daughters in Valle Arriba, a hilly, middle-class area full of brand-new apartment complexes. A group of nearly twenty friends were there, a cross section of Venezuelan professionals including two civil engineers, a petroleum engineer, a company manager, and a public affairs executive. They were all eager to enjoy Marvin's specialty: Mexican-style "tacos al pastor," or tacos with pork marinated in hot pepper sauce, cooked over a gas flame and served with onions, cilantro, and pineapple. The meal was a form of potluck, with everyone bringing something to the table. I was told to bring a bottle of locally made rum. Not wine or whiskey, because these are imported products that have become prohibitively expensive for most Venezuelans.

Marvin's tacos were a hit, but the conversation took a turn, as it usually does in gatherings of Venezuelans, to what everyone had to do to get the meal's ingredients. Finding the pork alone became a task that stretched over several days during which Marvin visited several supermarkets. The pork he eventually found was pricey. The cooking oil he used was part of a stash one of his friends had painstakingly accumulated over multiple shopping trips. The stories gave me a unique appreciation for the tacos I was eating, not to mention the guilt and shame I felt when I realized I had probably eaten more tacos than anyone else at the table. "These days the worst thing someone can do to you is to ask you to stop by the supermarket and buy some tomatoes or get soda, because going shopping has become a time-wasting transaction and you endure long lines of people," Marvin said.

I got a taste of that myself when I tried buying the bottle of rum for Marvin's party. I almost gave up after visiting three supermarkets where large crowds waited for at least an hour to reach the cashier. There was no cash register reserved for small purchases where I could pay for the bottle. On my way to lunch, desperate not to show up empty-handed, I asked a cab driver to take me anywhere I could buy rum without having to stand in line. Stumped, the cab driver asked the radio dispatcher for a place to take me, and he finally drove me to an obscure storefront where I found a bottle.

León, the Venezuelan pollster, made another interesting discovery about Venezuela's food scarcity levels. The worst cases of food shortages appear to happen in state-owned retail outlets like Bicentenario. Government store chains sell the largest amount of price-regulated goods. I witnessed this when I visited a medium-sized Bicentenario supermarket in the Las Mercedes neighborhood, on the east side of Caracas, on a Saturday afternoon after the crowds had left.

The view was depressing. More than half of the supermarket's aisles lay empty, and so did the wall-to-wall cooler displays. A whole wall of coolers was taped up with black plastic trash bags because the store had nothing to put in them. The floors looked dirty and soiled, as if hundreds of customers had made their way through the supermarket and no one had bothered to sweep and scrub the floors afterward. In the pasta and grain aisles, loose grains of rice littered the shelves, where ripped bags were strewn everywhere. The produce section had a few carrots that looked rotten; a family of fruitflies hovered overhead.

In a corner of the supermarket where the deli should be lay an empty and broken-down cooler with a photo of Chávez prominently displayed on the wall above it and a sign that read, "Please place the chicken in the plastic bags." But there were no bags around and certainly no chicken. I discretely took some photos with my phone, worried that store employees might see me and kick me out. But such precautions were unnecessary—the handful of employees in the store milled around the cashier area, talking among themselves, oblivious to their customers. It struck me that this was the lowest standard of retail service that companies like Farmatodo were fighting hard to avoid.

I experienced firsthand the powerful logic behind becoming a bachaquero in Venezuela when my notebook ran out after my first two weeks of interviews. Any ruled notebook would have been enough to continue my work, but I happen to favor Moleskine notepads, and I thought it would be a nice experiment to see if I could find one in Venezuela. Moleskine is a fancy Italian brand of hardcover notebooks bound in coated paper (I favor black) with a waistband that holds the book closed. And they're not exactly cheap. A reporter-type notebook of 3.5 by 5.5 inches can cost US$13 in the United States. I reserve Moleskine notebooks to jot down only important facts and ideas, like those for my book research. After a few calls to local bookstores I found nothing, but one bookstore employee gave me an interesting tip. A local clothing store called Neutroni sold similar notebooks very cheaply.

I visited the store in the Sambil shopping mall in Caracas, one of the largest malls in the country, to examine the notepads. The Neutroni notebooks turned out to be a very well made Moleskine knockoff. They have a similar binding and elastic band, including a small inside pouch that comes in handy for storing business cards. Inside the binding a note reads, "Designed in Caracas. Assembled in China." The price was 120 bolivars per notebook, or 67 U.S. cents.

I purchased twenty notebooks, more than enough to cover my book-writing needs, for the same price as one Moleskine in the United States. As I left the store I felt the temptation to buy more, but I relented. Yet the purchase got me thinking. One could easily drive to all three Neutroni stores in Caracas, buy every single one of the notebooks in the store, fly out of Venezuela, and sell them for several times the price it cost to buy them. If there were an infinite supply of those notebooks, a person could continue to take advantage of the price differential, cover travel costs, and make some money. The notebooks were so cheap that they became good gifts for friends.

During a later trip to Caracas in May 2015, I paid Neutroni another visit, hoping to buy more notebooks to hand out to friends. But when I reached the store, there were no notebooks left. A salesperson told me he had no idea if and when Neutroni would get more, maybe never, because the government was not making dollars available to import them anymore. Maybe someone decided to become a notebook bachaquero, bought them all, and sold them abroad for more money or, more likely, another Moleskine lover thought the notepads were a steal and took them all. Whatever the reason, without intending it, I contributed to a product's extinction in Venezuela.

3   LET THERE BE OIL

Life changed in Venezuela on July 31, 1914, when a hole in the ground—443 feet deep—spewed a dark viscous liquid at a rate of more than 250 barrels a day. Venezuelans knew this was their first major oil discovery, but they didn't understand what this meant for their future. Oil and Venezuela were so new that things and places needed names. That oil well became known as Zumaque, from the indigenous word for a shrub that grew nearby in Venezuela's northwest. A hill next to the well became *Cerro Estrella*, or Hill of the Star, named after the Star Drilling Machine, an early steam-powered driller that companies first used to drill for oil. The discovery belonged to the Caribbean Oil Company, a branch of Shell, one of several wildcatters that tried their luck in the mosquito-infested jungles of Venezuela. The companies drilled holes deep underground in a search for oil deposits that had lain undisturbed since the Miocene epoch, 23 to 5.3 million years before—a time when the earth cooled into ice ages and when humans finally split from their great-ape forebears.

Venezuela in the early part of the twentieth century was a vast undeveloped land where most people got around on horseback or mule. Its population was mostly illiterate, and agriculture made up more than half of Venezuela's economic activity. The Andean country was ruled by an iron-fisted strongman, Juan Vicente Gómez, a man who understood how to seize an opportunity when one came along. As the country's vice president, Gómez took power by force in 1908 when the president, his boss, took a trip to Paris reportedly to seek treatment for a nasty case of syphilis. Gómez sported a signature Hungarian moustache and loved spending time in his large hacienda. He was a bachelor, but that didn't stop him from keeping two mistresses with whom he fathered sixteen children. By some counts he fathered as many as seventy-three with several more women; no one really knows for sure. There was no real government and no clear rule of law. Gómez was the state; he was the law; he was God. And Venezuela was his personal Eden.

Oil became a godsend for Gómez. World War I was under way, and the navies of world powers had converted from coal to oil as a source of fuel. The oil industry had begun in Pennsylvania some sixty years earlier, and oil was no longer used just to light kerosene lamps. Henry Ford had been producing his Model T for six years when the Zumaque oil well began production. Crude was a prized resource that brought Venezuela instant wealth and gave Gómez enough power to rule the country in one form or another for twenty-seven years. He allowed foreign companies to drill for oil, paying nothing in taxes and royalties, and they backed his dictatorship. He would first grant oil concessions to friends, family, and business cronies, who would later resell them to foreign companies for a profit. This racket afforded him many friends and allowed him to build an immense personal fortune. By the time he died peacefully in bed in 1935, Gómez had become one of Latin America's richest men. He owned vast tracts of land and controlled paper, soap, and cotton production, to name a few industries. At one point, every time a Venezuelan ate meat, drank milk or lit a match, Gómez would grow richer.

He had little patience for dissent. Opponents would disappear or be tortured and poisoned in prison, because dictatorship seemed necessary at the time. Venezuela had just overcome decades of wars between ragtag caudillos in the 1800s that resulted in the semblance of government Gómez took over. He was meant to be the caudillo of all caudillos. U.S. president Woodrow Wilson once famously called Gómez a scoundrel. And oil companies liked it that way. In fact, oil executives insisted that Venezuela's government under Gómez become a landlord and that Gómez dictate all matters related to oil in Venezuela. Since the early days of the oil business in the United States, private property law allowed individual landowners to own the mineral rights under the soil. It became a headache for oil companies to negotiate with each and every landlord to drill on their land. The companies fought against a similar private property law in Venezuela and won. In their thinking, keeping in one's pocket a pliant and well-fed dictator who had the last word on a country's oil concessions seemed like an easier way to do business.

Gómez created the country's first army to protect the central government's power. He empowered the treasury to collect all state revenues, paid off Venezuela's foreign debt, and stuffed the government with loyalists. But his most significant legacy became the petroleum law of 1922, a piece of legislation that oil companies and their lawyers had drawn up. The law allowed companies to exploit unlimited amounts of oil-rich land during long periods. When Gómez died, Venezuela was a rich oil enclave that was run more like the dictator's personal hacienda than a nation. Oil revenue supplied two-thirds of the state's income and made up more than 90 percent of the country's exports. In roughly twenty years, Venezuela had gone from an obscure agricultural backwater somewhere in the Andes to the world's largest oil exporter and the second-largest oil producer after the United States. Gómez left a lasting mark in Venezuelan politics too. As Venezuelan historian Elías Pino Iturrieta argued in his 1985 essay "Killing Gómez," a little bit of Gómez became ingrained in every generation of Venezuelan leaders and state bureaucrats that followed: "Every five years, with each new government, our life is determined by the rule of Gómez-like figures . . . who model themselves after him, holding power and distributing favors as [the dictator himself did] in the past."[1]

Oil wealth changed economic life for Venezuelans. It made it possible to build a network of roads that connected distant parts of the country for the very first time and to revamp the telegraph. Gómez created the country's first banks and gave Venezuelans a taste of what a wealthy dictatorship could do. During the 1920s state spending helped Gómez maintain his power by feeding layers of cronies beholden to his whims. The oil industry also paid very high wages to Venezuelans who, along with their forebears, had dedicated themselves to tending farms for several generations. Emerging was a new class of richer worker that earned more money than it knew how to spend. By 1930, as the world struggled with the Great Depression, Venezuelans began to experience an unusual phenomenon. The flood of oil revenue the country earned every year caused the bolivar to appreciate against the dollar.

To make matters worse, the United States had allowed the dollar to weaken against other currencies during the Great Depression. This made the bolivar one of the world's strongest currencies. In the early 1930s a dollar bought 7.75 bolivars, but by 1934 a dollar was worth less than half that amount. The bolivar appreciated nearly 70 percent during the 1930s. Venezuela had gotten lucky, enjoying enormous oil riches just as the rest of the world struggled with a global economic debacle.

A strong bolivar was hell for Venezuelan farmers of coffee and cocoa, the crops that were once the nation's top exports. Those businesses died as their products became too expensive for foreigners to buy. Manufacturing products in Venezuela became impossibly expensive. But a strong currency was very popular politically. It was a boon for Venezuelan consumers, who could suddenly afford to import what they used, wore, and ate every day. Imported goods and a taste of modernity became commonplace in this new oil fiefdom. And there was no turning back. Everything from business costs to product prices to worker's salaries suddenly depended on an overvalued bolivar. Rural landowners sold their unproductive lands and sought new fortunes in commerce, finance, and urban real estate speculation—everyone was headed to Caracas and other major cities anyway. Peasants sought work in oil fields, but most migrated to cities looking for a new way of life. The once rural nation quickly urbanized. Housing in Caracas became scarce, and prices for real estate in this poor country competed with housing in the world's famed metropolitan areas. Venezuela was experiencing the first pangs of what would become known as Dutch disease, the phenomenon that occurs when the success of one natural resource ruins the rest of a country's economy.

When U.S. president Franklin D. Roosevelt read in a State Department brief how expensive Caracas had become he thought officials were mistaken. In a June 1939 memo Roosevelt asked Harry Hopkins, one of the architects of the New Deal and one of his closest advisers, to double check the State Department's calculations. "Will you get for me a memorandum on the relative cost of living in Caracas, Venezuela, as compared to Washington D C—in terms of American dollars? The State Department tells me that for a given income of say $2,000 in Washington, the same person would have to be paid about $5,000 in American money in order to live in the same way in Caracas. I don't believe it," Roosevelt wrote. "In having this looked up, don't let the State Department know about this query."[2] The response came a week later from the Department of Commerce's Willard Thorp, one of the economists who designed the Marshall Plan. His six-page memo lays out in crude and unusually precise detail Venezuela's first experience with an economy overrun by oil wealth. "Caracas is one of the most expensive places in which to live in the world," the memo began. Thorp informed the president that due to an overvalued currency the cost of a single room, with a shared bathroom, including meals cost $1,740 a year in Caracas, while a survey of the cost of living for U.S. federal employees showed that housing and meals cost $690 a year in Washington DC. "There is a housing shortage at the present time and many Americans are obliged to wait from two to three months to find a suitable home" in the South American city, Thorpe wrote.

That was not all. Water was unsafe to drink and had to be boiled daily. Renters had to pay the additional expense of installing electrical fixtures in Caracas homes because owners rarely did. "Toilet articles, soaps, medicines, and pharmaceuticals cost from 75 to 200 per cent more than in the United States," Thorpe added. "Automobiles, an essential in Caracas, cost from 90 to 110 per cent above the list price in the United States." Clothes for women were also imported and sold for as much as a 200 percent markup compared with U.S. clothing stores. Getting a suit tailored cost seventy dollars in Caracas but, Thorp warned, "the sewing is poor." The most damning item in Thorp's memo had to do with Venezuelans' work ethic: "Servants' wages are lower than in the United States, but they are much less efficient and will do only one kind of work." Life in Caracas resembled that of an expensive and remote mining camp. And living in that mining camp had become pricier than living just blocks away from the White House.

* * *

Venezuela's days of economic plenty did not last. World War II disrupted global trade and in doing so pushed the import-dependent nation into economic disarray, plagued by product shortages. Venezuela quickly went from a nation with enough purchasing power to import fine wines to a place where people struggled to find car tires.[3] Venezuelan president Isaías Medina Angarita, a former minister of defense who had cultivated a reputation for fascist sympathies—some believed he was a fan of Il Duce—responded the only way he knew how: he set price limits for transportation services and everyday consumer goods. Business leaders didn't like it, but it was too late. Strong government intervention into economic affairs had arrived, and there was little the private sector could do. The state already ran banks, meat packers, even the soap production it had seized from the Gómez family and its cronies. Gómez's beloved hacienda, La Placera, ended up in state hands—decades later it would become the home of Venezuela's mint, charged with printing the country's currency. The government's role as entrepreneur began almost by accident, by the need to confiscate the ill-gotten wealth of a dead dictator. State ownership of these businesses seemed like the only way to ensure everyone benefited from Gómez's grand larceny.

People were calling for more state intervention anyway. Arturo Uslar Pietri, one of the nation's best-known intellectuals, had captured the popular imagination a few years earlier with his essay "Sembrar el Petróleo" (Sowing the oil) in a local newspaper.[4] In it Uslar Pietri warned Venezuelans of the corrupting power of oil riches that could easily turn the country into a "petroleum parasite." It behooved Venezuelans to invest the wealth that flowed from crude to become productive, to stimulate agriculture and build new infrastructure. He believed the way to do that was through state intervention. In subsequent writings Uslar Pietri argued that without a heavy state hand, Venezuela would become a "vast petroleum camp, populated by petroleum workers, bureaucrats, lawyers, doctors, and importers and the day that petroleum disappears we would find ourselves . . . in the situation of dying of hunger, in a desert planted with skeletons of cars, of old refrigerators and boxes of oatmeal strewn about."[5] It didn't seem possible to Uslar or anyone else that oil would last for generations and that the same catastrophic scenario could play out with the government firmly in control.

Medina's government was now in a position to fix a major wrong. Oil companies controlled a number of irregular concessions issued by the late Gómez. Foreign oil firms had grown accustomed to drilling wells and pumping oil without encumbrance by the state. But Venezuela's increasingly empowered citizens demanded better education, health, and other public services. Venezuela began talks with oil companies about finding a better way to divvy the wealth obtained from crude production. Venezuelans naturally wanted to get more money from their oil. Medina wrote a letter to Roosevelt seeking help in persuading oil companies to accept less favorable tax terms. Roosevelt obliged. U.S. administration officials even helped the Venezuelans find consultants that could aid the government in the negotiations with oil companies.[6]

Oil had raised the country's profile on the world stage. Venezuela became a key supplier of the oil that fueled the Allied effort during World War II, so much so that at one point German U-boats and Italian submarines were dispatched to the Caribbean to disrupt the energy supply of their enemies by torpedoing tankers carrying Venezuelan crude. More important, Mexico had nationalized its oil industry in 1938, and Roosevelt didn't want the same thing to happen in Venezuela. When executives at Standard Oil, the company founded by John D. Rockefeller, felt like opposing Venezuela's intentions, U.S. officials told the company not to expect any help from Washington in a dispute with the oil-rich nation.[7] Oil executives knew Venezuela was too important an oil patch to abandon, so they complied. It was the cost of doing business. Plus, oil companies had originally insisted on making the state the sole authority on oil affairs in Venezuela in the first place.

In 1943 Venezuela passed a new oil law that enshrined a historic, precedent-setting accord, known as the fifty-fifty principle, with oil companies. Under the new terms, Venezuela would earn the same amount of money as the companies' net profits through royalties as well as imposing income and other taxes on oil production. The law also forced companies to build gasoline refineries in Venezuela. The idea behind the deal was to make the state and the companies equal partners in the business. It helped that oil companies could discount the taxes they paid in Venezuela from those they owed the U.S. government, under double taxation rules.[8]

Companies gained something far more important too. The deal legitimized the illegal oil concessions companies obtained during the Gómez days, and it extended their validity by forty years.[9] Not all Venezuelans, however, were convinced this law was a good thing. A young firebrand lawmaker by the name of Juan Pablo Pérez Alfonzo, who would later become one of the biggest headaches for global oil companies, argued that the agreement was too lenient because it allowed companies to keep the riches they accumulated under Gómez. Still, the fifty-fifty deal became an important milestone in Venezuela's oil history. It taught Venezuelans that from that point on they could bargain with oil companies and tax them more heavily when the need arose. After all, it was easier politically to tax foreign companies than to impose higher taxes on Venezuelans. As scholar Terry Lynn Karl put it in her book *The Paradox of Plenty*, Venezuela had effectively become a petro-state.[10]

. The Medina years ended badly. In 1945 a group of disaffected officers, who believed the military was underpaid and ill-equipped, ousted Medina and kicked him out of the country. A revolutionary junta took over, a caretaker civilian government run by Rómulo Betancourt, a pipe-smoking lawyer and political leader of the social-democrat Acción Democrática party. The junta was not kind to the ousted Medina. It accused the former president of paying nearly US$7 million in bribes to politicians and journalists and even claimed to have found a photograph of Medina cavorting with naked prostitutes that was "too obscene for publication."[11]

The new government appointed Pérez Alfonzo, the lawmaker who so virulently opposed the fifty-fifty agreement, as the new development minister. Pérez Alfonzo, a slender man who in later years sported a clean-shaved head, was an unusually steely politician. He hailed from a well-off family that had initially financed his medical studies at Johns Hopkins University, but he cut his studies short when his family ran into financial difficulties. On his return to Caracas he became responsible for his ten siblings and, through much hardship, studied law instead. Life had taught Pérez Alfonzo to be exacting and frugal; by some accounts he was almost monastic. From his new perch Pérez Alfonzo argued that the fifty-fifty deal did not really give Venezuela half the profits from oil, and he set about levying new taxes on oil companies to fix that. That was not all Pérez Alfonzo wanted. He pushed for Venezuela to share in the profits oil companies derived from the refining, transportation, and sale of fuel as well. A shrewd Pérez Alfonzo realized that it was cheaper for oil companies to produce oil in the Middle East than in Venezuela. To address that, a delegation of Venezuelan officials traveled all over the Middle East with copies of Venezuela's fifty-fifty agreement translated into Arabic, promoting its adoption. Soon Saudi Arabia forced similar terms on foreign oil companies, thanks to Pérez Alfonzo's efforts. Venezuela's fifty-fifty arrangement had become the norm in the oil world.

As oil revenue thrived, Venezuelans demanded new entitlements. The new government decreed the reduction of domestic gasoline prices in 1945 and forced refiners and fuel distributors to absorb the cost.[12] The government also sacrificed revenue by cutting taxes on gasoline to make it more affordable. In the next four years, gasoline in Venezuela would become the cheapest in the world.[13] Venezuela also adopted universal suffrage, and in 1947 its citizens chose their first ever democratically elected leader, Rómulo Gallegos, a famed novelist. Gallegos kept Pérez Alfonzo in place and continued to tighten terms on oil companies. His mandate ended, however, in just eight months with another military coup orchestrated by the same officers who had ousted Medina just three years earlier. The overthrow became known as the "telephone coup," because Gallegos was notified by phone that the military had taken control of the presidential palace. The military was becoming an emboldened, unwieldy institution that like most Venezuelans, had learned to expect generous benefits from an oil-rich government.[14] But unlike most Venezuelans, the military had the guns to back up its claim on more power. Democracy was still not quite within Venezuela's reach.

The coup leaders persecuted members of Gallegos's administration and forced Acción Democrática politicians into hiding. Pérez Alfonzo was thrown in jail, where he spent several months, sometimes in solitary confinement. He was later exiled and took up residence with his family in Washington DC, where he scraped together an existence by renting his Caracas home and became a regular reader at the Library of Congress. Venezuela and the world had not seen the last of Pérez Alfonzo.

* * *

A military junta ruled Venezuela, but General Marcos Pérez Jiménez eventually emerged as the real power behind it all. Pérez Jiménez was a pudgy and stout thirty-six-year-old with a taste for pomp and grandiosity who became popularly known by Americans living in Venezuela as "PJ."[15] He rigged the results of the 1952 general elections—which he had lost—by reportedly calling for "a more correct count" and proclaimed himself Venezuela's president.[16] Not surprising, the dictator believed strongly that Venezuela was not ready for democracy.[17] When Pérez Jiménez took power, Venezuela enjoyed unprecedented wealth. World demand for oil had skyrocketed during the postwar economic boom. Geopolitical conflicts in the Middle East pushed oil prices higher. Iran's nationalization of the oil industry in 1951 and the overthrow of that country's Mohammad Mossaddegh two years later, as well as the closing of the Suez Canal by Egypt's Gamal Abdel Nasser, sent a torrent of petrodollars pouring into Venezuela. During the seven years through 1957—spanning most of Pérez Jiménez's time in office—no other country accumulated as much foreign currency as Venezuela other than West Germany, which had reaped the benefits of the U.S.-funded Marshall Plan.[18]

Foreign investment in Venezuela tripled during the strongman's regime.[19] Companies were free to invest, profit, and repatriate their money in hard currency with no regulatory hassles. The government extended loans to industry and agriculture, but Venezuelan business leaders favored simpler businesses, such as the retail industry, the construction business, or just importing goods from abroad. In 1953 *Time* magazine quoted a local banker as saying, "You have the freedom here to do what you want to do with your money, and to me that is worth all the political freedom in the world."[20] The golden rule seemed to be: Do business freely but don't mess with PJ. The communist party was outlawed, and so were worker strikes. Other opponents were killed, persecuted, or jailed under the orders of Pedro Estrada, Pérez Jiménez's chief of national security and head spook. Estrada's henchmen were known to interrogate the dictator's enemies by forcing them to strip naked and sit on blocks of ice for hours on end.[21]

The flow of petrodollars sustained a dizzying cost of living. An American earning US$1,000 a month (or US$9,000 in 2015 dollars) could barely get by.[22] A lowly cook's wage was estimated at US$10.50 a day (US$94 a day in 2015).[23] Ridiculously low income taxes had become another gift to Venezuelans courtesy of a nation that earned most of its income from oil. The maximum tax rate was 28 percent, but it applied only if and when someone's earnings reached the equivalent of US$8.4 million a year.[24] By some accounts, someone earning the equivalent of US$60,000 would pay as little as US$1,800 a year in taxes, a 3 percent tax rate.[25] The same applied to the oil business. Unlike his predecessors, Pérez Jiménez did not raise taxes on oil companies, choosing to increase oil output instead. A lack of oil industry oversight even allowed companies to declare less oil than the amount they really pumped and sold abroad.[26] To obtain more money, Pérez Jiménez eventually opted for the sale of more concessions to companies eager to expand their holdings of oil-rich real estate. It was a giant reversal from the days of the 1943 oil law that had stopped issuing new concessions.

Pérez Jiménez had grand ambitions. Venezuela's oil affluence made it seem as if the country could simply buy its way into becoming a modern nation. The despot was inordinately concerned with changing the face of Venezuela, and in a way he did. He renamed the country "Republic of Venezuela," from the previous "United States of Venezuela": he created new state-owned companies in the mining, steel, aluminum, and petrochemical industries, and he embarked on a massive public works program that included schools, hospitals, and low-income housing but favored freeways and luxury hotels. Everything was meant to look modern, imposing, and sleek to impress foreign visitors.

In late 1953 Pérez Jiménez held court at the inauguration of the Hotel Tamanaco in Caracas, a white-tie party where roughly two thousand guests reportedly sipped whiskey and champagne and dined on sixty-five hundred pounds of beef and fowl.[27] The total bill for the party alone was estimated at US$75,000 (equivalent to more than US$670,000 in 2015). The hotel itself had cost US$8.5 million to build (or US$76 million in 2015 dollars). Pérez Jiménez built roads and freeways and cut the ribbon on a 10.5-mile roadway that connected Caracas with its airport by the coast in La Guaira, complete with several viaducts, one of which was nine hundred meters long, and tunnels that cut through the mountains. The freeway was considered an engineering marvel at the time and reportedly cost US$5.6 million per mile to build (US$53 million per mile in 2015). *Popular Mechanics* once called it "the costliest freeway in the world."[28] After it was finished, Pérez Jiménez was known to drive his Mercedes-Benz two-seater sports car down the roadway. But his pet project became the Hotel Humboldt, a nineteen-story glass tower perched atop the Ávila, a mountain that flanks Caracas—more than two thousand meters above sea level. The hotel boasted an ice rink, and visitors could reach it only by riding an aerial lift with a scenic view of the city. The hotel was very unsuccessful commercially. It opened and closed its doors repeatedly over the years and is considered a costly white elephant.

The military also benefited handsomely under Pérez Jiménez. He built a brand-new military club, complete with marble floors, fifty guest rooms, a movie theater that seated 450 people, two pools, a gymnasium, Tiffany clocks—the list of features goes on.[29] The grandeur of the place symbolized the rising importance of the military in Venezuela's power structure. Those involved in the country's construction boom created overnight fortunes not least because government contracts involved large kickbacks, bribes, and other schemes.[30] Venezuela's transformation attracted hundreds of thousands of immigrants from Italy, Austria, France, Spain, and Portugal who sought a better life away from war-ravaged Europe. And Pérez Jiménez welcomed them because he believed most Venezuelans were a backward, uneducated people and the country would benefit from an influx of educated Europeans. Venezuela's economy could absorb so much cash and so many people because there was so much to do, so much to build. Venezuela was the place to be.

It all came tumbling down soon enough. Pérez Jiménez's pharaonic projects became costly and inefficient, and his administration was wasteful and corrupt. He eventually cut down on corporate subsidies, which angered the business class, and reduced social spending, which didn't help his popularity with low-income and middle-class Venezuelans. Poverty in rural areas was high, and so was inequality. In his last year in office the top 2 percent of Venezuelan society controlled half of the country's national income.[31] When in 1957 the dictator set in motion plans to remain in power indefinitely, it became too much for his enemies to bear. But public discontent was not enough to oust him. The end came only when the military—unhappy with a lack of promotions and access to power—turned on him.[32] All it took was a conversation, no need for guns and blood. In late January 1958, when his closest military aides asked him to leave, Pérez Jiménez and his family packed their bags and at 3 a.m. boarded a plane headed for the Dominican Republic. The departure was so sudden that on boarding they left behind a suitcase with US$2 million in cash.[33]

* * *

Those who had been jailed, exiled, and persecuted by Pérez Jiménez were left to pick up the pieces. The political parties that Pérez Jiménez had banned dusted themselves off and prepared for a new election. The big task ahead was guiding Venezuelans, who had known practically nothing other than dictatorship for generations, to embrace and respect democracy.[34] After all, the military, oil companies, the rich, and competing parties could derail a democratic effort if they believed they were not getting their due share of power and oil wealth.[35] The new political leaders also had to contend with a population that was accustomed to the grandeur of the Pérez Jiménez years. The question of how best to turn oil riches into sustainable economic development and a stable economy, less dependent on oil, was not paramount in people's minds. The enjoyment of cheap gasoline, low taxes, and an over-valued bolivar that made it easy for people to buy imported goods instead of locally produced ones, was taken for granted. And so was a government that doled out juicy contracts and other subsidies.

The key issue at hand for a nation accustomed to strongmen and recurring coups, was how to ensure political stability. The answer came in the form of a pact, known as the Pacto de Punto Fijo. The political agreement was struck between the country's three major parties, the social democratic Acción Democrática, the Christian democratic Independent Political Organization Committee, COPEI, and the left-of-center Republican Democratic Union, URD. Under the deal, the parties agreed to respect electoral results, distribute cabinet posts in a new administration equally among them, and to follow similar, business-friendly economic policies. The communist party was excluded because the world was already well into the Cold War. Excluding the communists would reassure the business sector and the United States that Venezuela's political establishment could be trusted. Years later that decision would come to haunt Venezuelan politics. The bigger problem, not evident at the time, was that the pact turned political parties into the gateway to government favors and oil riches.[36] The country's brand of democracy consisted of giving everyone a large enough share of oil riches to keep the peace. Oil was more important than democratic principles. Venezuela's political establishment was making the country ever more dependent on crude.

In December 1958, Venezuelans elected as their president Rómulo Betancourt, the pipe-smoking leader who had headed the civilian junta in the late 1940s that paved the way for the country's first and failed try at democracy. Betancourt had originally empowered Juan Pablo Pérez Alfonzo to ensure that Venezuela was getting its fair share of crude wealth by raising taxes on oil companies. He wasted no time in calling Pérez Alfonzo, who was then living in Mexico, and offered him the newly created post of oil minister. Soon after his return, Pérez Alfonzo was painfully reminded of what oil had done to Venezuela's work ethic. He awaited the shipment of his beloved 1950 Singer Roadster, a gift he had managed to give himself while still living abroad. The delivery was taking longer than expected. When he finally got a call about his car, the Singer had been sitting in a warehouse for two months. Pérez Alfonzo sent a mechanic to retrieve the car, but then it broke down on the way to Caracas. Unable to fix the problem, the mechanic arranged for the car to be towed to Pérez Alfonzo's home. The issue was simple: the engine had no oil, and the mechanic didn't think to check before driving it. Pérez Alfonzo's prized convertible was now a useless chunk of metal. The oil minister had the car installed in his garden as a reminder of how oil could foster a culture of neglect and waste.

Later in life, he famously called oil "the Devil's Excrement." "Ten years from now, twenty years from now, you will see. Oil will bring us ruin," he warned.[37] He understood how toxic mismanaged oil riches could be to a country, but he also believed that Venezuelans, not foreign oil companies, should control their oil and have a final say on how their industry was run. Pérez Alfonzo had wasted no time during his years in exile. He had studied the oil business closely for many hours at the Library of Congress, and he wanted Venezuela to control the production and sale of its crude. At the time, the Seven Sisters, the most powerful oil companies in the world, which included the Anglo-Persian Oil Company (which would become BP), Royal Dutch Shell, Standard Oil of New Jersey (later Exxon), and Texaco (Chevron), dominated more than 80 percent of the world's crude reserves. They largely decided among themselves how much oil to produce, how to produce it, where to ship it, and at what prices to sell it. They could set oil prices low and hurt the revenues of oil-rich countries. The countries that actually owned the oil had no say in the matter.

Making matters worse, the United States had decided to restrict imports of oil from Venezuela, while favoring Canadian and Mexican crude. Pérez Alfonzo sold Saudi Arabia, Kuwait, Iran, and Iraq the idea of a secret gentlemen's agreement to defend oil prices, create state-owned oil companies, and turn the fifty-fifty agreement into at sixty-forty split in favor of their governments.[38] When in 1960 oil companies decided to steeply reduce the prices paid for crude, Pérez Alfonzo and his Arab counterparts were ready. Pérez Alfonzo flew to Baghdad, where he met representatives from Saudi Arabia, Kuwait, Iraq, and Iran and signed the agreement to create the Organization of the Petroleum Exporting Countries, OPEC. From that point on oil companies would have to consult with exporter countries before setting oil prices. Pérez Alfonzo and Venezuela had just helped created the world's first cartel of oil exporters.

Back in Venezuela, Betancourt was riding a wave of economic growth of 5 percent per year, on average, during his mandate that lasted through the 1960s.[39] Skyscrapers and apartment buildings mushroomed in Caracas, and so did the tin-roofed homes of the poor on the hillsides flanking the city. The country's per capita income was the highest in Latin America, and the bolivar remained one of the world's strongest currencies. People continued to migrate from farms to cities, leaving Venezuelan agriculture in such a decline that the government was forced to import staples such as wheat, corn, rice, and even eggs.[40]

The communists who were excluded from Venezuela's pacted democracy and who felt alienated by the bonanza took up arms against the government, even receiving training by Fidel Castro in Cuba. They kidnapped cargo ships and soccer stars, and sabotaged the pipelines of an oil sector that by 1963 churned out 3.5 million barrels of oil a day, in spite of these attacks.[41] Gun-toting guerrillas didn't dissuade French fashion house Balmain and jeweler Cartier from opening glitzy Caracas boutiques, catering to a growing middle class, because in this country oil money flowed like water.[42] Caracas had such a chic and exotic reputation that it was mentioned in the classic 1963 James Bond film *Goldfinger* as the location of one of the gold-smelting plants belonging to the evil character Auric Goldfinger, a gold bullion and jewel dealer. In what would later become the norm, companies continued to invest in Venezuela because profits were easy, even in the face of political distress. By 1963, Sears Roebuck had eleven stores in Venezuela, each of which was bombed by guerrillas. Insurgents even burned down a US$2 million Sears warehouse. Sears became an icon of the capitalism the guerrillas wanted to eradicate. The problem became so big that the government perched soldiers atop steel towers outside Sears stores. But business boomed nonetheless. That same year, Sears' same-store sales in Venezuela were up as much as 30 percent from the prior year. The company was rebuilding the warehouse insurgents burned down, was opening a twelfth store, and had struck deals to manufacture furniture and stoves in Venezuela.

Manufacturing, a sector that benefited from subsidies and was protected by tariffs, was expanding at a clip of 7 percent annually.[43] Manufacturing accounted for nearly a quarter of all jobs in Venezuela through the mid-1970s.[44] Still, the Venezuelan economy—with a fractured agriculture sector—was not diverse and strong enough to employ most people, so the government's social spending provided subsidized services and jobs to middle- and low-income Venezuelans.[45] Spending on education, health, water, and sanitation, among other benefits, which totaled roughly 5.3 percent of government spending under Gómez's dictatorship, rose almost sixfold, to 31.4 percent of state spending by the early 1970s.[46] That level of spending was becoming counterproductive. During the five years ending in 1970, Venezuela was spending more on health per Venezuelan than many other developing nations. Yet infant mortality rose, and life expectancy worsened. Researcher Arnoldo Gabaldón called it "one of the strangest phenomena in the history of health. The more money is spent, the less progress is obtained."[47] Despite such problems, persuading Venezuelans to join a leftist cause was hard because oil riches appeared to give them plenty of purchasing power. The job of defending the government against the guerrillas kept the Venezuelan military busy enough not to focus on ways to overturn governments. When Betancourt handed over power to his successor, it became the first democratic handover in Venezuela's 133 years as a republic. Sixteen of the twenty-three previous presidents had been generals.[48]

Pacted democracy stabilized politics but also concentrated all power in the presidency. If democracy taught Venezuelans that cozying up to the main political parties was the way to access oil riches, they quickly learned that the president had the ultimate power to distribute favors and decide how oil money was spent. This concentration of power made sense to Venezuelans who had learned to follow the dictates of strongmen. Venezuela's oil-rich government could survive without taxing its citizens so it was no longer beholden to them. Oil largely did away with political accountability. Oil money purchased voter support, and in turn, citizens learned to lobby, cajole, and beg their government for a living.

* * *

Venezuela was unprepared for what occurred in October 1973. Arab oil producers declared an embargo of crude shipped to Western nations in retaliation for their support of Israel in the Yom Kippur War. The embargo, which lasted five months, pushed oil prices to highs never seen before. By the end of 1974 the price Venezuela received for its oil had risen 260 percent to US$14 per barrel in just twelve months.[49] The wave of petrodollars would triple the money Venezuela earned from oil to US$10 billion a year. Former oil minister and OPEC founder Juan Pablo Pérez Alfonzo was deeply troubled by what he saw. "The US$10 billion will crush us," he warned. "We have a president with a mountain of gold to dispense. Everyone will be thinking how to put his hand in the bag."[50] He seemed to understand what most Venezuelans couldn't grasp or simply didn't want to accept. The flow of dollars from oil was too much for Venezuela's small economy to absorb. It caused a form of economic indigestion. Industries were ruined, inefficiency ruled, and money was wasted.

Governments thought it was just a matter of getting the right people in power to spend the money more effectively, but that was an illusion, a myth, Pérez Alfonzo argued. "We're going in reverse, the more we spend," he wrote.[51] He favored cutting oil output and moderating state spending to give the country time to absorb so much wealth. Venezuela did ease oil output a bit, but Pérez Alfonzo's dire warnings went largely unheeded. The newly elected president Carlos Andrés Pérez asked congress for special powers to issue laws by decree to better handle the avalanche of money. Venezuela was in a state of emergency because it had too much cash. For the first time in the country's history Venezuelans were worried that so much money floating around would cause prices to spike for every product and service, leading to unmanageable levels of inflation.[52]

Pérez vowed to administer "abundance with a mentality of scarcity," but that promise didn't really go anywhere.[53] He had a grandiose vision of creating "La Gran Venezuela," the Great Venezuela. If Venezuela's last dictator, Marcos Pérez Jiménez, once thought the country could buy its way to modernity with petrodollars, Pérez believed he could purchase economic development just as easily and quickly. He decreed higher wages and salaries; he funded social services and pushed the government to create jobs in any way possible. In one egregious example of desperation to use cash, Pérez decreed that every elevator in government buildings would be manned by elevator operators, and he put bathroom attendants in all public restrooms.[54]

Under Pérez, money sloshing around Venezuela grew at three times the rate at which the country's economy expanded.[55] Venezuela couldn't absorb so much cash, so prices for everything increased. Inflation during Pérez's first year in office doubled to 11.6 percent. Hoping to fix the problem, Pérez decreed price controls for a host of goods with the aim of making them affordable to the poor. Inflation was so high in those days that Venezuelans suddenly realized in 1974 that for the first time the money they kept in bank accounts lost value. Inflation turned out to be higher than the rate banks paid customers for their savings. In some years, inflation was higher than the rate banks were allowed to charge customers for loans, a great incentive to borrow and spend money.[56]

If spending money made more sense than saving it, Venezuelans wasted no time in developing a taste for the finer things in life. The country became known for having the best French, Italian, Spanish, and Middle Eastern restaurants in Latin America, many of them run by famed chefs. Venezuela became one of the largest importers of premium alcohol, like whiskey and champagne, as well as luxury vehicles, like the Cadillac El Dorado.[57] Caracas became such a chic destination that Air France's Concorde supersonic jet opened a Paris–Caracas flight in 1976. "Paris–Caracas by Concorde. The easiest six hours you've ever flown," read an Air France ad that was widely reproduced in glossy magazines at the time.[58] That same year, the per capita income of Venezuelans rivaled that of West Germany.[59] In 1970 middle-class Venezuelans already amounted to 58 percent of the population.[60] Venezuelans quickly became known as "Saudi Venezuelans" for their apparently endless capacity to consume.

Pérez created the Venezuelan Investment Fund—the first such fund meant to save oil revenue—with the aim of preventing too much money from entering Venezuela. It was meant to save half the country's oil revenue, but the fund never received as much. Instead of saving oil money for times of low oil prices, the fund quickly became a petty cash fund the president used to lend money to friendly nations in Latin America and to spend as he pleased. Pérez doubled the state's payroll to more than three hundred thousand employees in five years.[61] He also passed a law banning unjustified firing of workers by companies who felt squeezed by the president's wage hikes. Venezuela's most powerful companies learned to depend on subsidies, low taxes, and cheap government loans to make them stronger. By 1975 less than 9 percent of the country's companies accounted for more three-quarters of the value of goods made in Venezuela.[62]

The president sank gobs of money into the mining and steel industries; he moved to nationalize the oil sector as well. The country had already passed laws in the early 1970s to take control of how oil was priced, explored, and marketed, just as OPEC founder Pérez Alfonzo had wanted. President Pérez also charged foreign oil companies for unpaid taxes and put an end date of 1983 to most oil concessions, after which oil fields would pass back to state hands. In light of this, oil companies ceased investing in a business they would soon lose anyway. By 1970, Venezuela—not foreign oil companies—retained 78 percent of oil business profits.[63] So when the country seized the assets of foreign companies in 1976, Venezuela finally took full control of its golden goose.

* * *

In the 1980s Venezuela became a mess. A global oil glut caused by less demand for crude prompted the price of Venezuelan oil to fall by more than half to US$14 a barrel in the eight years through 1988.[64] Since Venezuelans had grown accustomed to generous governments, politicians continued to spend even in the face of less money coming in. Venezuelans couldn't help themselves. They had learned to enjoy decades of steadily rising oil wealth and never really gave much thought to what would happen if oil prices ever dropped. The crisis fell on the lap of president Luis Herrera Campins, a former journalist, who was later remembered for leaving office without having enriched himself. He was a pudgy man who cut a rather monochrome figure—he was always seen wearing a black suit and tie.[65] Campins was far from frugal while in office, however. To allow more spending he quadrupled the country's debts with foreign and local banks.[66] And when that was not enough, he raided the coffers of state oil company Petróleos de Venezuela (PDVSA) and took nearly US$6 billion the company had set aside to invest in the business. Since its creation in 1976, PDVSA had managed to remain independent from politics and had grown to become Latin America's largest company.[67]

With fewer dollars flowing into Venezuela, Campins also ordered the bolivar's biggest devaluation against the U.S. dollar on February 18, 1983, "Black Friday." That same year, oil-rich Venezuela had its first taste of currency dysfunction. Venezuelans with savings to protect nervously exchanged their bolivars into any hard currency. Campins responded by imposing capital controls—in essence prohibiting people from exchanging their bolivars into dollars for the first time in the country's history. He created Recadi and charged it with controlling the sale of scarce dollars at two exchange rates, 4.3 and 6 bolivars per dollar. To save foreign exchange, he banned the importation of perfume and lingerie, even alcoholic drinks.

Venezuelans were unprepared for the sacrifice to come. They had become accustomed to a life of plenty. Most felt no need to create new things, to innovate, or even to produce most of what they consumed. People aspired to government jobs that allowed them a comfortable life with minimal effort. Campins realized this was a problem. And he launched a campaign to prepare Venezuelans for tougher times and to inspire them to become more productive. Posters plastered around Caracas in 1983 that proclaimed, "This is no way to build a nation. . . . Combat laziness," were meant to encourage a change in Venezuelans' carefree lifestyles.[68] It was a unique moment for the country, especially for Venezuelans who just a decade earlier had become accustomed to drinking scotch and purchasing any imported product they felt like buying.

Venezuelans who had grown used to lobbying politicians for their share of oil riches pressed Recadi just as hard to get dollars. They needed dollars to buy imported goods, to travel, to pay for food, and to purchase the raw materials factories needed to produce. The country had grown dependent on the rest of the world to feed itself. Recadi became racked with corruption under the mandate of pediatrician Jaime Lusinchi, who took power in 1984 and who became infamous for giving his personal secretary and mistress a say in key political decisions, including cabinet appointments. Venezuelans began buying cheap dollars from Recadi to pay for phantom imports and instead selling the currency in a thriving black market for several times more bolivars. Few Venezuelans realized this racket would become a new profession decades later. Venezuelans were experiencing the topsy-turvy reality that came with depending entirely on oil windfalls without saving for the future.

In early 1989, for the first time in Venezuela's history, economic troubles took a bloody turn. Venezuelans fed up with a broken economy took to the streets in violent protests that left hundreds dead. It all happened a few weeks after Venezuelans, desperate for a solution to the country's economic problems, elected Carlos Andrés Pérez once again to run the country. Voters reasoned that surely the man who had led the nation during its richest period would know how to solve things in its darker days. Most Venezuelans didn't yet understand that Pérez's fantastic spending spree and his decision to run through the country's savings fund in times of plenty was largely responsible for the mess they were experiencing. Things looked dire. Inflation had topped 35 percent in 1988, mostly because of the rising prices for basic consumer goods that became increasingly tricky to find.[69]

Venezuela lacked enough cash to pay for food imports. Campins had imposed price controls on a host of goods to control runaway prices, but this only squeezed manufacturers, who in some cases lost money.[70] Inflation in the late 1980s had also made it uneconomic once again for Venezuelans to save money in bank accounts. In 1989, products like bread, toilet paper, and soap, even sugar, flour, and milk, disappeared from stores and reappeared in a black market. Some businesses were caught hoarding goods in hopes of selling them at higher prices, anticipating that controls would soon be lifted.[71] The famed Saudi Venezuela was running out of money. By the end of 1988, Venezuela was so indebted that the government was forced to use nearly forty cents of every dollar obtained from oil sales to pay its debts.[72] Venezuela's government had run up sizeable deficits not least because it also covered the losses of state-owned companies. The various companies that dictator Pérez Jiménez created had become inefficient, money-losing behemoths stuffed with unproductive public servants. And the country's economy in 1989 went into its worst recession ever, with gross domestic product contracting nearly 9 percent.[73] Venezuela was forced to seek a financial lifeline from the International Monetary Fund and asked the U.S. government's help to renegotiate and reduce its outstanding debts. At the time the world thought Venezuela did not deserve help because its problems largely resulted from having wasted its wealth. Venezuela stopped paying its debts and eventually managed to persuade banks to reduce its US$20 billion debt load by 30 percent.

Contrary to what he had promised on the campaign trail, Pérez announced a package of tough economic measures, all of them taken at once. He dismantled Recadi and freed the bolivar's exchange rate, which meant that

Venezuela's currency would lose 61 percent of its value versus the dollar, making everyday staples that much more expensive.[74] Since state-decreed prices for consumer goods didn't make sense anymore, he freed those too and increased the price of electricity and gasoline by 100 percent, for the first time touching an entitlement that Venezuelans saw as a birthright. Prices for public transportation rose as well. Venezuela could no longer afford to subsidize such services. Pérez cut government spending while still allowing for some social programs, but the pain was too much for Venezuelans to bear. People took to the streets by the thousands to protest, riot, and loot for ten days. Protesters set fire to cars and buses, and they clashed with the military. When it was all over, the uprising that became known as El Caracazo had left three hundred people dead and material losses in the millions of dollars. During the eight years ending in 1989, poverty had increased tenfold.[75]

Most Venezuelans didn't understand the role economic mismanagement had played in their fate. The need for a government to set aside oil revenue for the future or spend moderately and sustainably over time was alien to generations of the country's citizens. The way they saw it, rampant corruption was ruining their country. And they were partly right. The end of Recadi opened up people's eyes to a culture of kickbacks, bribes, and commissions that regular people and companies paid to get cheap greenbacks. To cheat the government out of dollars, importers had overinvoiced the purchase of goods they bought abroad. The subsequent corruption investigation entangled company executives from Ford, General Motors, and other big companies that had allegedly benefited from Recadi's subsidized dollars. Former president Lusinchi and his mistress were accused of handing dollars to cronies, among other shady dealings. Both fled Venezuela, and Lusinchi spent the rest of his days living abroad, hounded by corruption charges.

President Pérez turned out to be no better. In 1993 the attorney general accused him of embezzling U S $17.5 million from a secret discretionary fund. Weeks later the Supreme Court agreed, and for the first time in Venezuela's history the court voted to impeach a sitting president. Pérez would later be prosecuted and sentenced to house arrest when found guilty of corruption. Selling dollars at preferential rates in Venezuela created an incentive for state officials to cheat and steal and for Venezuelans to bribe them. Even before Pérez's departure, Venezuelans were so fed up with him that when an unknown paratrooper named Hugo Chávez led a failed coup attempt against his government in February 1992, people cheered. It didn't seem to matter that after many decades the military was once again in the business of bringing down governments. Venezuelans missed the old days when oil riches were taken for granted. Chávez became known as the man who stood up to a corrupt party system that was already on its deathbed.

* * *

By the time Venezuelans elected Hugo Chávez as their president in 1998, the country had suffered a lot more pain. In the mid-1990s a banking crisis, brought about by loose bank supervision, wiped out a third of the country's banks and cost the government US$7.3 billion—roughly 11 percent of gross domestic product at the time.[76] As banks closed, thousands of Venezuelans were forced to wait for months to recover their deposits, and they did. Those with large amounts of money in their accounts—mostly companies—lost some of their savings.

The banking crisis further convinced Venezuelans that corruption was primarily responsible for tearing Venezuela apart. In 1994 the government once again rationed dollar sales through capital controls under an institution called OTAC, similar to the rotten Recadi, and inflation topped 100 percent in 1996, the highest the country had ever experienced. When Chávez was first sworn in as president, roughly 44 percent of Venezuelan households lived in poverty.[77] Venezuela was a country where the rich lived in heavily guarded luxury villas and drove around in BMWs while the poor carried water in buckets into their shacks.

Chávez, a forty-four-year-old, folksy, barrel-chested man with a gift for oratory, understood his audience well. "How can [this] be a democracy when 80 percent of the people live in poverty in a land with so much wealth?" he asked when he ran for office.[78] Chávez had risen from poverty and joined the army at a time when Venezuela was fighting armed leftists in the 1970s. During his military career he developed an interest in leftist thinkers and built relationships with Venezuelan guerrilla leaders through his brother Adán, who had leftist sympathies. He created a secretive movement with like-minded military officers who believed in the need for a left-leaning government in Venezuela. Chávez seemed an enigma when he first ran for office. He denounced "savage neo-liberal capitalism" but at the same time promised to respect private property and never to "expropriate anything from anyone."[79] He claimed to believe in democracy, but he became a disciple of Cuba's Fidel Castro (Chávez even hosted a seventy-fifth birthday party for the Cuban dictator). And he referred to Cuba's system as a "sea of happiness."[80]

Venezuelans wanted a firm hand that would upend the rotten state of things, and Chávez seemed like someone with the strength to do the job. Many longed for the days of dictator Marcos Pérez Jiménez, whose totalitarian ways kept crime in check and whose grand infrastructure projects had given Venezuela a new face.[81] Chávez did not disappoint those who wanted a new political direction. He got the nod from voters to draft a new constitution; he created a new congress stuffed with loyalists and, in a throwback to Pérez Jiménez, changed the country's name to "Bolivarian Republic of Venezuela," in honor of Simón Bolívar, the nineteenth-century independence figure who fought to rid the region of Spanish rule.

The roughly one-half of voters who had opposed Chávez's election distrusted what he called his Bolivarian revolution. Many felt irked by Chávez's out-with-the-rich rhetoric and his increasingly close political ties with Castro. The Cold War had been over for almost a decade, and Cuba was hardly a sound economic example worth emulating. Plus, Chávez surrounded himself with former members of the defeated Venezuelan guerrilla movements of the 1960s and 1970s. Opposition to Chávez turned into mass demonstrations when in late 2001 he used an enabling law given to him by congress to decree forty-nine laws, including a controversial land law and new hydrocarbons legislation.

The enabling law was similar to the one Párez obtained during the 1970s oil boom to pass a flurry of laws to better spend the country's oil money. Chávez's land legislation gave the state the power to seize land deemed idle and break up large landholdings into smaller plots that would be handed to poor farmers. The president argued it was a way to strengthen agriculture so Venezuela could finally produce what it ate; he called it food security. His opponents feared it was a first step in weakening private property rights.

The new hydrocarbons law was Chávez's way of getting a grip on the oil business. Oil nationalists who advised Chávez were unhappy with how the oil industry was run. For starters, PDVSA had become far too cozy with foreign oil companies. Since the 1976 oil nationalization, foreign companies had once again managed to run Venezuelan oil fields with very favorable tax terms. PDVSA had launched a program called Apertura Petrolera, or Oil Opening, in the 1990s to attract the money and know-how the sector desperately needed. The company had struck generous deals with foreign firms that paid them a fee for every oil barrel produced and covered their costs and investments. Nationalists saw this process as a disguised privatization of the business, but thanks to those deals Venezuela's oil production had risen above 3 million barrels a day—one of its highest levels in years.

The Chavistas, as Chávez supporters were known, saw high output as a problem, too. Venezuela was producing more oil than its assigned quota as a member of the OPEC cartel, and doing this not only undermined OPEC— Pérez Alfonzo's creation—but also helped depress oil prices. At the time, the PDVSA brass thought producing more oil to capture a larger share of the U.S. market was more important than trying to keep prices high. Plus, OPEC cartel members were known to cheat by producing more oil than their assigned quotas anyway and they lied about how much they produced. As an anti-OPEC oil minister in Venezuela put it in the late 1990s, OPEC had become "a gathering of Pinocchios."[82] Chávez, in turn, sought to cement relations with fellow OPEC members and did everything he could to strengthen the cartel.

PDVSA's culture itself became an issue for the Chavista nationalist thinking. The company enjoyed a level of autonomy from politics that made the left uncomfortable. PDVSA was run like any efficient, for-profit enterprise and was recognized as one of the best-run oil giants in the world. Employees saw themselves as a technocracy leading an oil company stuck in a developing nation, held back by a rotten political class. More worrying for the Chavistas, PDVSA had found ways to limit the amount of money it paid the government, its owner. And as a form of insurance against political meddling, the company kept little money in its coffers[83] and instead used its hefty gains to grow its business abroad, even buying Citgo, which expanded the market for Venezuela's oil in the United States. After all, in the 1980s President Campins had raided PDVSA's coffers to keep his spendthrift government afloat. Keeping large amounts of cash idle was dangerous. Venezuelan governments had never shown self-restraint or even an inclination to save money for when times got tough. Chávez's movement saw in PDVSA an elitism that needed to be brought to heel.

To better control PDVSA, in early 2002 Chávez named his allies to the company's board, including nationalist academics and generals, several of them with no experience in the business. The move cemented opposition to Chávez within the company. Employees took to the streets to demand Chávez stop meddling with PDVSA. Months later, Chávez's foes led a coup against the president that managed to unseat him for forty-seven hours before the military restored him to office. Opposition to Chávez became so entrenched that in December 2002, thousands of PDVSA employees declared a two-month oil strike that paralyzed Venezuela's oil industry. Venezuelan gasoline stations ran out of fuel, causing long lines. Crude exports fell to a trickle and caused the country to lose billions of dollars in business.

The strike radicalized Chávez and gave the president the excuse he needed to take control of the company. He ousted more than nineteen thousand employees he deemed enemies of the state for abandoning their posts and boycotting the industry. With his characteristic showmanship, Chávez fired oil executives on national television by announcing their names and blowing a whistle like a referee kicking players out of a soccer game.

Venezuelans, who by now understood that their currency became worthless when less oil money came in, began to turn their bolivars into hard currency deposits they could safeguard overseas. To stop dollars from leaving the country, Chávez fixed the bolivar-dollar exchange rate, just like previous governments had done. He created an entity called Cadivi to administer dollar sales, similar to the defunct Recadi, which had become notoriously corrupt. Since fewer dollars available for imports usually meant higher prices for products in Venezuela, Chávez decreed price controls for a host of basic consumer goods. Like Pérez in the 1970s and several other former presidents before him, Chávez thought price controls would keep inflation in check. His government forced banks to devote part of their lending to favored sectors like agriculture at below-market interest rates. He eventually imposed limits on bank lending rates across the board,[84] which, combined with high inflation, encouraged people to borrow heavily and spend their cash quickly.

Chávez was also very lucky. Despite his political troubles at home, prices for commodities, including oil, started rising, driven by growing demand from emerging countries, especially China. The resulting boom, which lasted a decade, multiplied the price of oil sevenfold to more than US$145 a barrel at its peak in 2008. The rise mirrored that of the 1970s that made Venezuelans famous for their spending excesses. It became a unique opportunity to finance Chávez's agenda. He created massive social spending programs, known as missions, beginning with Misión Barrio Adentro, which brought thousands of Cuban doctors to tend to Venezuelans in poor barrios. He followed with Misión Robinson, a literacy program, and eventually Mercal and PDVAL, state-owned grocery chains that offered subsidized food to the poor. All of them became very popular with Chávez's supporters.

From that point on, Chávez and his allies won multiple electoral contests with ease. Voters even approved a constitutional reform to allow the president the ability to run for office indefinitely, changing a key provision established following the Pérez Jiménez dictatorship. Venezuelans took advantage of dollars sold at preferential rates to import clothes, furniture, whiskey, and luxury cars like Hummers, and to travel to exotic destinations. Venezuela's economy soon began to show signs it couldn't handle the influx of so much cash. Demand for plane tickets was so high that it became hard to book a flight out of Venezuela during holiday season. In 2005 Air France began flying its 747-400 wide-body plane to Venezuela to accommodate the number of travelers flying to Europe.[85] Demand for cars grew so much that car assembly plants in Venezuela could barely keep up. Inflation stood higher than bank interest rates, so people borrowed money and spent on plastic surgery, travel, and entertainment.

Encouraged by so much cash, Chávez declared himself a socialist in 2005 and vowed to create what he called "Twenty-First-Century Socialism." Maybe a socialist system with the state in control of key industries would work in Venezuela if the state had enough money to pay for it all. In the 1950s dictator Marcos Pérez Jiménez sought to modernize the country, and in the 1970s President Carlos Andrés Pérez sought to build La Gran Venezuela. Now Chávez wanted to make a new type of socialism possible. That same year Chávez began to seize land from large farms, and paper and textile companies from their private owners. He nationalized scores of companies and created new ones. By 2009 Chávez had created, seized, or purchased 123 companies, most of which didn't operate. They simply existed on paper and never became operational.[86] When Chávez offered tax and financing benefits to companies run by worker cooperatives, their numbers swelled to 280,000 in 2009, up from 820 in 1999, when he took office. But most turned out to be unproductive shell companies people used to access subsidies and cheap cash.

Chávez raised taxes and royalties on foreign oil companies and used the new 1999 oil law to give them a choice: accept minority stakes in all oil ventures, with the state holding majority control, or face nationalization. The 1999 oil law was not meant to apply retroactively to existing projects, but Chávez forced the changes anyway. In their Marxist view, the Chavistas argued that the dominance of foreign oil companies was the real reason for Venezuela's economic backwardness. Only if and when Venezuelans controlled and ran the oil business would the country finally develop. When Chávez took power, however, the government already received more than half the profits from oil produced,[87] and that portion surpassed 80 percent as he raised taxes on companies. By the time Chávez died from cancer in 2013, Venezuela's government take—the amount of money the state took from every barrel produced—exceeded 90 percent and was considered one of the highest in the world. What's more, foreign oil companies never had a say in how Venezuelan governments chose to spend their money. The country's recurring bouts of economic indigestion had nothing to do with oil multinationals; it was squarely the responsibility of Venezuelan politicians. Venezuela's economic growth under Chávez through 2006 was mostly the result of higher oil revenues, thanks to a global oil boom, than from Chávez's economic policies.[88]

When the government's share from oil was not enough to cover Chávez's ambitious spending plans, he borrowed money just as Pérez did during the 1970s. Like Pérez, Chávez both ran through the oil money the state had saved in a rainy-day fund and lent money to friendly governments. He also shipped oil to his allies with generous financing terms in a bid to promote his ideas in Latin America. And while President Campins took PDVSA's cash reserves in the 1980s to keep his government afloat, Chávez ordered PDVSA to finance social programs, manage loss-making companies, and build scores of homes for the poor to the tune of billions of dollars every year.

Chávez's goals of agriculture self-sufficiency largely failed to materialize, but the country's import bill surged exponentially during his mandate. In 2014 Venezuela suffered food shortages, but its food imports amounted to four times those of Colombia and three times those of Chile, both far larger economies.[89] Social spending under Chávez helped the poor get by, while the money flowed. Like Pérez, Chávez banned businesses from laying off people with a law that forced the private sector to keep workers employed in tough times. The state also doubled its payroll. By 2008 one of every three workers was a state employee.[90] The military, an institution that never really saw much action in battle aside from the multiple coups it orchestrated, gained more power. Chávez and his successor Nicolás Maduro appointed hundreds of generals and officers to run state-owned companies and occupy posts in top ministries. Chavismo made the country and everyone living in it ever more dependent on crude.

The oil boom began to wind down in earnest after Chávez died in 2013. At the time of his death he was still popular. After all, Chávez's spending had helped reduce inequality to a level that placed it on par with Canada in 2011.[91] Enrollment in secondary education rose from half of Venezuela's children in 1998 to seven of every ten children by 2010, according to the United Nations Educational, Scientific, and Cultural Organization, UNESCO. And infant mortality fell from 20.3 per thousand births to less than 12.9 during the first thirteen years of Chávez's mandate.[92] Still, many people question this data.

But Chávez's economic legacy was less stellar. Oil production went from more than 3 million barrels a day when he took office to 2.7 million in 2013. He weakened businesses, made fewer real jobs available, and made Venezuelans more dependent on the state. The capital controls he decreed turned many Venezuelans into black market dollar traders. Price controls, coupled with rising inflation, caused food scarcity and encouraged thousands of Venezuelans to buy and sell consumer goods in a black market as well. Venezuela's subsidized gasoline prices, unchanged under Chávez, encouraged Venezuelans to smuggle fuel to neighboring countries for a living. And artificially low interest rates gave people an incentive to borrow and consume even more.

Inequality had increased once again in 2013, and the number of Venezuelan households living in poverty had reached 48.5 percent by the end of 2014, higher than when Chávez first took office.[93] Runaway state spending helped the poor for a time but made the economy less stable. In the end, Chávez recycled the failed economic policies of his predecessors with far more dire consequences. Time and again, Juan Pablo Pérez Alfonzo warned the country that too much money mishandled would bring it ruin. Venezuelans paid close attention when Pérez Alfonzo defended the country's oil riches or when he transformed the global oil business to their advantage, but no one listened to his calls for restraint. Men like Pérez Alfonzo have become inconvenient, troublesome, even unwanted in a culture of excess like Venezuela's.

Zumaque—Venezuela's famed oil well—still pumped twenty barrels of oil a day when it turned one hundred years old in 2014. Lawmakers held a special session next to the well and decreed a wage hike for government workers to celebrate the occasion. Politicians gave speeches that called on Venezuelans to enjoy their oil wealth guilt free. The celebration made one thing clear. In one hundred years of oil history, after decades of dictatorship, corruption, multiple coups, and economic dysfunction, Venezuela had learned nothing.

4   EVERYMAN

The San Ignacio Surgical Medical Center, on the ninth floor of the exclusive Copernico Tower in Caracas, is literally and figuratively the summit of plastic surgery practice in Venezuela. The lobby of the eleven-thousand-square-foot clinic boasts gleaming Portuguese and Italian marble floors. Offices and rooms offer imposing northern views of the Ávila. The center has three operating rooms, ten beds, and a staff of sixty people, including a roster of fourteen surgeons, performing an average of ten procedures a day. The clinic is the domain of Bernardo Krulig, a thirty-two-year-old plastic surgeon whose name is associated with the very best cosmetic surgery in the country. When actresses, beauty queens, socialites, and even leftist Chavista politicians need a facelift, liposuction, or breast implants, they call Krulig. The young doctor has benefited from exacting standards and name recognition (his father is also a renowned plastic surgeon) in a country that has grown obsessed with physical beauty.

Krulig's is the type of business in Venezuela that weathers economic down-turns. Oil prices may be rising or falling, the economy may be growing or in recession, people may be rich or poor, employed or jobless, but demand for Krulig's services, and for plastic surgery in general, is always high. "People in this country spend their money on three things: beauty salons, restaurants, and plastic surgery," Krulig told me matter-of-factly.

I visited Krulig's clinic on a Tuesday in late January 2015, at 7 p.m. because he had no time during the day. Krulig works thirteen-hour workdays, typically performing two procedures early in the morning and holding appointments in the afternoons. He mostly tends to the kind of customers that Venezuelan consumer surveys classify as the A and B socioeconomic groups, the top 2 percent of Venezuelans, the type of people who live in luxury homes and drive BMW or Mercedes-Benz cars. Krulig does late-night consultations for famous but less well off patients too—often for Chavista politicians who prefer to visit his office at 11 p.m. to avoid being seen. It is a grueling schedule that can test anyone's stamina, and their looks.

Krulig keeps up his youthful appearance with a regimen of Botox to prevent worry lines from forming on his forehead, but his devotion to his work pays off handsomely. At the time, he earned roughly 2.7 million bolivars a month, or as much as US$54,000, calculated at Venezuela's third official exchange rate,[1] and that didn't include his overall share of the clinic's profits, a business he co-owns with his mother and siblings. To put that into perspective, the median pay for plastic and reconstructive surgeons in the United States was US$350,000 a year (or US$29,166 a month) in early 2015,[2] slightly more than half of Krulig's earnings.

Of course Krulig, like many other high earners in Venezuela, cannot readily turn his entire income into dollars even at the government's easier-to-obtain official exchange rate. At the black market rate, Krulig earned US$15,000 a month.[3] Regardless of the dollar amount, his salary in bolivars was more than 552 times the country's minimum wage,[4] which put him right at the top of Venezuela's income scale. A U.S. plastic surgeon makes roughly twenty-three times the minimum wage.[5] For Krulig's U.S. colleagues to be in the Venezuelan surgeon's bracket, they would have to earn US$8.3 million a year, the type of money reserved for top Wall Street executives, A-list movie stars, and famous basketball players. "I could buy myself a yacht or a plane, but I don't have the time to use them," Krulig told me. "A plane would only gather dust in some hangar." In Venezuela, Krulig's professional skills are prized above all others.

Even as they stand in line outside supermarkets to buy a packet of sugar, Venezuelans aspire to undergo cosmetic procedures. Plastic surgeries in Venezuela more than doubled between 2011 and 2013, according to the International Society of Aesthetic Plastic Surgeons (the latest available data).

Venezuela was sixth in the world in the number of aesthetic surgical procedures, with the United States and Brazil—far larger economies—leading the pack. Looking one's best is deeply ingrained in the Venezuelan psyche.

It is normal for Venezuelans from almost any socioeconomic background, but especially for middle- and upper-class ones, to take time off from work to recover from plastic surgery operations. Young girls grow up aspiring to get breast implants, and they constantly ask their parents for a pair when they become teenagers. Venezuelan beauty queens have won a combined thirteen Miss Universe and Miss World titles, more than any other country. This has no doubt helped convince Venezuelans that the world as a whole holds them to a higher standard of beauty they must strive to meet. When the oil boom was underway in late 2006, banks large and small offered plastic surgery loans for everything from nose jobs and liposuction to cosmetic dental treatments. In 2014 local pollster Datos found that 86 percent of Venezuelans agreed with the idea that "looking good translates into having a good life."

It's not just culture that prompts people to borrow and spend on a bustier cleavage—it's basic economic logic too. Plastic surgery has become an investment in a country where inflation eats away people's earnings. Beauty is considered an important, if not the most important, asset Venezuelans can invest in. A corporate secretary will get breast implants as part of her professional career strategy, and in beauty-crazed Venezuela, better looks can help her land a coveted position. It helps that a breast implant surgery in Venezuela costs a fraction of what it does in other countries. Oil wealth has nurtured a culture where looks have paramount importance. And in Venezuela's mismanaged economy a cosmetic surgery—something considered banal in most other countries—has become a sound, even smart way to spend money.

In early 2015 Daniel Slobodianik, who worked for years as the official plastic surgeon for the Miss Venezuela competition, had a list of twenty patients waiting as long as four months for the right-size implants, partly because implants and medical materials have become scarce in Venezuela. A high demand for cosmetic procedures kept Slobodianik in business, and he figures demand will stay high for years. "I could put my desk in a dirt field, under a tree, and hang a shingle from a branch offering plastic surgery, and people would start lining up for consultations," he told me.[6]

Slobodianik's patients typically hail from the B and C socioeconomic brackets—middle- to lower-income groups. A large number of his patients seek his expertise to fix botched procedures previously performed by underground plastic surgeons. For years, Venezuelans' obsession with larger buttocks or breasts drove low-income Venezuelans to underground doctors who injected them with gel-like substances known as liquid biopolymers. The substance causes deformities and even death. Slobodianik and other colleagues launched a successful campaign to ban the practice in Venezuela, and he now devotes part of his business to serving patients that suffer from the lifelong ailments resulting from having polymers in their bodies.

Krulig uses cash from his personal Visa and Master Card accounts to buy German-brand implants and has managed to maintain an inventory of fifty pairs to keep up with demand. An avid Twitter user with more than eighteen thousand followers, Krulig once tweeted a photo of his implant stock to reassure potential patients that he was very much in business, but he underestimated the extent of the demand for implants. Dozens of people began calling, offering to buy his implants so they could undergo surgery with their own doctors. He has sworn not to tweet such things again for fear the government may accuse him of hoarding the product.

Venezuela's economic disarray has had a silver lining for Krulig's practice. Back in 2011 Krulig and his siblings bought the ninth floor of the Copernico Tower, and they took out a fixed-interest-rate loan for 38 million bolivars (US$4.2 million at the time) to help finance the purchase. The following year, Venezuela devalued the currency by 32 percent. And inflation surged dramatically, turning the loan's monthly payments into almost nothing. "Inflation helped us. My salary has grown tenfold," Krulig told me at the time. Financial success in a poor country involves some sacrifices, and in Krulig's case that comes in the form of personal security. Krulig insisted on driving me to my hotel as he turned off the lights and locked up the clinic at 8:30 p.m.—he was the last person to leave. Although my hotel was just a few blocks away, safety had become an issue in Caracas. Krulig's security measures were no joke. He drove a metallic blue Ford Explorer with level-four bulletproofing, enough to withstand the bullet from a forty-four-caliber magnum handgun or the spray of a twelve-gauge shotgun.

Krulig's work forced him to make personal sacrifices too. He is Jewish and still single in a country where many well-off Jewish Venezuelans have left. This, he said, has made his potential dating pool that much smaller.

He realized doing business in Venezuela is getting increasingly difficult, but demand for what he does is so high that he planned to continue working as long as conditions allow him to perform top-quality procedures. "The [profitability] numbers still make sense to me," he said.

* * *

Carlos García is the chef of Alto, a famed haute-cuisine restaurant that thrives in Caracas. Garcia's signature dish, the Guajiro-style suckling pig, helped Alto land a spot among the top thirty eateries in the Latin America edition of the website World's 50 Best Restaurants for two years in a row. Alto's location is as exquisite as its menu. It is housed on the ground floor of an apartment building in Los Palos Grandes, a traditional enclave of upper-class families known for the lush trees that line its busiest streets. A massive rubber tree gives shade to Alto's thousand-square-foot patio, where a reflecting pool adds to a Zen-like ambiance. The patio's floor tile design features Alto's logo, a rendering of a thin branch with six leaves that mimics the rubber tree's foliage, the work of an award-winning Venezuelan architect. Tall French-style windows lead to a dining area with high ceilings that seats forty-five people. Patrons can gaze through a glass wall at the kitchen, a spotless room of shiny stainless-steel appliances where Garcia and his staff, like surgeons clad in white, turn every plate into a colorful piece of art.

The word *alto*, which means "tall" in Spanish, is a fitting name for the restaurant, since everything about it suggests unattainable heights. It is the height of Caracas cuisine, meant for the Venezuelan elite, and is run by the tall García—six feet four inches—who learned his craft by working in some of the world's most exclusive restaurants. Caracas was a top destination for fine cuisine lovers in the early 1970s, when a decade-long oil boom turned the city into a sort of Paris of Latin America. In those years, oil wealth allowed Venezuelans to travel and develop a greater taste for imported delicacies. By the time oil prices plummeted in the mid-1980s, a new generation of Venezuelans had acquired a habit of spending their money on entertainment that gave them a unique experience and bragging rights.

García and a partner invested the equivalent of US$480,000 to open

Alto in 2007, a year when rising oil prices made Venezuela one of the world's fastest-growing economies. The restaurant did well its first two years with a steady clientele of bankers, stockbrokers, and other wealthy customers who often paired their meals with US$1,000 bottles of wine. A well-run restaurant in New York City can earn between 10 percent and 20 percent in annual profits, with a great deal of luck. Alto initially churned out 23 percent annual returns in a country where bar and restaurant profits can top 30 percent.

García's good fortune took a sudden turn in 2010, when the Chávez government blamed stockbrokers for the bolívar's continuing loss of value and forced the closing of fifty brokerage houses, wiping out the income of Alto's richest clientele. During the following three years power outages and water rationing became common, and so did food shortages. In 2014 street protests ensued. García decided to close Alto for two months starting in February 2014, after students threw rocks and Molotov cocktails at armed soldiers right outside the restaurant's main entrance.

On a Friday in early February 2015—a year after its two-month shutdown—a water tank truck blocked the restaurant's main entrance, an unusual sight outside a gastronomic jewel. Alto had begun paying for a truck to deliver ten thousand liters of water twice a day to replenish the building's water tank the restaurant shares with the apartments above. The local utility provides water service to Alto and its surrounding area twice a week only, but faucets run dry the rest of the week without the extra supply.

Keeping a Venezuelan fine dining establishment going in 2015 required resourcefulness. Alto hired a full-time employee who scoured stores and supermarket chains across the city for flour, rice, and milk. "We pay seven to eight times what those products are worth just to make sure we have them," the chef told me. García and his chef colleagues now do more than talk about food when they get together—they trade names of suppliers of milk, coffee, table linens, and tableware. García has managed to create his own supply chain of products, as it happens, in the case of chicken. Aurelio, Alto's bartender, was raising chickens under García's specifications on a small plot of land he owns on the outskirts of the city. Aurelio aimed to supply Alto's kitchen with ten to twelve birds a week.

For quality vegetables, García found an urban garden a few blocks from the restaurant that supplied him with spinach and beets. The chef purchased a van and hired a driver to make the forty-minute trip to the coast twice a week to purchase fresh fish. Sought-after game fish like red snapper had become too pricey, because fishing declined in Venezuela after the government banned the use of industrial trawling fishing nets in 2009. Sardines and croaker—a bottom feeder, considered the cheapest fish in the market—were new in the Alto menu.

Alto constantly changes its menu to adapt to the ingredients it can get, and this need has forced the restaurant to give a unique spin to local dishes. But some Alto patrons don't immediately warm up to the change. "Some customers say, 'Only poor people eat this type of fish,'" said García, referring to the croaker. "Or they say, 'I didn't come to Alto to eat pasta with sardines,'" another Venezuelan staple on the menu. The clientele has changed along with the economy. In its early years, Alto became a fashionable scene for thirty-year-old, yuppie financiers eager to dine on caviar and fois. Most of those customers left the country, however. The restaurant has come to attract moneyed locals of a different sort—forty- to sixty-year-old foodies more interested in taking a break from their stressful lives than displaying their wealth.

A labor law Chávez passed in 2012 made life harder for Alto to handle employees. The law established a five-day maximum workweek with two full continuous days off for all workers. García tried rearranging staff hours, but service suffered and he couldn't afford to hire more people. Eventually, he gave up and decided to close on weekends. "We are one of the few restaurants of our kind in the world that close on Saturdays and Sundays," García said.

On the bright side, this schedule gave García and his staff a better work-life balance. But with less money coming in, the chef sought ways to keep up employee morale. "People who work in the kitchen are motivated by fame, but the servers are motivated by tips," García told me. To compensate for the loss of business, Alto paid for one of its servers to take English courses and for another to become a barista. The restaurant also paid for employees to take drama and crisis management courses. And every week, Alto employees enjoyed free yoga classes and a weekend soccer team practice. Yet despite these troubles, Venezuelans' penchant for consuming and eating out helped Alto earn a respectable 13 percent return in 2014, even after having shut its doors for two months early in the year.

New bars and restaurants opened their doors in Caracas in late 2014, in the middle of food shortages and street protests that made headlines around the world. A cursory review of new eateries during my May 2015 trip turned out at least six new restaurants on the east side of Caracas that had been in business for six months or less, and sometimes they seemed to barely keep up with the flow of patrons. The Licoteca, a high-end liquor store that opened in early 2014, sold bottles of Sassicaia Grappa for the equivalent of US$1,459 each.[7] A salesperson told me that in 2015 demand for such bottles was down—the store managed to sell roughly a box of six bottles every month, mostly to local businessmen and foreigners.

A new café called Bistro del Libertador is a remarkable example of how Venezuelans of different political stripes share similar consumer aspirations. The bistro is in Plaza Bolívar, a pro-Chavista territory in downtown Caracas. The emblematic plaza has become a favored spot for Chavista rallies that denounce capitalism and elitism and rail against an affected Venezuelan upper class. The bistro is part of an effort by Chavista mayor Jorge Rodríguez to revamp the area, and the eatery does its best to capture the feel of a trendy café. It has black-and-white checkered floors, an exposed brick wall, and vintage lightbulbs hanging from the ceiling. Slow-moving waiters dressed in black polo shirts and white flat caps serve customers coffee and slightly crumbled chocolate croissants. The business is privately owned, but the municipality owns the building where it is housed.

Back in 2010 the late Hugo Chávez nationalized the building, arguing that small shop owners were ruining an area imbued with historical significance. In January 2015, just a month after opening its doors, the bistro had plans to set up a VIP room on the second floor, the type of exclusivity Chavistas have long denounced as a way to discriminate against the less well-off. Regardless, the bistro has become the place where Chavista politicians and sympathizers go to see and be seen. But the prices were not much cheaper from those of classier Caracas eateries. At the bistro's grand opening, a string quartet played on as Rodríguez, the mayor, told reporters, "We are now in a space that used to belong to the oligarchy."[8]

The Libertador bistro is not the only establishment with Chavista backing. Across the plaza at the restaurant Rialto—which opened its doors in September 2014—government ministers, lawmakers, and other high-level officials can enjoy plantain-filled gnocchi. And a few blocks to the east the café and leftist bookstore El Techo de la Ballena, the Whale's Roof, serves Chavista hipsters who ache for their own version of a Brooklyn hangout. Marxism, food shortages, and political upheaval cannot stand between Venezuelans and their willingness to enjoy a drink and a meal in style.

One thing does stand in the way of Venezuelans and their cherished consumer lifestyle: a weak purchasing power. Wages no longer keep up with a level of inflation in the triple digits.[9] And Venezuela's middle-income salaried workers are hurting the most because, unlike the rich, they do not earn far more than they can spend and, unlike the poor, they benefit less from government social programs.[10]

Mauricio Durazzi, forty-six, a materials engineer who teaches mathematics at the Instituto Universitario de Gerencia y Tecnología—a for-profit technical institute in Caracas—is one of the hundreds of thousands of middle-class Venezuelans who now struggle to make ends meet. Mauricio has taught for thirteen years and in May 2015 took home 11,500 bolivars (or US$61) a month, less than two minimum-wage salaries. And he is one of the most highly paid teachers at the institute. His wife, an accountant, earned 20,000 bolivars (or US$105) a month at the time.[11] With their three-year-old son, they managed to muddle through because they lived rent-free in a guesthouse on his parents' property in a middle-class neighborhood. They didn't have enough money yet to find a place of their own. Mauricio's salary was barely enough to pay for a private insurance policy that covered his wife and child. "These days I essentially work to pay for health insurance," he told me.

Mauricio got into teaching when he lost his job at a refractory brick plant, which closed following the 2002 oil strike that plunged Venezuela into a recession. In 2015 Mauricio taught all week from Monday through Saturday, earning roughly 60 bolivars (or 31 U.S. cents) per hour of class.[12] Private-sector companies cannot afford to keep raising salaries at the same rate as inflation. And while the late Hugo Chávez and his successor, Nicolás Maduro, have decreed annual increases in the minimum wage, the cost of living rises faster. Companies in the private sector are also known to pay minimum-wage workers slightly above the minimum so they are technically not obligated to give workers the 30 to 40 percent annual increases in the minimum wage decreed by the president, a strategy companies often use to keep payroll costs in check.

Elio Ohep, the director for the Instituto Universitario de Mercadotecnia, a technical institute similar to the one Mauricio works for but with a larger student body, told me the government limits how high institutes like his can raise tuition. Plus, the government has put a 30 percent ceiling on profits. In the 2014–15 school year, Elio's institute managed to increase the wages of staff by no more than 20 percent, even as inflation reached almost 70 percent. Elio earned 50,000 bolivars (US$263) a month[13] in May 2015 and had other benefits like insurance, a yearly bonus equivalent to three months' salary, and free cell phone use, yet he struggled to keep his household budget in line. Elio explained the business of technical colleges to me at 6 a.m. on a Saturday, as he shopped for groceries in the Quinta Crespo market, a type of farmers market in a sketchy part of town. He said he could save 30 percent on his grocery bill by shopping there.

Professors at Venezuela's largest universities earn more or less the same as Mauricio, far from enough to make a living.[14] In April 2015 the economics studies unit of the Venezuelan teachers' federation estimated that the basic basket of goods—a set of consumer products a family of five needs to get by—cost Venezuelans more than six minimum-wage salaries.[15] That was a big problem for a number of families in which only two adults work to provide for the rest of its members, children and the elderly. Doctors recently graduated from medical school and working as residents in state hospitals earned even less than many teachers: 5,800 bolivars (US$30) a month as a basic salary, which, including yearly bonuses and other benefits, amounted to roughly two minimum-wage salaries.[16]

Venezuela's economic craziness has reached a point where doctors, teachers, and architects earn less than cabdrivers. Yon, a thirty-eight-year-old former cop who now drives a cab for many company executives earned 20,000 bolivars in a bad week in May 2015 and as much as 100,000 bolivars in a good one, which means he easily earned several times what Elio made in a month. Cabdrivers are unencumbered by hefty payrolls and other costs—aside from the upkeep of their vehicles—and they can set their rates as inflation creeps up, a luxury not available to salary-earning employees working for a company or the government. "I have a better income than a professional or a doctor," said Yon, the father of two teenage daughters, one of which was attending university to become a dentist. If Venezuela's economy continues on its current path, Yon's daughter may find that she spent years studying to end up earning less than her cabdriver father. Such insane distortions explain why as many as fifteen thousand doctors left Venezuela in the past decade to seek better job opportunities abroad.[17] By some estimates, roughly 1.2 million of Venezuela's best-trained professionals have migrated to the United States and Europe in recent years[18]; many more Venezuelans, especially the young, ache to make a living abroad as well.

To make up for their meager paychecks, Venezuelans have turned to debt. With inflation having reached triple-digit territory in 2015 and banks unable to charge customers more than 29 percent annual interest rates by law, Venezuelans would be crazy not to take on more debt. Venezuelans have lived through periods when bank interest rates sat below inflation, first in the late 1970s, then in the late 1980s, and again in the latter part of the 1990s. Generations of Venezuelans have learned that taking out debt makes more sense than saving money.

In Venezuela's upside-down economic reality, most financial experts in 2015 were telling people to become more indebted. After all, the higher inflation goes, the less their debts are worth over time. "If you're not borrowing, you're not understanding anything," Luis Vicente León, head of pollster firm Datanalisis, told hundreds of gathered spectators at his annual conference Consumer Trends in Venezuela 2015, held in May. "Take all the money the bank is willing to give you," he said, but he warned people to make sure such debt was used to purchase productive assets. He added, "If you're just covering your household's spending gap, you are digging your own grave. You are living artificially."

The incentive to consume is so great in Venezuela that people may not be getting the last part of that message. Credit card debt, adjusted for inflation, jumped nearly 50 percent in 2014 alone.[19] Cardholder debt at the end of that year stood at 18 percent of all bank lending, double what it was a decade earlier.[20] This was not particularly high by international standards, but the rate of growth had financiers and economists worried that people were taking on too much debt too quickly. Even more distressing, Datanalisis found that poor Venezuelans classified in the socioeconomic D group are the people most likely to use credit card debt to make up their consumption habits, the type of consumer most likely to experience trouble paying the money back.[21] As León put it, "The credit card is what keeps consumption alive in Venezuela."

Felix González, a Venezuelan personal finance coach and the author of *No Fear of Debt: Personal Finances in Times of Crisis* and *Personal Finances in Times of Revolution*, has made a career out of teaching readers and students how to manage their personal finances in Venezuela. González tries to wean his students from the Venezuelan habit of using credit cards to maintain their lifestyle. "One thing is to take on debt to buy a home or a car. Another thing is to use a credit card to buy a sixty-inch flat-screen television because it's the biggest one in the market," González told me. "Consumerism has gotten worse in the last ten years."

But González also encourages Venezuelans to make their country's crazy economic incentives work for them: Take on more debt but not in excess; try to find a way to earn hard currency and save it overseas, and take advantage of government subsidies as much as possible. In a world where gasoline is cheap, own a car. If the government wants to sell goods at subsidized prices, buy as many as them as you can. If Venezuelan politicians want to sell dollars at preferential rates, purchase as much as is legally possible. González essentially tells Venezuelans to do what they have learned to do during the past century—find ways to make a living out of a generous, oil-rich government.

To make sense of Venezuelan economic thinking, many turn to Axel Capriles, an economist and Jungian psychologist, who has long studied how oil has shaped economic behavior in Venezuela. Capriles relies on common archetypes from the country's culture to better describe how Venezuelans think and live. In his book *La Picardía del Venezolano* (The craftiness of the Venezuelan), Capriles explores the picaresque nature of Venezuelans and their tendency to look for shortcuts to get ahead economically.

The sixty-one-year-old therapist suggests that a popular cartoon character best captures the idiosyncrasy of the Venezuelan trickster: a white rabbit known as Tío Conejo, or Uncle Rabbit. Tío Conejo was conceived by Antonio Arraíz, a poet and storyteller who spent five years in prison for opposing the twenty-seven-year dictatorship of Juan Vicente Gómez. Arraíz's book *Tío Tigre and Tío Conejo* became a hit when it came out in 1945, ten years after the dictator's death. Tío Conejo was a rogue but a charming one at that. His adventures usually consisted of outsmarting a fierce tiger, known as Tío Tigre or Uncle Tiger, who constantly sought to devour him.

Tío Conejo became such a fixture in children's literature that the Venezuelan government used the character in literature meant to teach values to children through local fables. In one of his adventures, Tío Conejo tricks the tiger into getting stung by bees. In another, the devious rabbit escapes the tiger's clutches by making false promises of a place where the hungry feline could feast on fat cows instead. Tío Conejo resorts to tricks, subterfuge, and outright chicanery to get his way and satisfy short-term needs. Or as Capriles puts it, Tío Conejo, like most Venezuelans, seeks to outsmart the powerful and "only aspires to survive."[22]

Slyness has become a mechanism Venezuelans use to circumvent the rules of an all-powerful government and a corrupt bureaucracy. The Venezuelan trickster gleefully flouts everyday norms such as traffic laws, respecting a queue, or punctuality, and by doing so insures a better quality of life at the expense of others. Capriles calls this cultural trait "anarchic individualism." The flouting of norms occurs in other Latin American nations too, but Capriles argues that in Venezuela it comes from a psychology of abundance that leads people to think that wealth does not need to be created, just tapped. And to tap that wealth you need be to savvy and cunning. Venezuelans have not warmed to the idea of a frugal approach to managing wealth, because they believe oil provides plenty to make everyone happy. The Venezuelan quest to make a living doing as little as possible, Capriles argues, has not only become ingrained in the country's value system, it is a prized, even celebrated feature of someone's personality.

To illustrate his point Capriles likes to tell the story of an informal social experiment he conducted when living in Zurich. He would ask Venezuelans living there to describe someone who is the opposite of being a trickster. Invariably they would describe "a fool," "someone stupid," or "someone who lacks spark." Asking a similar question of the Swiss would yield very different answers: "a gentleman," "honest," "a virtuous person." During a phone conversation, Capriles pointed out to me that after years of dictatorship and rising and falling oil riches, Venezuelans have learned to live in the moment. Early in the twentieth century, Venezuelans learned that a dictator could always take away their livelihood; in more recent decades they found their wealth could evaporate when oil prices fell. These lessons help explain why fiscal restraint is anathema to Venezuelans. Why restrain spending? What purpose does that serve? Venezuelans have learned to think that rising oil prices will eventually make everything all right. As Capriles told me: "Venezuelans live day to day until they run out of money. They have no real budget; the forced restraint comes when the money runs out."

Success in business in Venezuela is also not associated with innovation or sacrifice but with sheer luck and having enough cunning to extract a share of oil wealth from the government. Rafael Di Tella, a Harvard University economics professor, has found that corruption and wild economic swings due to rising and falling oil prices have helped shape Venezuelan beliefs regarding entrepreneurship.

Di Tella argues that in an oil-rich country where a company can make a fortune during times of high oil prices and end up broke when oil prices fall, "the connection between effort and reward is lost."[23] In other words business success comes from good fortune, not effort. As Di Tella puts it, being rich is equated with "success in capturing [oil] rents and belonging to the elite, rather than on working hard in competitive industries." Di Tella and his colleagues performed a statistical analysis to study the correlation between economic performance, corruption and crime, and political beliefs in Venezuela. They found that bouts of inflation and unemployment and the perception of widespread corruption have helped make Venezuelans more receptive to leftwing, antimarket ideas such as those advocated by Hugo Chávez.

Luis Vicente León's polling firm, Datanalisis, has found examples of a deformed view of entrepreneurship. León notes that oftentimes unemployed or underemployed Venezuelans, when polled, classify themselves as independent entrepreneurs because they trade dollars illegally or they smuggle price-controlled goods or gasoline across the border. If they engage in legal business, entrepreneurship involves making money by importing a product and simply selling it at a hefty markup in Venezuela. Venezuelans admire economic success, but innovation, production, and economic sacrifice are not concepts that most of them readily embrace.

* * *

Picture Venezuela's everyman. The average Venezuelan is a twenty-nine-year-old man, because the country's population is young and men slightly outnumber women.[24] We will call him José Luis González, since *José*, *Luis*, and *González* happen to be the most common first and last names.[25] José Luis lives in a city, but he is far from rich. He lives with his family of five in a cinder-block home with a rickety roof, high up on the slope of a hill in a poor barrio where homes are tightly packed against one another.[26] If José Luis were lucky, he would live in a sturdier abode lower down the hill, where homes are nicer and the people are slightly better off and live in less cramped surroundings, but statistics are not on his side.

He has indoor plumbing, but water service is spotty,[27] which forces José Luis to fill large plastic buckets with water so the family can endure the days when taps run dry. Trash accumulates a few feet away from his home because trash collection in the area is unreliable.[28] As for electricity, it's free. José Luis, like many of his neighbors, has illegally tapped into the grid. The sewer system in the area also handles the excess runoff water, so it is easily overwhelmed when it rains, but José Luis's home has a septic tank.[29] He has no fixed phone line at home and uses a prepaid cellular phone instead. Everyone in his family has one.[30]

One of José Luis's major assets is a television set, a large flat-screen, and he has a DirecTV antenna jutting from his roof. Practically all the neighbors have one thanks to a prepaid service popular in low-income neighborhoods.[31] In fact, José Luis watches almost three hours of television a day, his primary source of entertainment.[32] He has a DVD player, a stereo, and a washing machine at home.[33]

José Luis doesn't own an air conditioner yet, but buying one is a priority.[34] Consumer surveys typically classify him as belonging to one of the poorest two socioeconomic groups, D and E, which together make up nearly 80 percent of Venezuelans.[35] Annual surveys show that people like him have three major purchase priorities in mind: a cellular phone, an air conditioner, and a television, in that order.[36] Buying productive assets like a car is less pressing, partly because he cannot afford large-ticket items.

His family lives off a monthly income of roughly two minimum-wage salaries, a chunk of which he earns doing janitorial work for a state-owned company. The most likely alternative job for José Luis would be hawking goods on the streets or driving people around on a motorcycle, or in a moto taxi—a popular mode of transportation in cities like Caracas. He cannot aspire to better employment because he has barely a ninth-grade education. José Luis and his family benefited from Hugo Chávez's social programs. His sister is a single mother who has received a stipend through the Misión Madres del Barrio, a social program that gives cash transfers to mothers in need. His grandmother joined Misión Robinson, a program that taught young and old how to read and write. His family also benefits from the free medical services provided by a local Cuban doctor, as part of Misión Barrio Adentro, a medical initiative.

José Luis's diet consists mainly of rice, corn flour in the form of Venezuela's tortilla-like *arepas*—which he consumes daily—chicken, and pasta.[37] He drinks coffee with almost every meal. Occasionally he will have meat, but no fish. Fish is mostly for rich people.[38] His mother and sister prefer to buy their food in modern supermarkets and only do part of their grocery shopping in stores near their home. They also buy price-controlled products in the local Mercal and PDVAL, the government chains of grocery stores created by Chávez. The growing scarcity of certain staple goods has forced José Luis and his family to visit large government-owned supermarkets farther away from home.[39] Sometimes it seems as if state-owned chains are the only ones well stocked with otherwise scarce goods.

His mother and sister supplement the family income by reselling goods with price controls like shampoo, toilet paper, corn flour, and deodorant at several times their original price. The family goes shopping together because stores ration how much of a good they sell per customer, and they try to buy a lot of everything so they can endure future shortages. They often stand in line for hours next to hundreds of other people, most of whom buy enough to consume and resell as well.[40] Venezuela may be running out of cooking oil, coffee, and powdered milk, but the old wooden cupboards in José Luis's home are stocked with enough food to last the family several months.

An increasing number of Venezuelans see shopping not as fun but as a stressful activity.[41] For people like José Luis, however, scarcity is also an opportunity. He could leave his job to work as a bachaquero—a reseller of price-controlled goods—full time, because an increasing number of people like him make more money as bachaqueros than by earning a minimum-wage salary. If José Luis lived in a border town, he would be tempted to smuggle goods like milk and gasoline across the border, where he can get several times the price he paid for them. Typically, street vendors make up almost 40 percent of those who work in Venezuela, and government employees make up a third of those employed, but how many bachaqueros are out there is a mystery for now because it is an illegal business and most of them avoid census takers.

When it comes to politics, José Luis has continually backed Chavismo for years, because his family has benefitted from social programs. Voters like him saw themselves reflected in Chávez, and his rhetoric of economic redistribution resonated with them. Plus, under Chávez the oil boom helped reduce poverty,[42] even if it proved short-lived. José Luis is not educated enough to fully understand concepts like democracy, socialism, inflation, or devaluation. Datanalisis estimates that nearly six of every ten Venezuelans lack enough formal education to achieve abstract thinking. "Most Venezuelans are susceptible to emotions, not rational thoughts," when it comes to politics, Datanalisis's León told me.[43] Indeed, Leon's polling firm found in 2010 that while Venezuelans approved of Chávez's Twenty-First-Century Socialism, nine out of ten people reject the idea of adopting Cuba's political and economic model.[44] What they like and crave is government assistance, and like previous generations, they will continue to support whoever promises to give them a larger share of oil wealth.

Few Venezuelans are as pro-Chavista as Humberto López is. The fifty-two-year-old bearded mechanic has something distinctive about him. When dressed in military fatigues complete with a starred beret, he resembles the iconic Ernesto "Che" Guevara. His Che persona has earned him the name "the Venezuelan Che" and a place within Chavismo as a star political organizer. Che, as he calls himself, is also a reputed top leader of the *Colectivos*, pro-Chavista armed groups that control various barrios and help rally—some say intimidate—voters to the ballot box. I met Che on a Saturday in January

2015 at the westernmost stop of the Caracas subway line, a place where few middle- and upper-income Venezuelans dare to tread. True to his persona, Che showed up in military garb, driving an olive-green, open-top 1951 Willys MB jeep. He chain-smokes cheap cigars he gets for free from a friend at a nearby market. His live-in girlfriend, Jenny, rode shotgun after having gone grocery shopping for coffee, Che's other daily addiction. I hopped in the back, and we sped off to the Barrio Nuevo Día, where he lives. Everyone in the streets shouted his name, soldiers saluted him, and he waved to his fans as we rode along. Riding with Che is almost as safe as riding inside a bulletproof car because no one dares mess with him.

Che lives in a modest two-story dwelling surrounded by rickety shacks with tin roofs on the side of a mountain that overlooks the famed La Guaira freeway that dictator Pérez Jiménez built. Che's assets are his home, which he inherited from his father, what looks like an abandoned home next door to his own, a savings account (he doesn't disclose how much he has saved), his jeep, tools he keeps in a shed, and two used Yamaha Virago 1000 motorcycles, which he says he managed to buy by saving the per diems he got from various minimum-wage government jobs. He also does some occasional work as a mechanic. In early 2015, however, a rotisserie chicken restaurant owner was paying him 10,000 bolivars (US$200 at the time) a month,[45] just to be seen in his restaurant, where he sat, smoked, and drank coffee. "I attract a certain clientele and criminals think twice about robbing his restaurant," he told me.

Che was a loyal follower of the late Chávez, and he blames Venezuela's economic ills on President Nicolás Maduro, who he sees as too soft on companies and the rich. Che is a firm believer that Venezuela's economic problems are caused by greedy business leaders who purposefully sabotage the economy to run Chavistas out. "We're in an economic war," Che said, referring to food scarcity. "And when you're at war, you bring out the military. Take the companies, militarize the economy!" Che didn't finish high school, but claims to read Marx and other thinkers on which he bases a mélange of ideas similar to the ideological mix Chavismo calls Twenty-First-Century Socialism.

He proudly claims he doesn't stand in line to buy groceries. Jenny, who is twenty years his junior, does the shopping for him. "I'm not a Cuban. I don't stand in line," he told me curtly, referring to the problems Cubans face every day. When he needs a spare tire for his motorcycles or any other scarce item, he picks up the phone and calls his Colectivo pals who solve the problem for him. "We don't threaten people to get what we need," he said of his Colectivo friends. "Some [armed] groups do it, but we don't." Che has subscription television at home and pays his electricity bill, though most of his neighbors don't. He told me he doesn't use toilet paper and has some handy only for visitors. Venezuelans should take advantage of food shortages to stop eating things that are bad for them, he said, like too much meat.

Che claims he has never benefited from government largess, but like many Venezuelans in the D and E segment, those closest to him have gained from social programs. Jenny finished her high school education thanks to Misión Robinson, and she studied law for free at the Universidad Bolivariana de Venezuela, a university founded by Chávez in 2003 that is known for enrolling all students, regardless of their prior education or academic scores. At the time of our chat Che was pulling some strings to get her a job as a lawyer in a government office. Jenny's mother managed to get a two-bedroom apartment assigned to her by the government even though she is a retiree living by herself (government apartments are usually assigned to families). Che assured me he did nothing to help her get a new home but admitted that she did mention to housing officials that he was practically her son-in-law and "that may have helped."

Ramón Barrios, the retired policeman who allowed me to examine his stash of price-controlled goods, lives just a few miles east of Che in La Pastora, a low-income neighborhood of ninety thousand people considered a stronghold of anti-Chavismo. He is a community organizer for Venezuela's opposition political party Un Nuevo Tiempo. He has a pension as a retired policeman and a minimum-wage job at the Caracas Metropolitan Legislative Council that provides extra income. Barrios's three-story makeshift home is in the lower part of his community, where years ago water service ran uninterrupted. But on the day of my visit he opened the tap of his kitchen sink and nothing came out. Electricity is also spotty. When I visited his home, Barrios invited a group of like-minded neighbors and party allies to share their experiences with me.

Barrios has known economic hardship, but he is relatively lucky for someone in his situation. He lives alone in a large house, so he is not forced to live in an overcrowded space with a large family, like many of his neighbors. Yet it was hard for him to make ends meet as inflation continued to climb. Barrios is diabetic and is covered by four different medical insurance policies. One of them he gets as a retired policeman, another he receives in his current job, and the insurance policies of his two sons provide coverage for him too. Still, he told me he gets his glucose meter, manufactured in Havana, from the Cuban doctors of the Barrio Adentro program for free. This drew howls of laughs and some reproving comments from his friends and neighbors, who also oppose Chavismo. Barrio Adentro is meant for those poorer than Barrios.

Barrios is an anti-Chavista activist who hasn't come to terms yet with the close relationship between Venezuela and Cuba. He doesn't like that the Castros have sent thousands of Cuban doctors to tend to Venezuelans. But scarcity and rising prices for medication are powerful enough forces for Barrios to briefly suspend his ideological inclinations. "What do I care if the doctor is Cuban? I have no beef with the Cubans. I don't like their regime, but that is something else," he told me. When Chavistas are no longer in power, Barrios believes, Cuban doctors should be given fifteen days to leave the country, but for now they may as well prove themselves useful. "One has to be an all-terrain type of person," Barrios said. "I believe in survival. I do what I can to survive."

FIG. 1. Some Venezuelans may not have running water or shoes to wear, but they won't miss their DirecTV programming.

FIG. 2. An empty Ford dealership is one of dozens that dot
Caracas at a time when car assembly plants lie idle for a chronic
lack of parts.

FIG. 3. Venezuelans stand in line to buy scarce groceries with price controls. In some cases people have been known to stand for hours for the chance to buy sugar, flour, or toilet paper.

FIG. 4. (*above*) Ramón Barrios, a retired policeman, shows his stash of price-controlled staples. He accumulated his food hoard over weeks of patiently standing in line to shop.

FIG. 5. (*right*) Venezuelans get not only rice but also a healthy dose of propaganda from the government.

FIG. 6. Humberto López, "the Venezuelan Che," waxes wise about the state of Venezuela's "economic war." His solution: have the military take over all privately owned companies, including food giant Polar.

FIG. 7. Che, with one of his most prized assets, a 1951 Willys Jeep, admits that getting parts for the car is a nightmare in Venezuela.

FIG. 8. (*above*) Rosa Meza lives in her two-bedroom apartment courtesy of the Chavista revolution. The government suspended her mortgage payments and those of all her neighbors. She doesn't know if she will ever have to pay for her home again.

FIG. 9. (*right*) The low-income family apartment complex, OPPPE 36, where Meza lives became famous for its shoddy construction. A year after it was finished residents complained of cracked walls, a broken elevator, pests, and sewer water seeping through the walls.

5 FUNNY BUSINESS

Alberto Vollmer, the forty-six-year-old chairman and chief executive officer of Ron Santa Teresa, still remembers a stark lesson his father taught him when he was just a boy. It was February 1983, and Venezuela's economy was in the midst of a currency debacle remembered as Black Friday. The bolivar suffered a massive devaluation against the dollar on the back of plummeting oil prices and a debt load the country could barely pay. People desperately tried to convert their bolivars into foreign currency. It was all very confusing to the young Vollmer, who turned to his father for an explanation as they made their way to Hacienda Ron Santa Teresa, their palm-tree-lined estate in the nearby Aragua valley.

"How bad is this crisis, and how long will it last?" Vollmer recalls asking his father. The older Vollmer said tough economic times could go on for many years. But he told his son not to dismay. This is both good and bad for the country and the family business, he said. When Venezuela's economy does poorly, local producers like Santa Teresa thrive. And when Venezuela's economy prospers, things don't go well for Santa Teresa's rum making. It seemed counterintuitive, but the reasoning was simple. When oil prices were high and Venezuela's economy flourished, a strong currency allowed Venezuela to cheaply import foreign goods such as whiskey, a pricier drink that Venezuelans favored over rum as a symbol of social status. This typically hurt Santa Teresa's rum sales.[1] And when oil prices plummeted and the economy soured, cash-strapped Venezuelans switched back to drinking rum. The explanation left a lasting impression on Vollmer, and it gave him an early appreciation for how tricky it was to do business in his native country. Vollmer's experience as head of a top rum maker offers a unique view of the pitfalls and outsized opportunities of doing business in an oil-dependent country like Venezuela.

The Vollmer family's rum-making tradition stretches back several generations to 1885, when Gustavo Julio Vollmer y Rivas, the first Vollmer born in the Americas, bought Hacienda Santa Teresa and revamped its rum-making operation. Gustavo Julio was the son of Gustav Julius Vollmer, a German émigré who had arrived in the South American country sixty years earlier from Hamburg and married Francisca Ribas, a cousin of Simón Bolívar, the famed South American hero. It was on Santa Teresa's land that Bolívar in 1818 ratified the abolition of slavery.

Santa Teresa had been producing rum for more than fifty years when oil was discovered in Venezuela in the early 1900s. The business managed to survive through the economic and political troubles that plagued the country for the next century. In 1999, as Chávez came to power, Alberto Vollmer and his brother took over the day-to-day operations of Santa Teresa and found a company nearing bankruptcy. It suffered from crushing debt and was quickly losing market share to competitors. The brothers restructured the business, cut costs by more than half, eliminated nine out of ten of the company's product lines, and saw sales rise 36 percent to roughly US$30 million by 2004.[2] It was a unique turnaround, but it was far from enough.

Vollmer, who wears jeans to the office and once worked as a photographer during his college years, saw the need to pair business success with a concern over social issues. A disaffected poor majority had voted Chávez into power, and the president's soak-the-rich rhetoric seemed to resonate with most Venezuelans. Vollmer saw an opportunity when a multitude of five hundred pro-Chávez families squatted on part of his land. He offered the group a deal: he would cede the land and a housing plan to accommodate a maximum of one hundred families, if the government paid for construction of the homes and the basic infrastructure needed to make it a residential area. The move earned him the respect of Chávez's leftist sympathizers.

Years later, when a local gang member was caught stealing in Santa Teresa,

Vollmer offered him a way out: do three months of unpaid work in Santa Teresa to mend the offence instead of handing him over to the police. The incident gave birth to Alcatraz, a project that uses rugby playing and training in various skills to draw troubled youth out of gangs and reinsert them into productive society. Vollmer's efforts were even captured in a business case study, "Ron Santa Teresa's Social Initiatives," published in 2005.[3] Harvard University's business school and others have studied the case as a fresh approach to managing political and social adversity.

In 2007 the World Economic Forum recognized Vollmer's social work by naming him a young global leader. In an attempt to build bridges with his government, Vollmer appeared on television with Chávez—a man who liked to brand business leaders as "parasites" or "bourgeois oligarchs." Chávez called Vollmer a true revolutionary. This didn't sit well with many of Vollmer's business leader colleagues, who thought that extending a hand to Chávez was a bad idea.

Vollmer's social work did not guard his business against Chávez's nationalization drive. In 2007 Chávez decreed the seizure of 131,000 acres of farmland in a bid to diversify planting of vegetables and corn. Two years later the military descended on the sugar-cane-rich Aragua valley to seize fields, forcefully oust sugar cane growers, and take their equipment. It was part of a Chávez plan to promote Venezuela's food self-sufficiency. The policy stripped Santa Teresa of 3,212 acres—a third of the estate. The seizure took away 20 percent of the agriculture-ready land on which Santa Teresa planted some of the sugar cane needed to produce molasses, a key ingredient in rum. The government called the seizure a "land rescue" and has yet to pay Santa Teresa for the land it took. As of May 2015 the case was still being dealt with in the courts.

The land law also forced Santa Teresa to devote another 20 percent of its farmland to planting corn instead of sugar cane, a directive that other growers in Aragua were also forced to follow. By early 2015 what used to be a key area of sugar cane production in Venezuela had little more than seventy-one hundred acres of sugar cane planted, a fraction of the area devoted to the crop before the land seizures began. The region went from producing more than a million tons of sugar cane a year to little more than 177,000 tons in 2014. Venezuela's overall sugar cane output in 2014 stood at 5.97 million tons, roughly 26 percent less than when Chávez came to power in 1999.[4] The change not only made it harder for Santa Teresa to obtain molasses but also decimated the country's sugar output. In 2009 Aragua supplied roughly two-thirds of the sugar Venezuela consumed, while the rest came from abroad. Six years later, with a much higher demand for sugar, that relationship was inverted. Venezuela now imports roughly two-thirds of the sugar it consumes, with the rest produced locally. Meanwhile, the government's corn and vegetable harvest goals have failed to materialize. State harvests are notoriously unproductive due to poorly tended lands or a lack of money to plant crops in the first place. Sometimes the modest harvest they yield is stolen.

Every step of producing rum gives Vollmer multiple headaches. But the country's economic troubles helped rum gain ground against whiskey. Santa Teresa's performance is astounding for a company doing business in a country plagued by inflation, various exchange rates, social upheaval, scarcity of raw materials, and a land-grabbing government. By 2014 the rum maker had managed to more than triple sales in ten years to US$100 million a year. Venezuela has long been one of the top ten markets in the world for scotch, but whiskey has become prohibitively expensive for most Venezuelans. Indeed in 2014 Diageo, the world's largest producer of spirits, reported it sold half the volume of scotch in Venezuela that it did the year before. Meanwhile, in June 2015, Diageo had seen sales of its Cacique rum double by selling not only a higher volume but also charging more for each bottle.[5]

Vollmer and his competitors deserve some credit. More than a decade ago Venezuela's rum makers launched a successful campaign to give local rum the designation of origin "Rum of Venezuela." The designation gave local rum producers an incentive to adhere to standards such as aging the rum for at least two years. The aim was to distinguish Venezuelan rum as a premium product in the same league as scotch. Vollmer says some consumers are now beginning to see premium rums as a good alternative to whiskey. Overseas, Santa Teresa has gained a reputation as being one of the best rum makers in the world, taking laurels at global spirits competitions.

Santa Teresa's main problem now is that it lacks enough raw materials to meet demand for its rum. "We're producing at 70 percent of our capacity," Vollmer told me in May 2015. The production challenges Santa Teresa faces are almost unthinkable for rum producers in other countries. A shortage of molasses is the main problem. Most of the sugar cane Santa Teresa needed

for its molasses came from the Aragua valley's harvest. Since the land take-
overs decimated the country's sugar cane production, Santa Teresa often
struggles to find molasses in other parts of Venezuela. Vollmer said Santa
Teresa suspended the distillation process for two months in 2014 due to a
molasses shortage.

Santa Teresa also has a hard time finding enough glass bottles for its rum.
The trouble started in 2010 when Chávez ordered the seizure of the glass-
making plants owned by U.S. glassmaker Owens-Illinois, which supplied
70 percent of the market. The government justified the takeover, arguing
that the company's dominance could cause problems in the future, but since
the state took over the company—now renamed Venvidrio—the supply
of bottles has been spotty. Smaller glass producers have gone bankrupt or
operate far below capacity because the government won't sell them dollars
to pay foreign suppliers of soda ash, a basic ingredient in making glass that
can be obtained only overseas.

This left the glass industry in 2015 operating at 60 percent of its capacity.[6]
The glass bottle problem became so great that in 2014 Santa Teresa stopped
production of its Rhum Orange, an orange rum liqueur made from two-year-
old rum and macerated orange peel, that came in a slender fifty-centiliter
bottle. The bottle maker went bankrupt, and no other domestic glassmaker
managed to produce a similar one. Vollmer found a glassmaker in Chile
that produced a few bottles, but the lack of dollar availability put an end to
that supply relationship. State glassmaker Venvidrio promised to produce
a similar bottle in 2015, but Vollmer wasn't holding his breath. "We'll see if
it really happens," he said.

Santa Teresa has also suffered shortages of corrugated cardboard boxes to
pack its bottles, the ink used for labels, and even the supply of bottle caps,
which became a problem when the usual supplier lacked the resin necessary
to produce them. Santa Teresa tried to import the caps, but the government
would not sell the company enough foreign exchange to pay for them. In
early 2015 Santa Teresa was forced to hold an inventory of no more than two
weeks' worth of the inputs it needs to keep production going, instead of the
several months' worth a rum producer usually maintains.

The government allows exporters like Santa Teresa to keep 60 percent
of the dollars they obtain from selling their goods abroad; they must

sell the rest to the state. However, Santa Teresa can't readily use its dollars to import the bottles, caps, and other materials it previously bought locally. The company uses its hard-earned foreign currency to develop new markets overseas. Vollmer jokes that his company is really in the extreme sports business because of the risk and uncertainty involved in every step of producing a bottle of rum. "This is a country where producing and adding value is practically prohibited, because of its economic policies," Vollmer told me.

Santa Teresa nets a 12 percent annual profit, but estimating costs can be tricky. Given the spotty nature of dollar availability in Venezuela, Santa Teresa has imported some inputs at various exchange rates. Finding scarce molasses far from Aragua can increase freight costs too. Due to inflation the company ups worker salaries every six months. Vollmer cannot say with absolute certainty how much the company earns in sales each year, and his US$100 million estimate was a conservative one that assumed a complex combination of exchange rates. High inflation also forces the company to keep its cash holdings low because Venezuela's currency loses value daily. The company keeps large debts in bolivars, since fixed-rate local debt loses value over time. Vollmer calls it "generating value through debt." Fortunately, Santa Teresa has managed to increase its rum prices freely, as liquor prices are not regulated. This advantage allows the company to keep up with rising costs as much as possible.

Vollmer's father was partly right when he told his son bad times could be good for Santa Teresa. The company can still make a profit despite incredible odds. But the boom-and-bust nature of Venezuela's economy has taught most people that producing is too much of a headache—importing goods is an easier business. Or as Vollmer puts it: "We're a nouveau riche country that never really had to work for what it has."

Since oil riches changed the country's entrepreneurial spirit in the early 1900s, Venezuela's strongest economic sectors, aside from the oil business, have stayed largely the same. Venezuela is a service-heavy economy where industries such as retail, real estate, telecommunications, and banking make up nearly half of the gross domestic product (GDP),[7] while manufacturers like Ron Santa Teresa, car assembly plants, and food producers amount to little more than 13 percent of G D P. In fact, under Chavismo manufacturing has lost importance in the economy, while the weight of imports doubled to 50 percent of G D P in the fourteen years through 2012.[8] Chavismo and previous governments never consistently tried to diversify the economy away from the oil business. The Chávez government has sold some companies U.S. dollars at preferential rates, doled out juicy government contracts to the well-connected, and forced banks to lend cheaply to favored sectors, but most companies were left to fend for themselves for more than a decade in an increasingly tough economic climate. Manufacturing also lost importance in the Venezuelan economy under Chávez, partly because the government seized scores of companies and ran most of them into the ground, and partly because excessive regulations made the economy less stable. Stringent regulations as well as price and capital controls cause many companies to lose money and, as such, make companies more dependent on the government's good graces to stay in business. Venezuela has become a place where the strongest companies survive, those who are the most politically loyal to Chavismo profit handsomely, and the rest learn to adapt to new and increasingly complex problems; otherwise they fail. And too many of them fail. The National Council of Commerce and Services, or Consecomercio, a commerce trade group, reported in early 2016 that fifty-eight thousand companies—most of them small—closed their doors in 2015 alone, because they could no longer operate in Venezuela's heavily regulated economy.

In a world where buying a disposable razor is almost impossible, brand loyalty has become irrelevant. Venezuelans accustomed to buying brand-name products have been forced to become less picky in the face of scarcity. And this is a problem for companies that for many years devoted millions of dollars in ads to persuade consumers to buy their brand of toothpaste or deodorant over that of competitors. Companies that have problems producing a good can suddenly lose the customer loyalty it took them years to build. Even in the face of scarcity many companies continue to advertise with the hopes that they can remain at the top of consumer minds until such time as they can resume their normal production cycle. "There no longer is such a thing as brand loyalty in this country," pollster Luis Vicente León told me. His polling firm Datanalisis found in August 2014 that nearly eight of every ten consumers no longer felt inclined to go the extra mile to find their preferred brand of food, household cleaning goods, or personal hygiene products.[9]

That makes sense, because in Venezuela customer choice is gone. In May 2015 for instance one could find only Colgate toothpaste in Venezuelan stores. All other brands seemed to have disappeared. Major consumer brands continued to advertise heavily in Venezuela, however, and some made sure to strike an inspiring tone in a time of crisis. At the airport in the city of Maracaibo, Coca-Cola campaign posters gush, "Happiness is your destiny" and "Optimism is always part of your luggage." That is quite a message for a country where travelers usually return home with their bags full of milk, shampoo, or the deodorant they can't buy in Venezuela.

Getting dollars at preferential rates from the government is key for companies to keep up production. The company that manages to get access to the dollar spigot can produce enough of a product and quickly grab market share away from competitors. In other words, the restrictive economic policies of Chavismo have not only forced Venezuelans to adjust their consumer habits but also created winning and losing companies.

Take the business of razors. In the battle between Procter and Gamble's Gillette and the Energizer-owned brand Schick, dollar availability made it possible for P & G to gain ground. In 2014 Energizer had trouble getting enough U.S. dollars and raw materials to supply Venezuela with Schick razors, so it quickly lost customers. By the end of the year, P & G had gained an additional 5 percent of market share in just months, and its Gillette brand controlled nearly 75 percent of the razor market.[10] In the game of getting access to U.S. dollars, companies like P & G and other large consumer product makers have developed close relationships with the government. But other companies are not that lucky or are simply unwilling to get too cozy with Venezuela's leftist politicians to obtain the necessary foreign currency, so they are forced to pare down or stop production of a product line and lose business.

Over coffee, Melquíades Pulido, the former president of the Venezuelan American Chamber of Commerce, explained to me why—despite such troubles—foreign companies refuse to abandon Venezuela. "This is a tremendous consumer market," he said. "Many companies will endure this tough situation as long as they can to stay here." Companies are used to making higher sales and profits in Venezuela than in many other markets, partly because they face less competition in their industries but in large part because of Venezuelan consumer habits. Pharmacy chains like Farmatodo for instance can earn 15 percent returns in Venezuela, nearly three times the rates of return for Walgreens and CVS in the United States. The hefty demand for products of Venezuela's credit-card happy consumers make it worthwhile for consumer goods and telecommunications companies to stick around, even when the economy sours. Telecom giant Telefónica, which claims more than a third of Venezuela's mobile market, has been known to earn higher revenue per phone user in Venezuela than in Brazil or even Germany, both far larger economies.[11]

The success of such companies is hard to believe for most people, when they hear news about foreign companies suffering heavy losses in Venezuela due to currency devaluations. In recent years, Ford, P&G, and even Telefónica have taken billions of dollars in charges in their financial statements because Venezuela's recurring devaluations make their bolivar sales worth less. And the Venezuelan government doesn't supply dollars for them to repatriate their earnings. P&G, a company with a sixty-five-year history in Venezuela, took a US$2.1 billion charge in July 2015, in large part due to Venezuela's weaker currency, yet the company told its shareholders it will continue doing business in Venezuela "for the foreseeable future."

Since they cannot convert their local sales into hard currency, foreign companies like DirecTV and Avon have taken to buying office buildings in Caracas with their bolivars.[12] Managing and maintaining those buildings is costly, but companies find the expense is preferable to letting their bolivars sit in bank accounts, where they lose value over time. Pulido points out that some of these companies managed to make fabulous profits in previous years, and even though doing business in Venezuela is increasingly costly and a hassle, the cost of leaving the country and dismantling their operations can be higher. Those who leave lose an important customer base, and it would be even more expensive for them to try and come back when the business climate improves. A marketing executive of a world-renowned soft drink company told me, "As a company in Venezuela you try to create new products that are not subject to price controls, you try to cut costs, you do anything you can do, but the last thing you do is leave Venezuela." Still, investing too much money in Venezuela can be tricky, a lesson that many industries, including car assembly plants, know all too well.

Chevrolet's car dealership on the busy Francisco de Miranda Avenue in Caracas stood abandoned in May 2015. Its two-thousand-square-foot showroom had no customers, no salespeople, and no cars. Desks lay piled on top of one another in rows. An idle mop leaned against a wall nearby. Next door, the Hyundai dealership was similarly empty. Its lone employee, a security guard, stood watch to prevent vagrants from breaking in. A sign on the window read, "We sell cars on consignment." The empty car dealerships that still dot Caracas in 2016 are a strange sight in a country where people see cars not only as a status symbol but as a form of investment in times of high inflation.

Buying a new car in Venezuela has become nearly impossible because car assembly plants don't produce enough and Venezuela's government regulates the prices of cars. To skirt price controls, cautious buyers and sellers of used cars meet in secret to execute transactions. The popular car website tucarro. com offers plenty of cars but no prices, just cellular phone numbers buyers can call for pricing details.

The government became fed up with the odd workings of the automotive industry in Venezuela, where car prices in bolivars rise along with the price of a dollar, so bureaucrats decided to regulate prices back in 2014. In times of robust economic growth, excess demand forces car buyers to get on waiting lists for vehicles and even pay hefty under-the-table commissions to salespeople to expedite their car purchases. For most buyers, having to negotiate the price tag of a car with a car salesperson is usually a hassle, and it is even more so if potential buyers have to bribe salespeople too. And when a new car rolls off the lot it's worth more money because people are willing to pay more for new cars when demand for them is through the roof. The real reason behind these anomalies is simple: the government's massive spending creates a demand for cars that assembly plants struggle to meet. Some expand their capacity, but others choose not to, because they never really know how long the burst of excess demand will last. No one wants to be left with idle capacity when oil prices decline and Venezuela's consumers no longer have enough money to spend.

Regulating car prices when the economy sours makes things equally problematic. At a Chevrolet dealership in Caracas in May 2015 I got curious stares the moment I stepped through the door, pretending to be a car buyer. There were no cars in the showroom, and Dayana, one of the three salespeople who spent their time reading newspapers, gave me a pity smile when I asked how to buy a vehicle. It had been two months since they sold a car, and they expected to get more in a month or two. After a brief chat Dayana gave me a card and told me to call her in a month to see what she could do for me. She didn't have to spell things out. It was obvious to me that she expected to be compensated for "helping" me buy a new vehicle. The government has set arbitrary prices on cars and this creates an even higher demand for them just as it happens with food. For instance in March 2016, the law forces a car dealership to sell a Grand Cherokee for no more than 12.5 million bolivars (or US$12,500).[13] That is such an unrealistic price that people pay far more under the table for that car. Vehicles leaving the factory floor on their way to dealership are guarded by members of the military that have instructions to deliver the car to a specific buyer that has prepaid for it. However buyers end up paying several times the official price because they've had to come up with enough extra money to bribe the salespeople and the military officers that deliver their car.

* * *

The *arepa*, a thick, round, tortilla-like patty made from corn flour, is traditional fare in every Venezuelan meal. People eat arepas for breakfast, lunch, and dinner and as a snack after a late night out. Venezuelans stuff arepas with cheese, pork, chicken, avocado, and a host of other ingredients, and they've given names to each variation, the most famous of all being the Reina Pepiada—loosely, "voluptuous queen"—in honor of a Venezuelan who was crowned Miss World in 1955. Arepas are to Venezuela what hamburgers are to the United States, a part of the country's cultural identity. They also happen to be big business.

Venezuelans make arepas from Harina P.A.N., a brand of flour so popular it is used as a neologism to refer to all corn flour, like calling all copy machines Xerox. The company responsible for such a successful product branding is Empresas Polar, a food giant that produces dozens of other products like mayonnaise, ketchup, and margarine, as well as the country's most popular beer brands and soft drinks. Polar also handles the bottling for Pepsi-Cola. Yet Harina P.A.N. has been the company's most emblematic product line for decades. Lorenzo Mendoza and his family own the company that began as a brewery in the early 1940s and has since grown to become the country's biggest private sector employer. The Mendozas also ranked number 690 in the 2015 Forbes list of the world's billionaires, with a net worth of US$2.7 billion.[14]

Polar's Harina P.A.N. came out in 1960, and for the first time made it easy for Venezuelans to make arepas. Before that, making the staple was a labor-intensive process that involved grinding corn into thick dough. Polar's flour just needed some water, and presto, the dough was ready. In 2015, however, Polar was losing money on every bag of Harina P.A.N. it produced. In fact, Polar began losing money on Harina P.A.N. in 2006, three years after Hugo Chávez imposed price controls on corn flour and other basic foodstuffs. In other words, the country's most emblematic food product produced losses for Polar for nearly a decade.[15]

Manuel Larrazábal, the CEO for Polar's food unit, walked me through the numbers in a glass-walled conference room at Polar's headquarters. The cost to Polar of producing a one-kilogram bag of flour was 16 percent higher than the price it could charge for the product. By Larrazábal's estimates, the company lost US$13.7 million annually from the sale of Harina P.A.N. in Venezuela.[16] "This is the moment when we're losing the most money, no doubt about it," he told me. The price for Polar's flour sat frozen for so long, and the government sanctioned price adjustments have been so meager, that the product has become almost worthless. "They have turned arepa flour into the new gasoline," Larrazábal said, referring to Venezuela's world-famous subsidized gas, the difference being that the state pays for the gasoline subsidy, but with Harina P.A.N., the money comes out of Polar's pocket.

Harina P.A.N.'s price of 19 bolivars (or ten U.S. cents) per bag,[17] made the flour cheaper than practically anything for sale in Venezuela. For the price of a cup of coffee, a consumer could buy two kilos of Harina P.A.N., enough to make forty arepas. For a more mind-bending example, the price of an arepa with cheese sold on the streets bought four kilos of Harina P.A.N., enough to make eighty similar arepas in the first place. That's because the law does not regulate prices for a cup of coffee or cheese arepas, so they rise with inflation. To show the public its predicament, in 2015 Polar released a television spot pointing out these distortions. "The effort of the Venezuelan workers who produce your favorite brand deserves a fair price," the ad said.[18]

Demand for Harina P.A.N. continues to rise because its low price makes it a target for smugglers but also because Polar's flour is the only brand

Venezuelans seem to find in stores. Harina P.A.N. production usually supplies half of the 1,250 million tons of flour Venezuelans consume every year. But Larrazábal pointed out that at the time the latest customer pantry check surveys showed that more than 70 percent of households carried Harina P.A.N., which means Polar's share of the market dramatically increased. Polar's competitors are producing far below capacity, and there's a very good reason for that: they are all controlled by the government. The state now owns eighteen corn flour industrial plants it seized from various companies. The government also controls Monaca, a corn flour producer owned by Mexican tortilla maker Gruma that used to satisfy 20 percent of flour demand. Government-controlled plants are plagued by slowdowns, shutdowns, and the lack of raw material. To the government's embarrassment, Polar's Lorenzo Mendoza has often publicly asked president Maduro to let Polar run the flour factories the government can't seem to run on its own. Maduro has never responded to that offer.

Polar's competitors don't produce enough because they also lose money. Polar did increase Harina P.A.N. production capacity in 2014 because the state promised to raise the price of flour enough to make it profitable if Polar brought new capacity online. When the company did so in August 2014, the state increased the price of flour roughly 50 percent, making the product profitable again for the first time in years. But corn growers then demanded a price increase for their crop too, and two months later the state increased the price of corn—Harina P.A.N.'s main ingredient—by 218 percent, making Harina P.A.N. unprofitable again. "The only way to increase installed capacity is allowing for profitability. There's no other way," Larrazábal argued.

A bigger problem is that Venezuela doesn't produce enough corn to satisfy the country's consumption. Even after the government nationalized lands and forced sugar cane producers like Ron Santa Teresa to plant corn instead, the plans for self-sufficiency have gone nowhere. The state imports six of every ten tons of corn Venezuelans eat. "If the government stops importing corn we don't eat arepas," Larrazábal said. To make matters worse, the government sells the imported corn to flour producers like Polar at roughly three times the price it pays to import it,[19] a rich business for Venezuela's socialist government. Polar asked the government to sell imported corn at lower prices to make flour production viable, but the government refused to do so.

Polar has been forced to pay for Harina P.A.N.'s losses with the money the company makes from other products. But in 2015 Venezuela's government banned Polar from selling other variants of Harina P.A.N., including a whole-wheat kind with extra fiber, arguing that such products were only meant to skirt price regulations. It didn't help at all when Polar noted that the company had been producing other Harina P.A.N. variations years before the government began regulating food prices. Or as Larrazábal told me: "[The government] says we already make a lot of money selling beer and other products." The thinking within Chavismo is that the Mendozas are rich enough and can afford to endure tough times with little access to foreign currency, paying more for raw materials and absorbing losses on their flagship product.

Distributing Harina P.A.N. to customers is a nightmare for Polar too. The company boasts the best distribution network in the country, reaching thirty-seven thousand points of sale across Venezuela, but in the face of food shortages the state began forcing Polar to divert truckloads of Harina P.A.N. from other parts of the country to the politically important capital, Caracas. Polar was also forced to redirect its flour distribution to state-owned supermarket chains. The idea was to give shoppers the perception that only government-owned grocery chains could deliver the food they need. And it's also why bachaqueros do their shopping primarily in state-owned grocery chains—because the government does what it can to keep state supermarkets well supplied. Of course redirecting food is a poor substitute for more production, especially when demand keeps rising because unrealistically low prices foster smuggling.

Another company in almost any other country would have stopped producing Harina P.A.N. years ago. Why endure the hassle if a government is so intent on forcing Polar to produce at a loss? Doing away with the country's most beloved product, however, would alienate millions of Polar's customers. But more important, stopping production could prompt the government to nationalize the company as Maduro, and Chávez before him, has threatened to do multiple times. Polar is already under constant government scrutiny. Larrazábal ticked off a list of half a dozen regulatory bodies, including the tax agency and the price regulation agency, that send inspectors to Polar unannounced almost daily.

During the week before my visit, Polar had undergone fifteen inspections from various government offices. In fact Polar keeps a count, available publicly on its website, of how many times the government has inspected its operations. From early 2008 through late-February 2016, the company tallied twenty-eight hundred inspections for Polar's food unit alone, or twenty-nine inspections per month. "We like to say that Polar is like Disney World," Larrazábal joked, "because everybody comes to visit." So far, Larrazábal proudly told me during our chat, not a single inspection had managed to find irregularities. In fact, Larrazábal noted how government inspectors are often awed by Polar's modern-looking installations. When they use the restrooms some are surprised to find Polar lavatories have toilet paper available. Sometimes, Larrazábal said, government inspectors have been known to offer their résumés to any Polar employee who looks like a manager in a position to help them. "Inspectors really understand what is going on in this country," Larrazábal said.

Polar has taken a unique, and quite courageous, stance toward state harassment: transparency. Unlike any other privately held company, Polar publishes on its website monthly, biweekly, and weekly reports detailing how much raw material it holds, how much of each food product it produces, the inventory it keeps on hand, how many tons of goods it distributes to clients, who their clients are, and how many trucks it uses. Polar's numbers tell a sobering story of what it is like to do business in Venezuela. On January 29, 2016, the company kept enough food inventory to last 1.1 days nationwide. The most it kept on hand was two days' worth of canned tuna. And a week earlier, Polar had no more than seven days' worth of white corn to produce Harina P.A.N., because getting enough corn is a problem in Venezuela. The tight inventory could force the company to stop producing if it ran out.

In late January 2016, Polar's Pepsi plant reported a tight four-day inventory of sugar, which Polar imports because the country's sugar output suffered when the state took over lands in the Aragua valley. If rum maker Santa Teresa has trouble getting molasses, Polar struggles to find sugar for soft drinks too. Polar alerted the government in 2015 that it needed to import more sugar on a regular basis or its Pepsi operation could suffer. Getting dollars to import raw materials is also an issue. In late January 2016, Polar had more than 360 requests to buy a total of US$78 million in foreign currency to pay overseas suppliers. Polar has had to wait as long as 460 days for the government to approve a dollar purchase request and as long as 738 additional days, or more than two years, to actually get the cash.

The most brilliant aspect of Polar's policy of transparency is that the company also publishes data on the products it fails to produce and why. In a country where the government has stopped making information available regularly to avoid the embarrassment of admitting high inflation and food scarcity, Polar's numbers are a not-too-veiled kick in the shin to a notoriously inefficient government.

Polar's worker absenteeism problems—a common issue Venezuelan companies face because firing workers is costly—resulted in the company failing to produce 62,211 kilos of mayonnaise and 86,000 kilos of flour during the two-week period ending on January 24, 2016. How about the power failures so common in Venezuela? Polar failed to produce 473.3 kilos of various products in those same two weeks because of recurring power outages and low voltage problems. That's not all. At Polar's Minalba bottled water plant, which has been in business for more than half a century, output was cut by 40 percent, or 3.32 million liters of water, in January 2016 because the company lacked packaging materials. Power outages at Minalba accounted for an additional deficit of 3,053 liters.

Time is also wasted in getting products to consumers. Polar needs government authorization before dispatching trucks carrying merchandise. Polar has to notify the government of every truck's cargo, its origin and destination, the truck's plate number, even the name of the truck driver. Polar must then wait for the government's nod for each truck to go on its way, but sometimes government officials take too long to approve shipments. This caused Polar an accumulated 582 hours of shipment delays during a two-week period in late January 2016, the equivalent of almost a month in lost time. Tracking truckloads of goods is meant to stop Polar products from ending up across the border or in the hands of the bachaqueros, who resell these goods for a living. "The government says we're in an economic war," said Larrazábal. "Then every Venezuelan must be an economic warrior, because people mostly behave in economically rational ways, especially in times of crisis."

Venezuela's National Superintendency for the Defense of Socioeconomic Rights, also known as SUNDDE, is the scourge of companies, shop owners, smugglers, bachaqueros, and anyone else involved in a legal or irregular line of work. The regulator is the government's big stick for those perceived to stray from state economic directives, and it helps enforce Chavismo's economic logic. The SUNDDE's job is ambitious: it aims to regulate Venezuelan consumption patterns, keep an eye on the cost structure of companies, and fix the maximum profits they can earn. Venezuela's government has decreed that no business can earn more than 30 percent returns on top of its costs, and in 2015 the SUNDDE was beginning to enforce this rule.

But the SUNDDE's purpose surpasses the technical into the political and ideological realm. In its 2015 and 2014 year-end reports, SUNDDE officials summarize their work and goals as fighting the "economic war that the parasitic bourgeoisie has declared against the people,"[20] and "to continue building the bolivarian socialism of the twenty-first century as an alternative to the savage and destructive capitalist system." As far as SUNDDE officials are concerned, Venezuela's runaway inflation and scarcity of products "have no rational economic explanation." This falls in line with Chávez's famed remark that "being rich is bad." For a time, the late president tried to popularize the idea that being an entrepreneur was suspect, even though his government made it possible for several well-connected Venezuelan business people to become astronomically rich. Under Chavismo, becoming rich is perfectly legal and possible as long as one does not criticize or otherwise interfere with the government's political goals. Many wealthy Venezuelans have learned to survive by either helping Chavismo or staying away from politics. Those hostile to the government get regular visits from the SUNDDE.

The SUNDDE's force of more than twenty-seven thousand volunteer inspectors, also called "People's Inspectors," are split into "fighting cells" that check every step of a product's journey from its arrival in Venezuelan ports or its production in a factory through the distribution chain until it reaches store shelves. SUNDDE officers, wearing their emblematic red-and-beige vests, run joint operations with the Venezuelan military to arrest street vendors found to be reselling goods with price controls, seize the inventory of companies accused of hoarding products, and arrest company executives considered economic saboteurs. SUNDDE operates in a legal world where, according to Venezuelan legal experts, an inspector's word can be enough to merit someone's arrest. It was SUNDDE inspectors in a joint operation with intelligence service agents who arrested Farmatodo pharmacy chain executives in February 2015 and accused them of economic boycott for not having enough cash registers operating in one of the chain's stores.[21]

In the first two months of 2015, Venezuelan authorities arrested more than twenty executives, mostly from supermarkets, pharmacies, and meat distributors, on similar charges of destabilizing Venezuela's economy. In one notable case, the government arrested the manager and legal representatives of Dia Dia, a supermarket chain that served more than 1 million customers in low-income neighborhoods, after an inspection found it held too much inventory.[22] The executives were jailed at Venezuela's intelligence agency head-quarters, and the chain was placed under the management of the state-owned food distribution company PDVAL. Dia Dia began as the social entrepreneur-ship project of José Vicente Aguerrevere, a mechanical engineer with an MBA from Harvard, who studied food chains in Latin America for a model that would offer low-price goods to poor families who shop for groceries every day. Dia Dia earned him recognition as a social entrepreneur by the World Economic Forum. Aguerrevere was not arrested and now lives in Boston.

Many believe the SUNDDE's role is to find people to blame for the coun-try's economic ills. The professional background of the agency's staff suggests that politics is the primary concern of those in charge. In the year and a half since President Maduro founded the agency, the SUNDDE had four different chiefs—all of them with a history as Chavista political activists. SUNDDE's first superintendent was Andreína Tarazón, a telegenic twenty-five-year-old law graduate who worked as a political organizer for the United Social-ist Party of Venezuela during her college years. But she had no experience working in the private sector or anywhere else to merit her appointment as a top regulator. Tarazón concurrently held the post of Venezuela's minister of women. She held both posts for five months until she was replaced at the SUNDDE by Dante Rivas, thirty-nine, a geography graduate with a face for television, who in the previous two years had served four months as min-ister of the environment, nine months as the head of the national institute of transport, and six months as minister of commerce. He left SUNDDE after two months on the job when President Maduro named him chief of Venezuela's passport authority. His replacement at SUNDDE, a lawmaker, lasted nine months at the agency. Maduro, like the late Chávez before him, is known to cultivate popular, young politicians and shuffle them from one post to the next, hoping fresh blood will fix inefficiency and corruption. But the president's SUNDDE appointees have all lacked business experience and would have a hard time reading a balance sheet. Plus, they rarely stay long enough to understand how any company or industry works.

SUNDDE's army of inspectors is similarly ill-equipped for the job. Many of them have little more than a high school education, a few have accounting or law degrees, and they lack the experience and training to understand a company's inventory management, much less its cost structure. José, a lawyer for a dairy producer in Venezuela that once was owned by a multinational corporation, told me how SUNDDE inspectors show up at least once every two weeks and always ask for the same information: the company's installed capacity, how much it is producing, and how much inventory it has. José said most inspectors don't seem to understand what they're asking anyway.

When SUNDDE announces a call to recruit new inspectors, scores of unemployed homemakers, former teachers, and law students are known to apply, thinking a job as a SUNDDE volunteer can lead to some government perk or benefit, or a permanent position in the government. Many repeat Chavismo's leftist mantra even if they don't exactly share that ideology, because they understand the keywords they need to get the job. Those who get hired are sworn in next to a statue of Chávez, where they promise to do what is necessary to protect the poor from capitalists. They are then sent to inspect the operations and finances of multimillion-dollar companies like Polar. This scenario explains why government inspectors often show up at Polar with their résumés on hand and would jump at the chance to work in the country's best-managed company.

* * *

Few businesses in Venezuela are as profitable, peculiar, and unpredictable as banks. Venezuelan bank profitability is considered an anomaly around the world. Wall Street bankers would sell their mothers and their souls to make their banks half as profitable as their Venezuelan counterparts. Of course, U.S. banks' total profits in dollars are larger than those earned by Venezuelan financial institutions, especially at a time when the bolivar is worthless, but the profit margins of U.S. banks are far lower.

Rolling Stone magazine once called Goldman Sachs a "great vampire squid wrapped around the face of humanity" for its relentless search for profits,[23] but Goldman's margins in 2014 stood far below those of top Venezuelan financial institutions. Venezuela's Grupo Banesco, the largest bank in the country by assets, lacks Goldman's size and global reach, but its annual nominal return on assets was more than six times that of the Wall Street firm.[24] Grupo Banesco's nominal return on equity—a measure of how much profit a bank earns for every dollar or bolivar shareholders invest in the business—was nearly eight times that of Goldman.[25] This vast difference in the profitability between Venezuelan and U.S. banks is a recurring phenomenon. More to the point, Goldman Sachs' famed chairman Lloyd Blankfein at sixty years old finally became a billionaire in 2015 with a net worth of US$1.1 billion, according to the Bloomberg Billionaires index.[26] But back in Caracas, the fifty-six-year-old Juan Carlos Escotet, the founder of Grupo Banesco, is already number 534 in the Forbes list of the world's billionaires, with a net worth of US$2.6 billion.[27] Yet few people outside Venezuela know Escotet's name. Needless to say, Venezuelan banks are more profitable than their peers in the rest of Latin America too, including far larger banks in Brazil and Mexico.

Such a rich performance by financial institutions in a developing country as troubled as Venezuela is hard to fathom. True, adjusted for inflation, Venezuelan bank profitability is far less than what it initially appears for its shareholders. But Venezuela's financial system traditionally enjoys far higher margins than most others around the world. The key source of Venezuelan bank profits is the difference between the low interest they pay for deposits and the high rates they charge their customers for loans. That interest differential is and has historically been wider in Venezuela than nearly anywhere else. This became the case the moment private banks in the oil-rich country were first allowed to set their own interest rates in the late 1980s.

But Venezuelan banks don't rely entirely on a boring business like borrowing and lending to make money. Banks in this country have been known to speculate heavily on real estate and resort hotels during construction booms, and they lend money to the businesses of their own shareholders and executives. Such risky endeavors would not be tolerated in other countries, but in Venezuela bank regulation has traditionally been less strict. Banks are the economy's plumbing system. And in a country with so much flowing oil money, those who control the plumbing can make a lot of money on commissions and on unorthodox but profitable side deals. When inflation creates poor lending conditions, banks still lend money to Venezuela's crazed consumers, but they invest heavily in government bonds and securities that can offer steady, almost risk-free returns. And in times of exchange controls, they have been known to deal in black market dollars too.

Venezuelan banks have learned to adapt to extremely adverse conditions to make money. "The source of bank profits is always changing," Oscar García Mendoza, who served as the chief executive officer of Banco Venezolano de Crédito for thirty-one years through 2014, told me in a telephone interview. "As a banker in Venezuela, if you want to run a simple business, you will never be successful," he said.[28] When trading black market dollars for clients using dollar-denominated bonds and gold was not yet punishable with jail time under Chávez, García Mendoza's bank did a brisk business helping match dollar buyers and sellers and charging a fee for the service. Still, he made sure to retain a team of savvy lawyers who could get the bank out of a tight spot if such business ever became an issue with the government.

Under Chávez, García Mendoza's bank, unlike its competitors, developed a reputation for not participating in the wholesale buying and selling of government-issued dollar debt—a very profitable and legal business at the time. Many banks eagerly bought state-issued dollar-denominated bonds, paying for them in bolivars at the official rate of 2.15 bolivars per dollar, only to resell them to local investors at more than twice that rate, pocketing the difference. The scheme worked because Venezuela's exchange controls created a hunger for anything that could be sold for dollars, especially government IOUs. It was a fantastic business. The government managed to get financing, the banks made gobs of money, and customers got access to dollars.

But those who participated in that scheme were forced to keep a far too close relationship with the government, something that made García Mendoza and his bank directors uncomfortable. "Benefiting from such a great business with the help of the government is never free," said García Mendoza, because bureaucrats and politicians always want something in return from banks that earn hefty profits. Some banks often engaged in unsavory business practices too, García Mendoza said. He remembers a customer who sought a loan from a competing bank to finance the renovation of a building he wanted to sell. The bank president allegedly offered to approve the loan if the bank was able to get a cut from the building's eventual sale.

Under Chávez's socialist government, banks continued to make gobs of money. For starters currency controls forced Venezuelans to keep their money in the country, which flooded the banks with cash. Unlike most financial institutions, Venezuelan banks don't need to borrow money from investors or other banks to do business; almost all their funds come from inexpensive customer deposits. And the same capital controls spawned a lucrative foreign-exchange trading business for banks that lasted many years. Chavismo set minimum and maximum levels of interest rates banks had to pay and charge customers, but the margin between the two is still wide. Chávez forced banks to devote nearly two-thirds of their loans to state-favored activities like agriculture and tourism at below-market interest rates.[29] At the same time, however, his government issued billions of dollars in government debt, and trading those instruments became a rich side business for financial institutions. Under Chavismo the weight of the financial-services sector in the country's economy more than tripled to nearly 8 percent of GDP in September 2015.[30] Banks have long sought close ties with the government as a way to stay alive and profitable over time. And Venezuelan politicians have learned to keep a cozy relationship with banks because they control the country's economic plumbing.

A year after I moved to Venezuela, I caught president Hugo Chávez during a public appearance and asked him to explain how he reconciled his leftist rhetoric with economic policies that helped banks make so much money. His usually jovial facial expression darkened for a moment, but he then sounded a conciliatory tone. "The idea is that all businesses in this country make money," he said and walked on.[31] The truth is that the more restrictive policies become in a country like Venezuela, the greater the incentive for banks to engage in risky side businesses to make a profit, because the excessive flow of oil money is still there thanks to the government's uncontrolled spending of oil money. Venezuelan banks are not run-of-the-mill, small-town, mom-and-pop banks. Venezuela's flood of riches has turned banks into a deformed, steroid-injected version of what a normal bank should look like. Bankers feel entitled to charge high interest rates and fees because inflation and the bolivar's devaluation eat away their gains. In times of high inflation, banks also lose money in real terms on every loan or credit card they issue, so they seek to trade profitable government-issued IOUs. And they engage in real estate and foreign currency speculation, because too many petrodollars make the bolivar overvalued too. In fact, speculation and loose lending were behind the failure of several banks during the Venezuelan banking crisis of the late 1990s.

The fabulous profits of Venezuelan banks can be dangerous. Banks in Venezuela are well capitalized and were growing at a fast clip in 2015,[32] but their owners were not investing enough in continuing to capitalize their businesses, which could lead some to become insolvent eventually. That's hardly a surprise. Why would a banker invest to grow a business when inflation is trending higher than the profits bank shareholders earn? Having banks that invest too much money in government paper can also become a problem if Venezuela's government stops paying its debts. As García put it, banks that become too cozy with the government "are trying to save a business but risk losing a country." Worse, if Venezuela suddenly eliminates exchange controls, savers could choose to pull out their bolivars from banks en masse to exchange them for dollars, a nightmare scenario for the country's financial institutions. Venezuelan banks are an example of the wild-west business practices of an oil-rich enclave where wealth and profit go to those with enough wits and a sense of timing to make a fortune.

The jet-setting banker Víctor Vargas is the type of businessman who thrives in this upside-down world. His Banco Occidental de Descuento, or BOD, Venezuela's fourth-largest privately owned bank,[33] took spot 1,407 in the 2015 Forbes list of the world's biggest public companies, valued at US$12.9 billion. Vargas grew up in an upper-middle-income home and married into a banking family that launched his financial career. In the 1990s he created and sold banks, and took advantage of Venezuela's banking crisis to snap up BOD, a regional bank with a roster of oil industry clients. Years later, when anti-Chavista oil workers sought to oust Chávez by going on strike, Vargas reportedly opposed the move and in doing so gained the government's trust.[34] He soon developed a reputation as "Chávez's banker," primarily because his bank dealt heavily in buying and selling government-issued dollar debt. In 2006 nearly four of every ten dollars his bank earned came from buying and selling securities, mostly government paper.[35]

As his business thrived under Chavismo so did Vargas, whose taste for luxury became legendary among the reporters who covered banking industry events where Vargas would hold court, donning fine suits and expensive watches. He is known to closely guard his net worth, but his lifestyle tells his story.

Vargas's life has no time zone, as he shuttles between his various homes in Caracas, New York, Miami, Palm Beach, and the Dominican Republic. In late 2004 his Dominican home became the venue for a lavish reception for 1,570 guests catered by New York's Le Cirque, when his daughter married Luis Alfonso de Borbón, the great-grandson of the late Spanish dictator Francisco Franco and second cousin of Spain's King Felipe VI.[36] A polo fanatic, Vargas owns the Lechuza Caracas polo team, famed for a stable of purebred steeds he flies around the world to play in top tournaments. The Spanish-language magazine *Hola!*, which closely follows the lives of royalty and the super-rich, often features photos of Vargas and his family spending summers in Spain's exclusive port of Sotogrande,[37] where he is often spotted aboard the *Ronin*, a 190-foot-long yacht he purchased from Larry Ellison, the founder of Oracle Corporation.[38] When jaded Venezuelans see Vargas's wealth they assume it flows from government favors, the easy riches they dream of achieving one day. Yet Vargas takes exception to the idea that he owes it all to Chavismo. In a rare interview with the *Wall Street Journal* in 2008, he tried to set the record straight for those in the media who marveled at his lifestyle but did a poor job of tallying his assets: "I've got three planes, two yachts, six houses," he noted. "I've been rich all my life!"[39]

The widely held belief in Venezuela that the ultrarich owe their success to government favors is best exemplified by the rise of Wilmer Ruperti, a fifty-five-year-old oil tanker captain turned shipping tycoon. Ruperti, a stout man fascinated with all things related to Simón Bolívar, owned a small shipbroking firm in Venezuela when in 2002 oil industry strikers sought to end Hugo Chávez's government.

The son of an immigrant Italian cook who arrived in Venezuela in the 1950s, Ruperti had worked for years as a ship captain in state-owned company Petroleos de Venezuela (PDVSA) before striking it out on his own in the 1990s. Ruperti's business made money by contracting ships for as little as US$5,000 per day, then turning around and chartering them to commodity trading clients for as much as seven times that amount.[40] When the oil strike crippled Venezuela's fuel supply, Ruperti moved quickly to charter three Russian tankers to bring in fuel he sold to Venezuela's government, and he talked shipping companies and insurers into allowing ships to dock in Venezuelan ports, something many were afraid to do because of the ongoing political upheaval.

The Chavistas saw his intervention as crucial in bringing an end to the strike. Years later Chávez honored Ruperti's efforts with the Star of Carabobo, a high government distinction. Ruperti's quick thinking during the crisis netted him a cool US$16 million,[41] but his biggest reward was earning the trust of PDVSA, which would often turn to Ruperti for its shipping needs after it dismissed thousands of employees—including those in its shipping arm—for taking part in the strike. By 2008 Ruperti's business owned nineteen ships and was worth, by Ruperti's own estimates, roughly US$1.4 billion.[42]

Ruperti is often considered Venezuela's version of Aristotle Onassis, not least because of his flamboyance. At a Christie's auction in 2004 he paid US$1.6 million for two pistols once owned by Simón Bolívar.[43] Years later Chávez displayed the pistols on national television and thanked Ruperti for donating them to the country.[44] Ruperti is known for flying in a private jet, driving a bulletproof BMW, and keeping two South Korean bodyguards with deadly knife-throwing skills,[45] like something out of the James Bond movie *Goldfinger* in which an evil Korean named Oddjob kills people by throwing a razor-sharp bowler hat like a deadly Frisbee. In the last decade Ruperti founded television channel Canal i and later married Venezuelan soap opera star Anastasia Mazzone, a woman twenty years his junior. "A lot of people think I'm a devil, but it's not true," he told the *Wall Street Journal* in 2006. "I sleep easily at night and morally I'm satisfied."[46] Ruperti's gold-plated life is just a taste of the riches that flow from an industry that is Venezuela's wellspring of riches and folly: oil.

station premises, but the thirty thousand liters of gas he sells every day—fuel is sold by the liter in Venezuela—amounted to less than 3,000 bolivars in sales in May 2015, enough to buy two movie tickets, a popcorn-and-coke combo to consume at the theater, and a bite to eat afterward. PDVSA wires Pepe two lump-sum payments every month; one is a subsidy that covers Pepe's payroll for eight employees, worker benefits, and maintenance costs. The other is supposed to be Pepe's "profit" for handling the gasoline giveaway. "None of this makes sense," Pepe told me, and added that as of May 2015, a cash-strapped PDVSA owed him two months of cost subsidy. "Gasoline prices must rise. There's no other way out."

Venezuelans consume gasoline with the same abandon reserved for drinking large amounts of Coca-Cola or water. And it makes sense because in Venezuela a gallon of either of these drinks is far more expensive than a gallon of gasoline. The average Venezuelan consumes 40 percent more gasoline than people in any other country in Latin America.[2] Venezuelans love 4×4 sport utility vehicles, Hummers, and fast cars. Dilapidated gas-guzzlers from the 1970s still make the rounds as taxis in Venezuelan streets. Yachts, boats, and jet skis overrun the crystal-clear waters of Venezuela's beaches. Beachgoers clad in bikinis and swim trunks anchor boats offshore and stage massive parties, the floating equivalent of tailgate gatherings—complete with DJs, bass-thumping loudspeakers, and plenty of rum and whiskey—that also burn obscene amounts of gasoline. Jet fuel is also ridiculously cheap. It all made sense to me when I departed Caracas after one of my research trips. I boarded an Airbus A321 bound for Colombia, but nearly two-thirds of the plane's 194 seats were empty by the time we took off. I asked a flight attendant if this passenger load was normal, and she nodded and told me sometimes flights would depart with as few as three passengers on board. Airlines flying to Venezuela don't care if their flights are empty on the way out, because they refuel their planes with cheap jet fuel in Venezuelan airports, a great way to save money.

Cheap gasoline has given birth to *pimpineros*, curbside sellers of gasoline smuggled across the border to Colombia, where gas goes for dozens of times the price in Venezuela. *Pimpinero* comes from *pimpina*, the name given to the plastic containers used to carry fuel. Small-time bootleggers will fill pimpinas, stow them out of sight in their vehicles, and drive them across the border to Colombia, undetected by Venezuelan soldiers who keep an eye out for smugglers. Some people fill their motorcycle tanks, ride across the border, empty the tank, and sell the gas, keeping just enough for the return trip home. By some estimates, as much as 14 percent of Venezuela's gasoline ends up across the border.[3]

Smuggling causes shortages of gasoline in Venezuelan gas stations. In Maracaibo, the capital city of the oil-rich state of Zulia near the border with Colombia, lines of cars often snake out of filling stations. Sometimes pimpineros will sell liters of gasoline in plastic bottles just blocks away from Maracaibo gas pumps. As with shampoo and detergent, shortages have gotten so bad that a pimpinero need not cross the border to resell fuel but can easily do so inside Venezuela. To prevent smuggling, Venezuela's border states have been placing electronic chips on vehicle windshields to track the consumption of trucks, buses, and regular passenger cars when they refuel, to make sure they don't purchase too much gas. Of course regular Venezuelans, pimpineros, and bootleggers are the small fish. Members of the top brass in Venezuela's military are reputed to control the really big business of smuggling whole gasoline tank trucks across the border undetected. Profits from gasoline smuggling are large enough to grease the palms of soldiers, custom officials, and anyone even mildly involved in the gasoline value chain. Even top executives of PDVSA, responsible for supplying the country with fuel, have been tied to smuggling rings. In January 2015, Gladis Nubia Parada, PDVSA's chief of the domestic fuel market division, was arrested and later charged with allegedly diverting fuel to border zones.[4] Sometimes it seems as if nearly everyone is tempted to get a cut of the gasoline giveaway.

Venezuela began enjoying the cheapest gasoline in the world in the late 1940s. By then Venezuelans had come to realize that living in an oil-rich country could involve perks like cheap gas. For years prices for gasoline in Venezuela were higher than in non-oil-producing nations, something Venezuelans believed at the time was outright unfair. Why not enjoy one's own wealth? Venezuela's government decreed cheap gasoline prices in 1945, and four years later, a gallon of gasoline sold in Caracas for less than half the price it did in New York. Venezuela's domestic gasoline prices had become the cheapest on the planet,[5] a distinction the country has held on to, on and off, until today. The amount of money PDVSA receives from selling gasoline at home is not enough to cover the cost of producing that gasoline in the first place. By some estimates, PDVSA gives up US$12.5 billion in earnings every year in subsidizing the country's gas-guzzling habit.[6] That is enough money for Venezuela to build a brand-new gasoline refinery every year with a capacity to turn three hundred thousand barrels of oil into gasoline every day,[7] enough to satisfy nearly half of Venezuela's daily consumption. It is a lot of money for a country that is running out of toilet paper because it doesn't have enough cash to produce it. This has become a bigger worry in 2015 and 2016, when world prices for oil have fallen, dramatically cutting Venezuela's oil earnings.

Desperate to save money, Venezuela's government launched a campaign in January 2015 to prepare Venezuelans for the first gasoline price increase in decades. Ads with the specious slogan "Energy for the People" ran on television and in local newspapers. In one of the television spots three carpenters discuss how to price a rocking chair that cost 2,500 bolivars to make. When one of them suggests they sell the chair for 100 bolivars, the others explode in indignation. "In Venezuela something similar happens with gasoline," the ad says. "The price is thirty-five times less than what it costs to produce it."[8] The message that pricing a good below cost makes no sense is an interesting one, coming from a government whose policy of price controls forces many companies to lose money on the goods they produce, and whose leaders regularly denounce profit as evil. The idea of raising gas prices to at least cover the cost of gasoline production is a logical one, but economic logic, just like milk or sugar, is in short supply in Venezuela. Nearly every Venezuelan, from cabdrivers to company executives, agrees that gasoline is far too cheap. But when confronted with the prospect of higher gas prices, many of them immediately come up with ideas about how the government should spend that extra money. It doesn't seem to dawn on most people that raising gasoline prices to cover the cost of producing it means that this money cannot also be used to pay for something else. Venezuelans have grown accustomed to having their cake and eating it too.

Those who have lived long enough don't believe the Chavista government will ever get rid of the gasoline subsidy. And they may have a point. In February 2016, President Maduro decreed the first gasoline price increase in twenty years. Maduro raised the price of 95-octane fuel to 6 bolivars per liter, a 6,185% increase. The price hike seemed large in percentage terms, but it was a pittance. At the black market rate, a gallon of gas was worth two U.S. cents at the new price, still the cheapest gasoline in the world by far. Venezuelans can still pay for gas with their spare change. The reason behind the timid increase is the widely held belief in Venezuela that any politician who dares increase gasoline prices substantially is politically dead. Most Venezuelans attribute the El Caracazo social uprising of 1989 to the government's decision to raise fuel prices. El Caracazo left an impression on a generation of Venezuelan politicians who now equate sound gas prices with uncontrollable social upheaval. It also doesn't help that Venezuelan leaders almost always think of increasing gas prices only when the country faces an economic crisis, a time when making gasoline pricier can cause more discontent.

Venezuelans want their gas and they want it cheap for a very good reason: oil looms large in their country. Venezuela has more readily accessible oil than any other nation in the world. Proved oil reserves—those reserves of oil that can easily be exploited with available technology—stand at nearly 300 billion barrels. Venezuela's reserves are larger than those held by Saudi Arabia and are enough to satisfy U.S. oil consumption for almost forty-four years.[9] Seen another way, Venezuela can keep producing oil at its current rate for more than three centuries.[10] But proved reserves don't fully reflect how much oil Venezuela has. The overall amount of oil resources in place in Venezuelan reservoirs—including oil that's harder to recover—is more than 1.2 trillion barrels, which is as much oil as humanity has ever consumed.[11] It is quite likely that other forms of energy will make oil obsolete before Venezuela ever runs out of the stuff. Venezuela also has the capacity to turn large amounts of oil into gasoline. The country owns the Paraguaná refinery complex on the northwest coast of Venezuela, a three-refinery facility, one of the largest of its kind in the world, with miles of pipelines and storage tanks that, when run efficiently, can process almost a million barrels of crude into gasoline every day.

Overseas, Venezuela owns the Houston-based Citgo, which controls three oil refineries in the United States, one of the largest refiners serving the world's largest economy. Venezuela's government also owns refineries in the United Kingdom, Sweden, and Scotland and in the Caribbean. This partly explains Venezuelans' sense of entitlement. In their thinking, a country with so much oil and such a powerful presence in the global energy business can afford to give Venezuelans cheap gasoline.

To better understand how Venezuelans view their oil wealth, just turn to part three of PDVSA's 2014 annual report. In the middle of a drab document filled with figures and jargon one finds a simple list of oil fields, each with a name, a date of discovery, how much oil each holds, how much it produces, and how many years that oil can last. It's like the inventory of a giant and exquisite wine cellar, with vintages and the total number of bottles in store.

For instance, the field called Melones ("melons"), in the northeastern state of Anzoategui, was discovered in 1955, when Venezuelan dictator Pérez Jiménez ruled the country and Elvis Presley made his television debut. If Melones continues to produce at its current rate of twenty-six thousand barrels of oil a day, it has enough oil to last 116 years.[12] The oldest "vintage" in store is the Lagunillas field, discovered in 1913, the year the Ford Motor Company unveiled the first moving assembly line. Lagunillas has sixty-two more years' worth of oil to consume. The offshore version of Lagunillas, a portion of the field that lies under Lake Maracaibo, will produce oil for sixty-six more years. The Maracaibo basin gave birth to the country's oil business. Oil from Lagunillas helped fuel the advance of the Allied forces during World War II. The Cerro Negro field, discovered in 1979, is the most productive, pumping 431,000 barrels a day, and has the most in store, enough to last 767 years.[13]

Like wine, oil has different properties that are dependent on the region where it's produced. Sweet and light crude from Maracaibo is more liquid and has less sulfur, which makes it pricier. It's also the type that is quickly running out. Crude that is heavier, like a paste or a thick sludge, and loaded with sulfur, like the Cerro Negro kind, comes from a region called the Orinoco Belt, the world's largest oil patch, a flat, wild territory of roughly twenty-one thousand square miles that stretches east to west along the Orinoco River, one of the longest in South America and known for its crocodiles and piranhas. It was the fresh waters of the Orinoco that convinced Christopher Columbus, during his third voyage to the new world in 1498, that he had found a new continent. Orinoco crude is filtered and blended with the sweeter kind to improve its value and to move it through pipelines to the coast where it is loaded onto ships, the longest of which, if set on end, would rival the height of the Eiffel Tower in Paris.

Venezuelans keep a close eye on the value of their vast oil cellar by tracking the price of an "oil basket" that incorporates the different types of crude they own and sell and is published weekly in newspapers and on websites. In this country, to enjoy wealth, all Venezuelans have to do is tap it, like wine straight from a barrel. When the price for the oil basket is high, Venezuelans gleefully anticipate lots of money flowing into their economy. And when the basket price is too low, Venezuelan presidents jump on planes to lobby their fellow members of OPEC to reduce oil production so they can prop oil prices back up again. Venezuela lives and dies by the price of its oil basket.

State-owned giant PDVSA, which controls the country's vast oil empire, has become as unusual as the country's own economy: it controls the richest accumulation of oil in the world but doesn't have enough cash to pay its bills. The company has earned more than US$100 billion from oil sales annually in recent years and has sold every barrel of crude for at least twice what it cost to produce it,[14] which means the company typically mints money every time it pumps a barrel of oil. Yet PDVSA takes months, even years to pay its suppliers and has accumulated billions of dollars of unpaid bills to the point that now its own contractors lend money to the troubled company. French oil-services firm Schlumberger, which provides the drilling and well services Venezuela needs to keep pumping crude, has given PDVSA a US$1 billion revolving credit line that the company can use to pay for its services.[15] In other words, Schlumberger has lent PDVSA enough money for the French firm to get paid for the work it does in Venezuela. It is difficult for a company like PDVSA to justify such a credit line from a supplier when it normally earns more than eight times that amount in a month.

The oil giant owes billions of dollars to bondholders and foreign banks too.[16] It owes money to the Chinese government, which fortunately wants to be paid in oil, not cash; otherwise PDVSA would struggle to pay back the Chinese. Paying the salaries of its own workers has become such a challenge that PDVSA also borrows money from Venezuela's central bank, which prints fresh bills to help cover PDVSA's cash shortfalls.[17] Thus PDVSA had failed to wire Pepe—the gasoline station manager—the money he needs to pay his staff.

PDVSA is cash poor because it has become a giant piggy bank for Venezuelan politicians. The company pays for Venezuela's social spending plans—called missions—that have become popular with the Chavista movement's low-income supporters. These include Misión Barrio Adentro, a network of thousands of Cuban doctors in poor barrios; Misión Alimentación, or Food Mission, which offers subsidized food to Venezuelans; and more than two dozen similar programs and other spending funds Venezuela's president can tap to pay for pet projects.[18] PDVSA prioritizes social spending over paying its bills and investing in oil. And the money spent on the government's social programs is over and above the taxes and dividends that PDVSA already pays the government every year.[19] PDVSA has consistently spent more money on social programs during the five years ending in early 2015 than it did on operating and oil exploration costs combined, and on the equipment it needs to increase oil output over time, the main reason for the company's existence in the first place.[20]

The company does other things oil giants don't usually do. PDVSA produces corn, rice, meat, and milk and plants sugar cane but doesn't produce enough food to make a difference in Venezuela's consumption. PDVSA produces lumber, roof tiles, and cinder blocks to build the homes the government gives the poor almost for free. And unlike the business of pumping crude, the company loses money on these activities.[21] Keeping those loss-making businesses going, however, provides jobs to thousands of workers and Chavismo's political supporters.

PDVSA is also very generous with Venezuela's political friends. It has sold oil with very favorable financing terms to a group of eleven neighbor countries—all of them close political allies, like Nicaragua under leftist leader Daniel Ortega, and Cuba under the Castro brothers. Countries typically pay half the bill up front and have up to twenty years to pay the rest with an annual interest rate of 2 percent.[22] No financial institution in the world offers countries such generous terms to pay their energy bills. Plus, the more oil PDVSA sells under those terms, the less money it gets upfront for the crude it pumps. This situation is especially painful for the company as it struggles with cash problems in a time of low oil prices. In 2015 and early 2016 PDVSA was forced to cut back on its shipments of generously financed oil to its friends.[23]

Petro diplomacy is also costly because countries often fail to pay PDVSA the billions of dollars they owe. In July 2015 a troubled Jamaica struck a deal to pay US$1.5 billion to cancel its outstanding oil debt of US$3.2 billion with PDVSA, meaning the island paid Venezuela 47 cents out of every dollar it owed.[24] PDVSA accepted these terms because it needed the cash. Better to get cash now than none later. The Dominican Republic struck a similar deal and managed to get a 52 percent discount on its own energy debt with Venezuela.[25]

Under Chávez PDVSA also refinanced Cuba's oil debts, and the president even let Nicaragua off the hook for its own obligations with Venezuela in 2007.[26]

PDVSA's penchant for spending money on everything but producing more oil has its lenders worried. In early 2016, Wall Street analysts and owners of PDVSA bonds feared the company's cash problems could force it to stop paying its debts. The company's credit ratings—the equivalent of a consumer's credit score—are abysmal. Credit rating agency Fitch Ratings gave PDVSA a CCC credit score in March 2016 that suggested a very real possibility that the oil company could cease paying its debts sometime within the following two years.[27] More to the point, the price of PDVSA bonds gyrate wildly and in 2015 and early 2016 some of the company's debt instruments sold for as low as 30 cents, which means bondholders assumed PDVSA would surely default on its obligations soon and that's as much money as they would recover from their investment.[28] Lenders worry because PDVSA began having cash problems when oil prices were still high, and they naturally assume things can only get worse for PDVSA in times of low oil prices.

Fixing PDVSA's cash problems is not as easy as imposing higher taxes on foreign companies that operate in Venezuela. Under Chavismo the government already takes roughly 90 percent of the money obtained from selling every barrel of oil, up from 60 percent during the early years of Chavismo through 2006.[29] What is left goes to PDVSA's foreign partners. PDVSA's cut of the oil business—also known as "government take"—is already considered one of the highest in the world.

One would assume that a company sitting on the world's largest oil patch could solve its money problems by producing more oil. But PDVSA cannot increase oil output quickly, in large part because it hasn't invested enough in the business to increase its production capacity. The country produced 2.53 million barrels of oil a day on average in February 2016,[30] nearly one-fifth less oil than it did in 1999, when Hugo Chávez became Venezuela's president.

Plus, efficiency is not a PDVSA strength. As of early 2015, PDVSA was a bloated bureaucracy of nearly 150,000 employees.[31] That's almost twice the number of people employed by ExxonMobil, which produces nearly 66 percent more oil than Venezuela and is one of the most profitable, best-managed oil companies in the world.[32] PDVSA doesn't look good compared with state-owned peers either. The Saudi Arabian Oil Company, or Saudi Aramco, a company considered the best-run state-owned oil giant, employs less than half the number of people that work for PDVSA and produces more than three and a half times the number of barrels produced by the Andean country.[33]

Since Chávez fired more than nineteen thousand PDVSA oil workers and executives after the 2002 strike, his administration and his successor's favored hiring politically loyal people over those with technical expertise. Almost two-thirds of the company's workforce has worked at PDVSA for less than nine years, and roughly 40 percent are younger than thirty-five years old.[34] The company's culture changed as well, favoring politics over work. The color of the company's logo was changed to red to signal the arrival of an administration with a socialist bent. And its new slogan, "PDVSA now belongs to everyone," became a Chavista rallying cry. Workers were told to don red T-shirts and other political paraphernalia as a symbol of the company's cultural shift. Attending political meetings ahead of elections became mandatory for nearly all PDVSA employees, especially the company's president, board members, and managers, who could often be spotted sitting quietly at nationally televised events during which Chávez would speak for several hours. When top executives failed to show up to political rallies and chose to work instead, Chávez would often scold them on public television.

PDVSA arguably reached its highest expression of political engagement in November 2006, when the company's then-president and oil minister, Rafael Ramírez, a left-leaning oil engineer loyal to Chávez, told company managers in a secretly taped meeting just weeks before Chávez ran for reelection that the company's goal was to help get the president elected again. Ramírez is a man of impeccable revolutionary pedigree. His father once belonged to a Venezuelan guerrilla movement in the 1960s. PDVSA, Ramírez told the gathered managers, "is redder than red," referring to the colors of Chávez's political movement. And he warned oil company chiefs "it is a crime and a counterrevolutionary act, for a manager to seek to curb the political expression of our workers in support of President Chávez." The video of the speech was leaked soon after, and Venezuela's electoral authority fined Ramírez for his statements, but he ran the company under those parameters for a decade through September 2014.

A heavily politicized PDVSA has also bred corruption scandals. PDVSA's private planes have often become mere taxis that family and friends of company executives and other government officials have been known to use for leisure trips to places like Sydney, Hawaii, Paris, and Colorado.[35] Chávez was also known to lend PDVSA planes to political allies in the region, like Bolivia's president Evo Morales and Honduras's deposed leftist leader José Manuel Zelaya.[36] Abuse of PDVSA's fleet of planes is particularly notable, since Chávez, when first elected in 1999, publicly auctioned twenty-three state-owned jets to get cash for social spending and vowed that, unlike previous governments, he would not tolerate the abuse of government-owned planes by corrupt bureaucrats.[37]

The most salient case of graft arguably occurred when Argentine airport officials caught a Venezuelan businessman, Guido Antonini Wilson, carrying a suitcase with US$800,000 in undeclared cash in August 2007. The ensuing scandal revealed that Antonini was accompanied by PDVSA executives in a private jet chartered by Argentine government officials. A U.S. court eventually took up the case, since Wilson lived in Miami and Venezuelan government envoys went to U.S. soil to persuade Wilson to keep quiet about the origin and destination of the money. An FBI probe eventually concluded that Wilson was carrying PDVSA money intended to help fund the electoral campaign of Argentina's Cristina Fernandez de Kirchner.[38] Fernandez publicly denied the accusations. In a country with notoriously weak institutions, PDVSA has arguably become one of the most affected by a culture of free-for-all spending.

The oil company had better days. PDVSA came into being in 1976, from the assets the government nationalized from foreign oil companies. In the decades following its creation, PDVSA built a strong corporate culture fostered by Venezuelan executives who had previously worked for large oil multinationals such as Exxon, Chevron, and Shell. By the 1990s a series of polls by trade magazine *Petroleum Economist* showed that experts saw PDVSA as the national oil company with the best-run operations and finances.[39]

Top PDVSA executives educated in the United States—many with Ivy League degrees—ran the company with an eye on the bottom line. PDVSA became one of the most profitable and efficient oil companies, producing 3 million barrels of oil a day with a payroll of roughly forty thousand employees in the late 1990s,[40] less than a third of the workers PDVSA employed in

2015. The company was one of the most coveted to work for in Venezuela. Workers took their children to PDVSA-financed schools that offered top-notch teachers and educational resources. They enjoyed cheap shopping at company stores and membership in the company's resort-like clubs.[41] Upper-level managers in PDVSA were known to earn salaries that, converted into dollars, hovered around the mid six figures. They bought yachts and kept apartments in Miami. They were also known to abuse the use of the company's fleet of private planes.

PDVSA employees avoided Venezuelan politics. In the 1990s the oil company had become an institution that enjoyed far more credibility than Venezuela's corrupt and inept politicians. There was a purpose to this too. Venezuelan presidents had been known to raid PDVSA coffers to fund their political plans, so PDVSA executives tried to stay away from politics and keep as little cash on hand as possible, lest it become a temptation for spendthrift politicos. But the company's elite culture soon clashed with Venezuela's pervasive poverty levels. When Chávez first ran for office in 1998 he denounced PDVSA's sense of being a state within the state, and his rhetoric resonated with the majority poor, who felt excluded from the company's high-achieving culture.

PDVSA's poor management under Chavismo is best captured by its failed goals. PDVSA has spent years making bold but unrealistic corporate plans to increase oil output. In 2005 PDVSA's corporate strategy promised to almost double Venezuela's oil production to 5.85 million barrels of oil a day by 2012.[42] More than a decade after PDVSA published that goal the company pumped roughly 2.7 million barrels of crude a day and was no closer to achieving such ambitious targets. Venezuela's latest plans now promise to achieve the same output target in 2019.

In 2015 a new PDVSA president struggled to improve things. Eulogio Del Pino, a Stanford-educated petroleum engineer with a penchant for hiking up the Ávila for exercise, is a rarity in PDVSA. Del Pino, a plump man, has a competitive streak as well. In my years in Venezuela I would often see him hiking up the Ávila in the early mornings. He once boasted to me he could hike a three-hundred-meter stretch up the mountain in twenty-five minutes or less, but after running into him often, his pace convinced me that was just bluster.

In the oil industry, Del Pino gained a reputation as an able operator who did the tough business of trying to run PDVSA, while Ramírez took an increasingly political role. Del Pino developed a reputation for spending more time running the company than attending political rallies. And under his watch, PDVSA employees have been asked to wear formal attire to work and less informal red-colored clothing, a signal that in a PDVSA in crisis, business is becoming more important than ideology.[43] Del Pino worked to persuade foreign oil companies to invest fresh money into Venezuela's crippled oil industry, a tall order in times of critically low oil prices. By March 2016, Venezuela's oil basket fetched little more than US$25 per barrel.

On a Friday in January 2015 I paid a visit to the PDVSA president's office to meet Rafael Rodríguez, Del Pino's right-hand man. As I entered the building, a large billboard with the image of Chávez quoted his call for the advancement of the revolution. Chávez paraphernalia is still very much a part of the company's decor. As I waited for my meeting I perused a PDVSA in-house glossy magazine that quoted an employee thanking the revolution for hiring him to work in a new PDVSA-owned seismic company, a business for which he had no prior experience.[44] Rodríguez, a lawyer in his thirties, sported a checkered blazer, leather loafers, and what looked like an IWC Portugieser watch.

A large photo of Chávez hung behind his desk. Del Pino instructed him to ask me about my project and sound me out. The new PDVSA president and his team don't usually give interviews and have been known to avoid press conferences. And it's no surprise; at the time the local press often carried stories of how hard-core Chavistas were asking President Maduro to replace Del Pino with someone with a more revolutionary ethos. Rodríguez took the opportunity of our friendly chat to defend the company's role as a cash cow. PDVSA, he argued, cannot be compared with any other oil company. "Most oil companies respond to the interests of profit-seeking shareholders, but PDVSA responds to one owner, the state," he told me. By September 2015, Del Pino had taken the dual role of PDVSA president and oil minister, which forced him to become more directly involved in the political side of things. Turning PDVSA around will likely take many years.

* * *

Five o'clock on Thursday afternoons is swim class time at the Altamira Tennis Club. The six-lane semi-Olympic-sized pool, surrounded by tall palm trees and carefully manicured lawns, is teeming with children who are watched over by a laid-back coach. Uniformed nannies and waiflike young mothers idle by. The main building, however, has a faded art deco glamour. The covered terrace, the pool furniture, even the modular plastic trash cans look dated. The club, flanked by the ritzy apartment buildings of the La Castellana neighborhood to the south and an imposing view of the Ávila mountain to the north, has stood for years as a place where the Caracas elite mingle. The exodus of many moneyed Venezuelans over the past fifteen years has not been kind to the institution. Wealthy families who fled Venezuela's rising socialist government and worsening crime rates in the city sold their shares in the club to foreign companies that now use it as a perk for executives posted in Caracas. And the new owners see no need to upgrade the club's premises in a troubled country.

Sitting at a table by the pool I met Luis Xavier Grisanti, a long-time president of the Venezuelan Hydrocarbons Association, also known by its Spanish acronym AVHI, a hybrid between a trade group and a think tank for foreign oil companies in Venezuela. Grisanti, a Venezuelan with grizzled hair, has the air of a diplomat and was once Venezuela's chief envoy to the European Union, Belgium, and Luxembourg. He now holds one of the most delicate jobs of all, serving as the face of foreign oil companies doing business in Venezuela, which include some of the world's largest corporations, such as Chevron and Royal Dutch Shell. He also teaches petroleum geopolitics at the local Simón Bolívar University.

As an icebreaker, Grisanti told me of his recent run-in with four thugs who took him on a *secuestro express*, or express kidnapping, a type of quick abduction by assailants who carry off victims to ATM machines and force them to surrender large amounts of cash, an increasingly common occurrence in Caracas. Grisanti was taken for more than two hours while his wife negotiated with the men on the phone. He wouldn't go into too much detail, but he was thankful things ended well. "Fortunately they didn't know who I was. I told them I was a university professor, which is true," he said. As a former diplomat, Grisanti treads carefully when delving into the subject of what it's like for foreign companies to do business in Venezuela. He estimates that AVHI members have sunk as much as US$10 billion into the local oil industry over the previous nine years, and a total of roughly US$40 billion since

1992. Most of that money was not fresh cash but a reinvestment of the profits generated by their Venezuelan oil projects in the course of producing oil.

For foreign firms, sinking new money into a country considered high risk like Venezuela—where the government nationalizes company assets and changes contract terms unilaterally—requires safeguards. Why would they invest more in a business where they are minority partners, PDVSA calls all the shots, and their cash can end up being used for political purposes instead of oil production? Under Chávez, foreign companies saw their tax and royalty rates go up, and many were forced to relinquish control of the fields they ran. In 2007 Chávez even nationalized the assets of U.S. companies ExxonMobil and ConocoPhillips, both of whom disagreed with the new terms of doing business in Venezuela.[45] They both took the country to court to seek compensation.[46] Since then, PDVSA's foreign partners have invested as little as possible in Venezuela oil projects. If the government's own PDVSA doesn't see fit to invest enough money in the business, foreign companies reason they shouldn't risk their money either. In that sense, AVHI members followed a script similar to that of the owners of the Altamira Tennis Club, who saw no need to upgrade the club's premises and chose to keep them stuck in the 1950s.

In 2015 pumping oil in Venezuela was still profitable for foreign companies, but the terms of the joint ventures with the government—known as mixed companies—were very restrictive. Under Chavismo the executives of foreign firms have grown accustomed to sitting in board meetings of oil projects and simply listening to how state officials make decisions on anything from how much money to invest to how many workers to hire. They are expected to shut up, nod, and keep oil flowing.

In 2014, PDVSA hired British communications firm Bell Pottinger to survey the concerns of its foreign partners and their appetite to invest in Venezuela. The Bell Pottinger survey results didn't shock anyone. Foreign companies felt mistreated and had little interest in fronting more money when their knowhow and contributions were ignored. Chavistas saw them with suspicion, not as partners in a business.[47] PDVSA's Rodríguez was charged with liaising with Bell Pottinger, but both Del Pino and Rodríguez declined to share the survey results for this book. The truth is the PDVSA findings mirrored the results of a similar study conducted by Grisati's AVHI just three years earlier. The AVHI study showed that some of the largest oil companies in the world felt railroaded by Venezuela's government. PDVSA ran the joint ventures like an extension of the state company with no consideration given to partners who wanted to co-govern projects and have input on issues as basic as how to follow best practices in oil extraction, which PDVSA workers often violate. Even before Chávez, Grisanti told me, "PDVSA lacked a culture of knowing how to work with foreign partners."

Much of it has to do with ideology. Venezuela's oil nationalists see foreign oil companies as usurpers. Carlos Mendoza Potellá, the resident oil expert at Venezuela's central bank who was once the personal secretary of OPEC founder Juan Pablo Pérez Alfonzo, is no fan of the international oil companies Grisanti represents. His views are aligned with Chavistas when he says that international oil companies "don't see Venezuela as an oil superpower. They see [the country] as loot."

Nationalists like Mendoza Potellá were stern critics of a Venezuelan policy called Apertura Petrolera, or Oil Opening, in the 1990s that gave foreign companies low tax terms and freedom to run oil fields once again, something that had not been allowed since Venezuela nationalized the business in the late 1970s. The opening angered nationalists, who saw it as a backdoor privatization of the oil industry. Even Grisanti admits that some of the deals struck with foreign companies in the 1990s had "overtones of illegality." And Mendoza Potellá admits that PDVSA's plans to more than double Venezuela's oil production to 6 million barrels of oil a day by 2019 are unrealistic pie in the sky,[48] because the bulk of the money to make that happen must come from the same foreign companies Chavistas publicly label as enemies of the revolution.

After a long period of talks between the state and private companies in 2013 and 2014, PDVSA agreed to a compromise with some of its partners. Companies willing to invest more money in Venezuela could put the cash in a trust fund overseas that the partners, not PDVSA, control. This was meant to give them an assurance that Venezuela's politicians wouldn't run through that money as well. In addition, PDVSA has allowed partners to appoint key managers like the finance and procurement chiefs of oil projects, positions that PDVSA used to control in the past. And the state giant found ways to make business cheaper for partners, too. By May 2015 PDVSA had signaled a willingness to let partnerships exchange their dollars at a weaker official exchange rate, in essence making it cheaper for them to cover oil workers' salaries and benefits.[49] Under those terms, various oil partners, including the U.S. oil giant Chevron, had agreed to invest more cash. The risks such agreements run is that radical nationalists may take to denouncing them as a sign of government weakness.

Grisanti is enthusiastic about PDVSA's realization that it needs its partners. But by AVHI estimates, low oil prices in some cases still make it uneconomic for companies to sink more money into Venezuelan projects, and, in other cases, the returns are considered low for high-risk ventures in a politically unpredictable nation like Venezuela.[50] Grisanti thinks Venezuela may once again have to offer partners the type of attractive terms they enjoyed before Chávez raised taxes and royalties and seized their assets.[51] This welcoming of partners may be especially important if PDVSA wants to increase its capacity to produce oil in the Orinoco region, where producing crude is more costly. Foreign investors may also want to own higher stakes in ventures too.[52] The trouble is such changes would appear to Chavistas as the equivalent of handing over sovereignty to foreigners and letting them take Venezuela's oil for free. Grisanti and AVHI's corporate members understand that perceptions and the country's history matter very much in Venezuela's oil business. It is important for AVHI that any agreements do not come off as the ideas of paternalistic oil multinationals. As Grisanti told me: "For some people it is hard to understand that we are partners, that we're not here to confront one another."

* * *

At five thirty on a Wednesday morning in May 2015 I sat at the Maiquetía airport, next to bleary-eyed commuters waiting to board the first flight headed to Maracaibo in Zulia, Venezuela's historically oil-rich state. Outside the waiting area window, the jet bridge featured a billboard-sized ad with two large photos of Chávez and President Nicolás Maduro with an underscored phrase: "We sow oil, conscience, and *socialist values.*" The ad stretched along the bridge arm with images of oil workers, each overlaid with the words *Humanism, Loyalty,* and *Solidarity.* The government's prolific propaganda has sought to turn oil and the industry that produces it—the economic lifeblood of this country—into an instrument of political and social trans-formation. The workers that pump crude are revolutionary comrades, and the oil industry is more than a profitable business; it's a source of political patronage. The ad prepared me for what I was about to find during my visit to Maracaibo. Under Chavismo, PDVSA has taken on the ambitious mission of poverty alleviation. Anything that stands in the way of that goal—be it a sound corporate culture, best oil practices, responsible energy consumption, or an overall well-run oil industry—has become less important.

I was on my way to the city of Cabimas, a thirty- to forty-minute drive southeast of Maracaibo. After landing in the Maracaibo airport I boarded a car and crossed the 771-foot-long Rafael Urdaneta Bridge that links the eastern and western shores of Lake Maracaibo, a fifty-one-hundred-square-mile body of water slightly larger than the U.S. state of Connecticut. Small offshore oil rigs and platforms dot the lake's greenish waters. The lake suffers from an infestation of duckweed, a problem some experts attribute to the disposal of human waste and more than a century of oil exploitation.

Cabimas sits on the eastern shore and is home to roughly two hundred thousand people, a town of low-slung buildings and scorching humid heat. The average temperature year round is roughly 86 degrees Fahrenheit, but multiple gas flares from oil production make Cabimas feel hotter. The town became world-famous in 1922 when an oil well known as Barroso No. 2 blew out, yielding one hundred thousand barrels of crude a day. The wealth that flowed from that well changed the small town of roughly five thousand people. By the 1970s Cabimas had been transformed into a small city with enough of a sense of entitlement to fashion itself as a small cultural hub. At one point the town attracted international stars, such as world-famous tango singer Carlos Gardel. As the output of Barroso and other wells matured and waned, eventually so did the town's fortunes. The site of the Barroso well became a public plaza, and the theaters there eventually closed. In 2013, however, Cabimas opened a series of multiplex cinemas, a major event for a town where the last movie theater, La Fuente ("The Fountain"), had closed sixteen years earlier. Some in Cabimas still remembered the days when the first *Jurassic Park* movie premiered there.

Cabimas is the quintessential oil town. Part of the city lies under lake water level because of a phenomenon called subsidence, a sinking that happens after decades of oil and gas extraction. A wall of contention protects the eastern shore cities from being flooded by the lake. Cabimas is not next to or near an important oil field; it is itself one. Pump jacks, the hammerlike pumps that lift oil to the surface, oscillate next to apartment buildings, smack in the middle of residential areas. Natural gas flares jut out of the ground, their flames flapping above rooftops. Children ride bikes along fenced-off oil well stations that sit just blocks away from parks and grocery and liquor stores. Cabimas has 178 active wells pumping crude, which forces oil workers to drive back and forth around a city almost the size of New Orleans to check on production.

In 2015 Cabimas was already considered a marginal oil field that produced only as much as seven thousand barrels of oil a day; its productive life is nearing an end. Marginal fields require more money and special technology to coax the remaining oil out of the ground. The tricky job of running this type of operation in the middle of a city falls on Petrocabimas, a company run by PDVSA and a partner called Suelopetrol, the only Venezuelan privately owned oil company to have signed a joint venture with the state behemoth. Despite a century of oil history, Venezuelans have failed to create many private-sector companies with the capacity to run oil operations. Venezuelans have long seen the business of investing and running oil fields as something only the government and deep-pocketed multinationals can do. Suelopetrol is a rare example of a domestic success story in this business. Created in 1984 as a small services company that specialized in seismic imagery—the technology used to assess underground oil reservoirs—Suelopetrol had its start as a contractor for PDVSA.

The modest business was the brainchild of Henrique Rodríguez Guillén, a civil engineer from an upper-middle-income family in Caracas. Rodríguez had a good sense of timing. In the late 1990s, when Venezuela auctioned scores of oil fields to foreign companies, Suelopetrol struck a deal with German company Preussag Energie, which operated Cabimas. The deal gave Suelopetrol a modest 10 percent stake in the field, but it was a qualitative jump for Suelopetrol from an oil services contractor to becoming responsible for helping run an oil operation. This meant Suelopetrol would do the kind of work major oil companies like Chevron, ExxonMobil, and BP do in oil fields around the world. Suelopetrol grew in importance over time, eventually bought out the Germans in 2004, and in doing so became a partner with PDVSA. This move gave the company a seat at the table with the big names in the business. In 2016 Suelopetrol not only owns 40 percent of Petrocabimas but also has become a partner of Chevron to pump and blend heavy oil in the Orinoco region. Suelopetrol also explores for oil in Colombia and produces crude in a field in Texas.

In mid-May 2015, the staff at Petrocabimas faced a cumbersome problem. As many as thirty cars and pickup trucks—roughly a quarter of the fleet that oil workers used to inspect wells and oil tank sites—had flat tires or lacked car batteries. This made it hard to perform the routine security checks necessary to ensure the field runs smoothly. Buying the tires and car batteries was a challenge not least because they had become scarce goods in Venezuela. At the Duncan car battery distributor in nearby Maracaibo, dozens of people lined up around the block every morning before the business opened its doors. And there was no guarantee these customers would find a battery that fit their vehicles. Finding tires was an equally problematic task.

What made things even harder was the tedious approval process Petrocabimas managers had to go through to buy something as simple as a car tire. Almost every moderately large purchase had to get the nod from PDVSA, the majority stakeholder in the field. Managers at Petrocabimas spent several man hours persuading the PDVSA brass in Caracas to allow the purchase of these parts piecemeal, a couple of tires from one store, a battery from another, instead of having to make one full purchase. As things stood in Venezuela, no single distributor could sell Petrocabimas the tires and batteries it needed to get its trucks running again. To buy any product or contract out any service, Petrocabimas managers went through a process that lasted several months. They first had to announce a tender for the purchase or service, and they then had to get estimates from interested companies. The estimate was then reviewed by a costs engineering team, and if approved, the decision was passed on to the Petrocabimas board, after which it had to get a final nod from a separate board of PDVSA managers in Caracas. Some of these boards met only once a month, which means something as simple as getting a few cars fixed could take several months or a year, even though Venezuelan law states these procurement processes shouldn't last more than forty-five days. In a country with runaway inflation like Venezuela, prices change so quickly that an original estimate to service a car will expire in fifteen days of less. When that happens, the whole purchase process has to start all over again.

For years, PDVSA has kept a tight grip on the budget of oil projects like Petrocabimas. This means Petrocabimas has no say over how to best spend money to produce oil. The reason for that goes beyond sound fiscal prudence. During the Chávez administration, PDVSA changed its main focus from producing oil to paying for generous social programs for the poor and the salaries of a government payroll that increases in size every year. This leaves less money to invest in producing oil, which means that projects like Petrocabimas feel the pinch. PDVSA decides which, when, and how much Petrocabimas suppliers get paid. As of May 2015 the oil venture hadn't paid equipment suppliers for more than two years. Some suppliers had simply stopped working with Petrocabimas because they were frustrated with mounting unpaid bills. In one notorious example, one of Petrocabima's jackhammer pumps had been pumping crude for almost four years and the supplier of that pump hadn't been paid yet. This backlog was even more problematic in the face of recurring equipment theft. Petrocabimas and other joint venture companies had seen several vehicles in their fleet stolen by criminals that some people suspected were members the Colombian guerrilla groups that take refuge in Venezuela. Petrocambimas keeps pumps and pipeline parts, as well as electricity generators, locked inside metal cages to prevent theft. Thieves are also known to ride motorboats to offshore oilrigs in the middle of the lake to steal parts that they later resell as scrap metal.

Managing personnel is one of the most difficult aspects of the job. Under the Petrocabimas joint venture terms, Suelopetrol managers had no say over who and how many people got hired to work on the oil project. PDVSA made all the hiring decisions, which had led to what some managers saw as too much hiring for an operation the size of Petrocabimas. In 2006 approximately seventy-seven people ran the Cabimas operation; in 2015 Petrocabimas employed 250 people, but the field produced roughly the same amount of barrels it did nine years earlier.

Absenteeism is high, partly because PDVSA offers very lax medical leave conditions that workers often abuse. To point out how extreme things can get, a Petrocabimas manager recounted his own experience when he visited a PDVSA doctor to check on a minor vision problem. The doctor offered to write the manager a note so he could take as long as three weeks off work. The manager declined the offer, but many workers have found ways to extend their medical absences for months while still being paid. Keeping tabs on the number of workers at the site could be problematic as well. New workers that came with a recommendation from some high-up PDVSA figure in Caracas could suddenly join a Petrocabimas work crew. Suelopetrol managers were never consulted about these additions to the payroll, because PDVSA paid the salaries of these workers. This arrangement often caused problems at Petrocabimas, where workers would outright ignore the orders of managers appointed by Suelopetrol. Their loyalty lay with PDVSA.

Over the past decade, PDVSA has hired many inexperienced and poorly trained oil workers who profess allegiance to Chavismo. As a way to gauge political sympathies, PDVSA personnel evaluations in Petrocabimas and other projects monitor such things as social work and participation in political rallies organized by the government. The decor of the two-story Petrocabimas corporate offices offered a clue to this culture. Photos of Hugo Chávez, underscored with his political quotes and the blood-red color of his movement, were prominently displayed on nearly every wall. During major electoral events when large crowds are needed to show support for Venezuela's president, PDVSA sends the majority of Petrocabimas workers to Caracas by bus—a roughly twelve-hour trip—and leaves behind a skeleton crew to tend the oil fields. For a long time, PDVSA also asked Suelopetrol managers to show up to these rallies as well. Refusing to participate could be professional suicide for workers.

Personnel troubles have a ripple effect on Petrocabimas' levels of efficiency. Workers at Petrocabimas operating a drill could take 120 days to do the work a well-trained drilling crew could do in half the time. Even though PDVSA's personnel culture causes such problems, Suelopetrol couldn't do anything about the excessive amount of substandard hires, because the human resources manager was a PDVSA appointee. The Petrocabimas president and the general manager were also appointed by PDVSA. Indeed, Petrocabimas had a revolving door of presidents and managers. The company had three presidents in the year prior to my visit to Cabimas, and two general managers in the previous six months.

Lack of cash, low efficiency, and rotating management made it hard for Petrocabimas to maintain its operating goals. Cabimas once aspired to produce twelve thousand barrels of oil a day, but that aspiration was almost twice the amount of oil the field produced on its best day. Production costs were out of whack too. Roughly two-thirds of Petrocabimas' annual budget went to paying administrative costs, payroll, worker pensions, and benefits, and less than a third covered the equipment and services needed for actual oil production. Oil managers said that cost relationship should be inverted if the company aimed to produce more oil than it did.

Despite such problems, however, the cost of producing a barrel of oil in Venezuela is relatively low. Part of the reason is that oil in this country is readily accessible and there is no need to spend billions of dollars in exploration efforts to find it. Venezuela's oil fields are on land, not offshore, which usually makes costs skyrocket. Even Venezuela's thickest, most viscous oil is easier to extract than similar oil in other parts of the world such as Canada, where cold temperatures make oil as hard as rock, so it requires heavy machinery and giant trucks to exploit and transport it, as in a large mining operation.

Producing one barrel of oil cost Petrocabimas an average of US$24 in 2015, slightly above the national average but far below what it costs to produce oil in the United States, Canada, and many oil-rich countries in the Middle East and Africa, where war, theft, and terrorism can add a hefty price tag to every barrel produced. Venezuela's costs per barrel could be even lower. PDVSA forced its partners to pay workers in bolivars, but to do so they had to exchange their U.S. dollars at the 6.3-bolivar-per-dollar rate. If not for that restriction, costs at Petrocabimas could go as low as US$12 per barrel.[53] For context, Venezuela was selling its oil in May 2015 at US$56 per barrel, or more than twice what it cost Cabimas to produce oil. In other words Petrocabimas easily turned a profit for many years under Chavismo while oil prices remained high despite the field's notorious inefficiencies. Things looked dire for Petrocabimas in late March 2016, however, when Venezuela was selling its oil at an average of US$25 per barrel—almost what it cost Petrocabimas to pump a barrel.

There is a popular saying in the oil industry that is often attributed to John D. Rockefeller, the founder of Standard Oil, the company that later became ExxonMobil: "The best business in the world is a well-run oil company.

The second best business in the world is a badly run oil company." In Venezuela that phrase has a special resonance because the country's poorly run oil industry has managed to make gobs of money for years. Petrocabimas' operating troubles are an x-ray of sorts of what happens in nearly every other Venezuelan oil project, including far larger ones in the Orinoco region. Even the most powerful companies in the oil business that operate in Venezuela have had to endure the inefficiency, poor leadership, and thick bureaucracy that has become a hallmark of Chavismo's management.

Under the new trust fund accords that PDVSA struck with partners in 2013 and 2014, Suelopetrol agreed to invest US $625 million of its own money. Suelopetrol's money will be placed in a trust that Suelopetrol-appointed managers will handle. The deal also gives Petrocabimas the right to pay its own workers, a necessary step for the project to foster its own culture of worker excellence. The new arrangement is a chance for Suelopetrol to grow in importance too. In exchange for Suelopetrol's investment, PDVSA handed Petrocabimas control over Tía Juana, an adjoining oil field to the south, twice the size of Cabimas. Tía Juana employed four hundred people and was producing twenty-six thousand barrels a day in early 2015, more than three times Cabimas' output, with almost twice the number of workers Cabimas employed. Petrocabimas was still in the process of incorporating Tía Juana to its operations in early 2015, and its goal was to double the output of the Cabimas and Tía Juana fields by 2022. That is easier said than done, however. PDVSA ran Tía Juana on its own for years with no outside help. The state of the field when it was turned over to Petrocabimas offers a glimpse into the operating practices of PDVSA.

Suelopetrol conducted an evaluation of the state of Tía Juana once it was handed over by PDVSA.[54] The survey reviewed 3,290 wells, 65 stations that manage oil flow, and the rest of the field's infrastructure. The study showed overgrown brush in more than half of the oil well installations. Allowing vegetation to grow near oil wells can be a fire hazard. Keeping oil-producing areas free of wild vegetation is a basic best practice in any oil operation. The study showed oil spillage in and around 58 percent of the oil wells examined, too. The field's access roads were also invaded by brush and kept in poor condition, with little to no security features to guard oil operations. These conditions left the equipment at the mercy of thieves. Tía Juana's oil-pumping equipment was also found to be in a state of disrepair. In one instance a Petrocabimas manager used a smart phone to film a broken jackhammer pump that had not been oiled for at least six months and had parts missing but somehow continued to operate. In the eyes of this manager, the fact that the jackhammer continued to work after months of neglect said a lot about the quality of the pump's manufacturing. An abandoned pump that continues to produce oil by mere inertia also does much to explain Venezuela's ills. It reveals why Venezuelan politicians believe they can get away with investing as little as possible in the oil business. It also says much about why Venezuelans eagerly seek an easy, comfortable existence, doing as little as possible. This is a country where money simply oozes and bubbles out of the ground almost effortlessly, with very little human intervention.

7 MANGO MANAGEMENT

On Saturday, April 18, 2015, Marleni Olivo managed to hit Venezuela's president, Nicolás Maduro, on the head with a yellow mango. Olivo was attending a political rally in the north-central state of Aragua, where the president—a former bus driver—made an appearance driving a red bus with the window open, waving as he made his way through a packed crowd. The woman threw the fruit and struck the president right above the left ear. A video captures the moment when Maduro feels the impact and ducks, while one of his security guards tries to find the culprit in the crowd.[1] The mango had a message written on it with a black marker: "IF YOU CAN, CALL ME," including Olivo's phone number. The fifty-four-year-old Olivo was not some crazed fan or stalker of the president but a citizen desperate to obtain one of the government-built homes that both Maduro and his predecessor, Hugo Chávez, had been giving out for years to thousands of poor Venezuelan families practically for free as part of a plan called Gran Misión Vivienda, or the Great Housing Mission.

The mango incident came at a difficult juncture for Maduro. The president led an oil-rich country that paradoxically suffered from shortages of food staples, such as rice and chicken, and analgesics to treat basic fevers. Under Maduro, power outages and water rationing had become common in Venezuela and the country's annual rate of inflation, 68 percent in 2014, was one of the highest in the world. To make matters worse, the price Venezuela received for its oil had halved in the previous year to US$50 per barrel, which meant that tougher days were still ahead. The president's popularity ratings were near record lows. That same month, local pollster Datanalisis estimated that no more than 28 percent of Venezuelans approved of how Maduro managed the country, half the level of support he enjoyed just two years earlier when he took office. With congressional elections slated for later in the year, 46 percent of voters planned to support opposition candidates, with only a quarter favoring Maduro's socialist allies.[2]

Days later Maduro made light of the mango incident in a nationally televised appearance and said his aides had called Olivo on his behalf. "Marleni had problems with her home. I have approved it, as part of the program Gran Misión Vivienda. You now have your [new] apartment. They will give it to you in the next few hours," Maduro said, speaking directly to Olivo through the camera. Olivo's story made headlines around the world. "Woman Who Hit Venezuelan Leader with Mango Rewarded with New Home" read a story in the *Telegraph*, a British newspaper.[3] Comedian John Oliver on his show *Last Week Tonight* made fun of the case and of the fact that many Venezuelans emulated Olivo's example in the following days and weeks by throwing and handing over mangos to the president and his aides with written messages. The mango episode even inspired a free Google Play game app called Maduro Mango Attack, where players throw tropical fruit at the president.[4] The game reached one hundred thousand downloads by late May 2015.[5]

When Olivo finally spoke to the press she explained that she used a mango she had handy because she didn't have paper at the time to write the president a message. In fact, that same day, the president received more than four thousand pieces of paper with all kinds of petitions and requests for favors that followers gave to his closest assistants in hopes of getting help paying for a medical treatment or getting a home or a job.[6]

Seeking special favors from political leaders is common in nations with a largely disenfranchised population. But Venezuelan presidents with control over vast oil riches attract more favor-seeking citizens than most. When Hugo Chávez became president in 1999 he was often overwhelmed by the number of messages written in letters or on scraps of paper that his followers tried to place in his hands and stick inside his pockets as he walked by. Young and elderly women were known to pick fights with the president's bodyguards in their desperate attempt to ask their leader for a special favor. Just six months into Chávez's mandate a Reuters article called Chávez the "Saint of Miracles" for poor Venezuelans,[7] because his followers appeared to believe the president would solve their problems almost magically, if they could just place their message in his hands. At the time, the Miraflores presidential palace received eight thousand letters a day seeking favors from the president.[8] People would ask him to apprehend criminals, to give them a bag of cement, or to give someone a scholarship.

Chávez made it a point to grant those wishes in the most public way possible, announcing favors to handpicked followers in his weekly, televised show *Aló Presidente* ("Hello, President"). In 2000 he created the Sovereign People Foundation with its own budget to address these petitions whenever possible. A Venezuelan who suffered an accident could suddenly get full medical treatment, or someone with vision problems could fly to Cuba for an eye operation free of charge. Others managed to get a job at a ministry or at a social program managed by the government. During Chávez's later years, the luckier ones moved out of their dilapidated homes into government-financed housing units, a gesture of presidential generosity.

This personalistic approach to running a country has political benefits. It makes voters feel more connected to their leader, while the president appears to solve people's most pressing problems. It also foments the belief, prevalent in Venezuela, that the government has the power and wealth to fix virtually any problem. According to a 2011 poll by Latin American pollster Latinobarómetro, approximately 48 percent of Venezuelans believe the government can solve "all of society's problems."[9] That percentage rises to 81 percent when one includes respondents who agreed with the idea that the government can solve "most of society's problems"—that was nearly twice the average of similar responses in the rest of Latin America. But Venezuela's government is far from a magical problem solver. When the president assumes the role of top caregiver and job and home provider, problem solving becomes a lottery: some people get their issues addressed, and many others believe that one day they will get lucky as well.

Naturally there is a frenzied competition to bring problems directly to the president. Ordinary Venezuelans are not the only ones vying for attention. Under Chavismo presidents have been known to delegate very little, so multiple decisions require the ultimate presidential nod. If the leader's last word is needed for most decisions, however small, ministers stop thinking for themselves and they fight each other for face time as well. The long-term goals of government institutions take a backseat to the president's immediate desires. In a world where success depends on getting a piece of the president's attention, Olivo's mango idea was brilliant. It was a creative way to grab Maduro's attention long enough to get a problem solved. Maduro and Chávez have run the country by shifting their focus from one emergency to another, offering short-term fixes with little long-term planning, as if they were being hit on the head with mangos all the time—call it mango management.

This approach to running the country is not new in Venezuela, but it became a hallmark of Chavismo. Mango management affects the way the government spends money. To pay for projects on a whim, a president needs total freedom from budget rules. With this in mind, Hugo Chávez created the FONDEN fund to hold billions of dollars off budget that he could use at a moment's notice with little transparency or accountability. More to the point, Venezuela's treasury consistently underestimates how much money it expects to get from oil every year so it can budget as little as possible. This gives the president more cash to do as he pleases. By law the federal government must share its budget with municipal and regional administrations, so by budgeting less money, the president gets a hefty war chest for social spending at the expense of governors and mayors.[10]

Chávez's famous missions are the foremost example of mango management. By his own admission, Chávez created the programs in response to a political emergency: his poll numbers were too low at a time when his foes sought a referendum on his rule.[11] The missions were a band-aid measure. They became a parallel bureaucracy that superseded the power of the health and education ministries that Chávez didn't trust could spend the money effectively enough to turn his approval numbers around quickly. In the long run, however, the missions fattened the state's payroll and worsened the government's notorious levels of inefficiency and graft. But they did help low-income voters, and in doing so they made Chávez one of Venezuela's most popular presidents.

His social programs became so useful as a tool of patronage that Chávez and his allies became the country's dominant political force, easily besting their opponents in all presidential, congressional, and local elections as well as most referendums between 1999 and 2014. Through Misión Vivienda, Chávez handed out tens of thousands of homes to poor Venezuelans ahead of the December 2012 presidential vote. The housing program became instrumental in persuading Venezuelans to reelect the already cancer-stricken leader for another six-year term, just months before he died. The lack of long-term planning was evident. In the rush to get homes built, many housing units were poorly constructed. The country was also not ready for such a large-scale housing initiative. Venezuela soon ran out of construction materials such as steel and cement, which idled many projects for months on end. The state continued to build low-income housing after Chávez's death, and the shortage of steel became so acute in 2014 that the government began crushing abandoned cars and bicycles to obtain the steel rebar needed for construction projects.[12]

Chávez's social missions were poorly targeted too. A study of social programs conducted by Venezuelan poverty expert Luis Pedro España in 2014 concluded that nearly half of the roughly 2.5 million Venezuelans who benefited from Chavismo's social programs were not considered poor at the time.[13] For instance, España found that nearly half of the Venezuelans who bought subsidized food in state-owned supermarkets were people who were not the intended recipients of such subsidies. In the case of the subsidized apartments given to Venezuelans at below-market interest rates, nine of ten recipients were not considered poor either. Politics has much to do with the assigning of social benefits. España found that nearly four of every ten people who claimed not to benefit from missions felt excluded from them because they did not support Chavismo.[14]

Under mango management, politically popular spending is more important than investing in infrastructure and basic services. Take water for instance. Venezuela has the twelfth largest renewable water resource on earth,[15] but its cities—especially Caracas—suffer water shortages for long stretches. The reason is simple. The six reservoirs that feed Caracas cannot keep up with demand, and the government has not built a new reservoir in more than fifteen years.[16] Leaky and broken-down water pumps and pipelines explain why water pressure is low and taps often run dry in various parts of the city. The Tuy water supply system, considered the largest of its kind in the world, with a reservoir and forty miles of waterways, is now under construction to serve the city, but lack of funds has delayed its completion by more than a decade.[17] The rest of the country suffers similar problems. Indeed in 2014 roughly four of every ten Venezuelans did not receive steady water service every day.[18]

The electricity sector is also in shambles. Ever since Venezuela nationalized power companies in 2007, not enough money has been invested in new power generation capacity. The country's transmission grid is old and prone to failures.[19] Droughts have made it hard to generate power in a country where more than half of the electricity comes from hydropower plants. But the big problem is levels of consumption that are outsize for a broken economy like Venezuela's, a phenomenon caused by subsidized electricity prices. Every Venezuelan consumed on average 3,413 kilowatt-hours in 2012, roughly on a par with electricity usage in China, which has one of the fastest-growing economies in the world.[20] In April 2015 excess power demand had gotten so bad that the government declared a national power emergency and cut the working hours of government employees to less than six hours, hoping to use less air-conditioning,[21] and in early 2016 the government forced shopping centers and hotels to cut down on power usage during the day, forcing stores to close and hotel guests to spend hours with no power.

Inefficiency is a common side effect of mango management. Chavismo became more popular when the government seized companies and increased their payrolls, but the companies became less effective. Venezuela's largest steel mill, Sidor, is a case in point. In 2007, the year before Chavez took over the company, Sidor's forty-five hundred full-time workers produced 4.3 million metric tons of liquid steel.[22] Chávez seized Sidor, arguing that a state-led enterprise would do a better job of producing steel and caring for workers. Seven years later, the company had more than tripled its payroll to more than 15,500 employees, but its steel output, at 1.04 million tons, was less than a quarter of what it was before the state took over.[23]

Nationalizing companies was one of several measures proponents of Chavismo adopted in hopes of advancing their brand of socialism. Chávez tried persuading people to barter for products instead of using money.[24] He pushed business leaders to let workers co-manage companies at the board level by offering money to revamp their operations, a throwback to the self-management of Josip Broz Tito in Yugoslavia.[25] He created scores of companies, some of them in partnership with China, Belarus, and Iran, to assemble Iranian tractors, Chinese computers, and Belarusian mining trucks. Each failed economic approach gave way to another. By mid-2014 Chavismo had doubled the number of public-sector employees to 2.7 million in a span of fifteen years, according to the National Statistics Institute. In a clear indication that lessons are not usually learned in Venezuela, Maduro created a new mission called Efficiency or Nothing in 2013, charging eight hundred volunteer inspectors with rooting out graft and inefficiency in government institutions. Maduro's thinking was that he could fight the vices of bureaucracy with more bureaucracy.[26]

The foreign banks and bondholders who lent money to Venezuela fear mango management the most. Venezuela in 2016 is strapped for cash because oil prices are low and the country has lost billions of dollars of foreign exchange owing to far too many imports and too much waste and corruption. But Venezuela still has to pay its debts and import the food and other basic necessities people need to lead moderately normal lives. The country already struggles to import staples such as corn for arepas and sugar to sweeten coffee. Venezuela's creditors fear that the nation may eventually skip out on its debt obligations.

Bank of America's Merrill Lynch estimated the Venezuelan government's total debt load topped US$123 billion in 2015,[27] several times what the country earned from oil sales in that same year when oil prices plummeted. Indeed in 2015 and early 2016 Venezuela's oil company barely kept enough cash on hand to cover debt payments due in the year.[28] The need for cash was such that in April 2015 the country pawned nearly 1.4 million troy ounces of the gold bars its central bank keeps stowed as part of its reserves with Citibank for US$1 billion in cash,[29] and the country continued to liquidate the bank's gold reserves in the following months. President Maduro even flew to China seeking a financial lifeline from its ally and partner.[30] The country with the largest oil reserves in the world has been reduced to depending on the deep pockets of others to survive.

Observing Venezuela scramble to pay debts is like watching a tipsy tightrope walker cross the Grand Canyon with no safety harness. He might pull it off, but a sudden gust of wind would end it all. Bank of America reckoned that Venezuela was burning through its cash and assets at a clip of $20 billion a year in late 2015, and the country could do this for three more years but no longer. If oil prices stay low for a long time, and if bondholders and China choose not to renegotiate Venezuela's debts or lend the company any more money, soon the country may no longer be able to pay what it owes.

Everyday Venezuelans suffer the most from mango management, but most of them don't even know it. Venezuelans endure blackouts or days of no running water. They have trouble finding coffins to bury their dead because Sidor struggles to sell coffin manufacturers the sheet metal they need to make them.[31] And politicians pile short-term solutions on top of short-term solutions, putting price caps on coffins, on cars, and on bottled water, which makes it more costly to produce them.[32] Chances are no citizen ever wrote a message on a piece of paper or on a mango asking a Venezuelan president for a new water reservoir, better electricity infrastructure, more investment in the oil sector, or a well-run steel company. And since no one is hitting them on the head about it, Venezuela's shortsighted leaders have learned to neglect those issues until they become emergencies.

* * *

On a Friday morning in February 2015, Jenny called to tell me that Che— the star Chavista personality—was still sleeping because he was up late with friends. Che, Jenny, and I had plans to go to La Guaira to visit Jenny's mother, Rosa Meza, who I was told lived in a fully equipped apartment a block away from the ocean, courtesy of the Chavista government. I gave Che a few more hours of sleep and met Vladimir, a Venezuelan photographer, who agreed to accompany me on the trip. Vladimir and I jumped in a cab to Che's home, but the cabdriver only reluctantly made his way to a part of town where he ran the risk of getting mugged. Minutes later his nervousness turned into surprise, however, when he realized that Che, an icon of Venezuela's leftist revolution, would escort us to the coast, riding one of his motorcycles dubbed La Poderosa II (The Powerful II). With Che riding ahead, the trip became the safest ride my cabdriver had given any client.

Before heading out, however, Che took me aside for a talk. He was concerned about what exactly I was planning to write in my book. Driving me around the barrio, bringing me into his home, even discussing how he lives was one thing, but taking someone to visit his not-quite mother-in-law

(Jenny and Che are not married) was something else entirely. Che claimed he had never visited Rosa's home, and although he didn't say so, he appeared uncomfortable with the whole idea. I explained to him that visiting Rosa would give me a window into the life of someone who was lucky enough to get a government apartment under Chavismo. Chávez and Maduro funded famous social programs for the poor, but few people had managed to get a brand-new apartment. After a few minutes of private powwow, he appeared ready to go. Jenny seemed more eager to take me to her mother's home, probably because our trip would finally force Che to accompany her when she visits her mother.

We made our way down to the coast with Che speeding ahead down the freeway in what looked like a scene out of the 1969 road movie *Easy Rider*. Jenny rode in the cab with Vladimir and me and gave directions to the driver. Suddenly, a man riding a bike, a moto taxi, caught up to Che, inched close to him, and asked him to take a photo. The man pulled out a cellphone and took a selfie with one hand while he perilously held the bike's handlebar with the other in the middle of the freeway. He took the photo, waved to Che, and sped off. The drive took half an hour, and we soon reached a white, thirteen-story building, one of three identical ones in an apartment complex called OPPPE 36, in an area of Playa Grande just a few steps from the ocean and four miles from the Maiquetía airport. This is far from prime real estate. The beaches near the airport are dirty, and from the building's parking lot one can see and hear planes landing. But the most remarkable sight was the building itself. The apartment complex was roughly two years old but looked much older. Its facade had cracks in various places, and the paint was peeling. The lobby of the building had dirty concrete floors and an abandoned commercial space, with broken ceiling tiles, trash, and a small mountain of loose gravel on the floor, that no business had found fit to lease. The whole building looked like it was unfinished when residents moved in.

Jenny's mother, Rosa, a woman in her sixties, turned out to be a sweet woman who welcomed me into her home and immediately offered a cup of coffee. She lives in a second-floor apartment overlooking the parking lot. And that is fortunate because the building's elevator doesn't work, so residents have to trek up and down the stairs every day, which is a pain for those who live on the top floors. Her home is a spartan two-bedroom apartment with concrete floors and a small kitchenette equipped with Chinese Haier-brand appliances. The fridge, the stove, a washer-drier unit, and a water heater were provided free of charge by the government two weeks after she moved in.

The kitchen, living, and dining area turned out to be an open space furnished with modest wooden chairs and a dining table adorned with plastic flowers in a vase. Rosa told me that a Chinese construction company—one of several foreign firms the Chávez government hired to build low-income apartments—erected this building. Rosa and her neighbors received their apartments in October 2013, just two months before Venezuela's municipal elections. Many of the ninety-six families now living in the building came from the same shelter for homeless or displaced Venezuelans, where some of them lived for almost three years before they received their new homes.

News of Che's arrival, with a foreign visitor in tow, caused a bit of a stir in the building, and within minutes a group of people came to visit. A woman who identified herself as the building's government liaison said the building's residents were still waiting for the government to send them free furniture as well, but they had been waiting for over a year. The neighbors slowly opened up about the problems they faced every day with a building that was poorly constructed. The construction process itself was delayed several times and was paralyzed for eight months, partly because the light fixtures, electricity cables, and other construction materials were often stolen. And despite the government's intention to give them fully equipped and furnished apartments, it was better to have the families move in first because the furniture and appliances could have been stolen before residents showed up.

The building's elevator worked for a few months after they moved in, but it often suffered mechanical failures. The community pitched in to call a technician, and the man found that the salty sea spray in the area had corroded the elevator's motor and its guide rails. It appears the builders installed the elevator despite damage to the rails. The elevator had been out of service ever since. I excused myself to take a peek at Rosa's restroom, and I noticed the bathroom and the shower had no tile, the walls were cracked, and a hole in the floor to the left of the toilet—crudely covered with a piece of cardboard and tape—emitted a foul odor. Rosa and her neighbors later informed me the sewer pipes in the building often got clogged and this caused bad smells in people's bathrooms. The shoddy construction of OPPPE 36 began making headlines in local newspapers less than a year after the building was finished. Residents complained of poor trash collection, troubles with pests, even sewer water filtering through the walls.[33]

The quality of Venezuela's newly built low-income housing varies depending on who the builder was. Just across the street from Rosa's building sits the Hugo Chávez Commune, an area with seventeen hundred new apartments built by Turkish construction company Summa. The Summa units are gray-and-white four-story buildings, with modern architecture that looks luxurious in comparison with Rosa's. The housing complex has well-lit streets and grassy areas with brand-new jungle gyms where children play. Rosa and her neighbors said the government typically assigns the nicer apartments to members of the military and their families. Rosa knows this firsthand because her other daughter, Jenny's sister, is married to a member of the military and the couple received a government apartment in a nicer Caracas housing unit next to the country's top military base, Fuerte Tiuna.

The conversation with Rosa and her neighbors eventually turned to the issue of price. How much do they pay for their apartments? And do they have legal documents showing they own their homes? When the residents of Rosa's building moved in, many expected these to be a gift from the Chávez administration. After all, during Chávez's last years, the president often spoke publicly of giving apartments away to the poor. By 2013 Venezuela's government had handed out as many as 381,000 housing units over a period of two years, with no paperwork or legal title to the property.[34] Many families received only a certificate that established they were assigned their home but forbade people from selling or transferring the property to others. After Chávez died, President Maduro announced plans to legalize the holding of thousands of government-built homes and to make people pay for them. "No one is paying a cent here," Maduro complained in early 2013. "How will we sustain the spending and investment to build future homes? By doing magic?"[35] However, three years after that vow thousands still have no legal papers for their property.[36]

Five months after moving in, the families in OPPPE 36 confronted a nightmare scenario: they each received a notice from the state-owned housing bank BANAVIH informing them that they were considered to be in default and unless they paid up what they owed, they faced eviction in fifteen days. Rosa handed me the BANAVIH notice she received in March 2014. The letter informed Rosa that she was five months behind on her monthly mortgage payments of 878 bolivars, the equivalent of a third of a minimum-wage salary at the time.[37] BANAVIH demanded payment to "avoid the [ensuing legal] fight" and threatened a seizure and auction of the property.

Rosa assured me government officials did not properly explain to her and her neighbors that they had a mortgage to pay. But when I dug further into Rosa's folder of paperwork, I found a housing ministry document dated October 3, 2013, that laid out the loan's terms. Rosa's family income was estimated at 3,000 bolivars (or US$50 at the time),[38] and the value of the apartment was 340,000 bolivars (or US$5,666). Under the terms, the government assumed half the cost of the apartment as a subsidy and gave Rosa thirty years to pay the rest at a generous 4.7 percent fixed annual interest. This type of financing was extremely generous in a country where inflation hovered at 70 percent a year at the time. Under those conditions the government was already losing money. People were getting their homes practically for free.

It soon struck me that Rosa didn't fully understand the basic terms of the financial agreement. It's unclear whether government officials did not fully explain their obligations to Rosa and her neighbors or the building's residents chose not to pay, hoping Chavismo would eventually forgive their debts. Figuring out who did what is irrelevant in the end. Faced with eviction, the building's community quickly organized to protest and reached out to the authorities, saying they could not afford to cover mortgage payments. The OPPPE 36 eviction crisis happened to coincide with a spate of opposition protests against Chavismo that made headlines around the world in the early months of 2014. As Rosa and her neighbors tell it, soon housing ministry officers showed up, they conducted a study of the community's ability to pay, and they forgave the debt of a couple of families and told everyone else in the housing complex—to their relief—that all mortgage payments would be suspended until further notice. By the time of my visit, Rosa had been living in her apartment for almost a year and a half for free. Che shook his head when he heard the story and said people needed to pay something for the homes. "People like to say I deserve this apartment. Why do you deserve it? No you don't. People need to work," he said.

Despite the building's sad state, Rosa and those who live in it felt thankful and remained loyal to Chavismo. The building's government liaison attributed the shortages of basic food staples to the smuggling and reselling of goods that comes from "people's greed." The OPPPE 36 Chavistas I spoke to supported the government's efforts to impose fingerprint technology on all food outlets as a means to stop smuggling, a problem one of Rosa's neighbors believed was originally caused by foreigners, mainly Colombians who cross the border to buy cheap goods they can resell back home. The idea that foreigners are to blame is often part of the Chavista discourse. Naturally, none of the neighbors I spoke to at OPPPE 36 blamed the ongoing product scarcity crisis on the government's price control policies.

Rosa graciously offered us lunch, and over a plate of beans and rice, we discussed the country's problems. Che pointed out to me that despite these complaints people living in Rosa's building were worse off before they moved in. He argued that neighbors rarely take these complaints to the authorities, so the problems with housing become nothing more than rumor and innuendo. As we left, a woman walking up the stairs caught a glimpse of Vladimir's camera and angrily demanded to know who we were and what our business was in the building. Under Chavismo, writers or anyone with a camera or a microphone have become suspect, unless they happen to work for state-owned news outlets. Rosa quickly intervened and reassured the woman that we were there to interview her and came with Che. The woman gave Che a broad smile, but she still eyed Vladimir and me with suspicion.

* * *

Rosa's housing woes are just a glimpse of the poor quality of Venezuela's state-led construction ventures and how they result in waste. Indeed, Venezuela's government spending has become notoriously inefficient when it comes to providing citizens with goods and services. The World Economic Forum's 2015–16 Global Competitiveness Report puts Venezuela at number 140, or dead last, in its rankings of government wastefulness, which means that—by that measure—Venezuela has the most wasteful government on the planet,[39] far worse than African oil-producing nations run by dictators and kleptocrats such as Angola.

Venezuela also comes last in the World Economic Forum's ethics and corruption rankings, which are pieced together by looking at practices such as diversion of public funds and a culture of kickbacks and bribes.[40] In a subsection of that index that looks at the use of bribes and irregular payments in the previous year's 2014–15 report, Venezuela was number 137 of 144, tied with Angola. That is quite a feat. While President Chávez was not known for enriching himself and his family members, the thirty-seven-year regime of Angola's leader, Jose Eduardo dos Santos, has often been characterized as one of the most corrupt on the African continent. Dos Santos's forty-year-old daughter, Isabel, is now the richest woman in Africa, with a US$3 billion net worth that Forbes reckons was amassed by taking stakes in key industries with the help of her powerful father.[41]

Waste and corruption have saddled Venezuela with deficient infrastructure too. The World Economic Forum's last two competitiveness studies have shown that Venezuela has one of the most deficient levels of infrastructure in the world, and among oil-rich OPEC members, only Angola and Nigeria are worse off. However, Angola ended its civil war a little more than a decade ago, in 2002, and Nigeria suffers from ethnic religious strife in its oil-producing Niger Delta area and from recurring Islamic insurgency attacks. Venezuela is free from such complexities.

Venezuela's crazy economic nature is best captured by the World Economic Forum's ranking of the overall macroeconomic environment, which looks at a country's inflation rate, budget balancing practices, debt, and credit scores. In 2014–15 Venezuela ranked number 139 of 144, the worst macroeconomic environment among oil-producing nations, with the exception of war-torn Yemen.[42] And while some oil-rich countries in Africa are worse off than Venezuela in terms of an educated population, the sophistication of their businesses, and the availability of technology, Venezuela's crazy economy is considered less stable and has struggled with the curse of Dutch disease for nearly half a century longer than its African counterparts. In fact Venezuela suffered from Dutch disease for decades before the *Economist* magazine coined the term *Dutch disease* in the late 1970s to refer to the economic troubles the Netherlands suffered after it discovered natural gas in the late 1950s.

Nigeria, the Republic of Congo, the Democratic Republic of Congo, and Angola all discovered and began producing crude in the 1950s and 1960s, nearly half a century later than Venezuela did. It wasn't until the 1970s that Angola's oil output surpassed coffee as its main export, and Equatorial Guinea discovered crude only in the late 1990s. By the time Norway began developing its North Sea oil reserves in the 1970s, Norwegians were well aware that Venezuela's struggles with petroleum riches had become a morality tale they didn't want for themselves. At the time, the *Financial Times* newspaper had already taken to calling Venezuela's petroleum insanity the "Venezuelan Effect."[43]

Plenty of resource-rich nations around the world manage their spending better than Venezuela does. One of its neighbors, the copper-rich Chile, has carefully designed its budget for many years to keep spending in check.[44] To figure out the budget, a team of Chilean economic experts keeps an eye on the economy's growth and estimates how high copper prices can go. The South American country prepares four-year budgets instead of annual ones as a way to keep spending priorities grounded in long-term plans instead of sudden political whims. When the country receives far more money than originally expected, it squirrels cash away in two funds, one used to pay debts and cover deficits when copper prices are low, and the other to help pay people's pensions. What's more, Chileans from all walks of life understand the government's spending rules and how they help make the country's economy more stable. The World Economic Forum puts Chile as the twenty-ninth most stable economy in the world, a better macroeconomic environment than the United Kingdom.[45]

Similarly, Russia under Vladimir Putin has used a complicated formula that takes average oil prices for the last decade, the country's tax receipts, and a debt limit to decide how much the government can spend. Russia has also set aside oil money in two funds to save for future generations and to spend on infrastructure. The Norwegians are even more conservative. Norway allows only 4 percent of its giant oil fund, the largest and richest in the world, to cover government spending needs every year. This legal maxim has become so ingrained in society that everyday Norwegians have come to know it as "the budgetary rule." The International Monetary Fund estimates that in 2013 a total of eighty-one countries followed strict spending or debt limits to balance their budgets and another sixty-one nations practiced medium-term budgets that span several years as a way to prudently spend their money,[46] but Venezuela is not one of them.

Venezuela's oil-rich Middle Eastern counterparts—those not torn apart by armed conflict—have also done a better job of erecting stable, growing economies. Oil nations belonging to the Cooperation Council for the Arab States of the Gulf, or GCC, such as Kuwait, Saudi Arabia, the United Arab Emirates, and Qatar, who also happen to be OPEC members, still struggle to diversify their economies away from oil, but they have been far smarter and effective at spending on infrastructure and high-quality health and education for their populations. They have avoided the type of runaway inflation and devaluations that make it impossible for people in Venezuela to save money in banks, and that prompt them to desperately go into debt and spend on cars and other consumer goods to safeguard their earnings. And they have done so coming from similar starting points in their history. Qatar was a poor, pearl-fishing nation when it first began exploring for oil and gas in the late 1930s, a couple of decades later than Venezuela did, and its government is usually ranked as the best in the world, ahead of Finland and Norway, by the World Economic Forum owing to its levels of efficiency and transparency.

The government of the United Arab Emirates (UAE) is also considered one of the top six best-run public administrations in the world, according to the World Economic Forum. The UAE may be famous for its luxury skyscrapers, such as the fifty-six-story Burj Al Arab hotel that resembles a sail and sits on a manmade island, and the 829-meter-tall Burj Khalifa, the tallest building in the world, but it also boasts top-quality roads, seaports, and airport infrastructure, besting the United States and many countries in Europe.[47] Arab countries in the GCC are not without problems. They are not democracies, and their laws about human rights and labor rights leave much to be desired. Such conditions allow their leaders far more leeway to do as they please than in Venezuela, where politicians fight to get elected and reelected every six years. Venezuela's democracy tempts presidents to use oil riches to perpetuate their hold on power. This means that future Venezuelan leaders must balance electability with a long-term view of the country's development and have a deep sense of discipline to responsibly manage the nation's economic affairs.

* * *

On October 10, 1999, at 4 a.m., a plane carrying Venezuelan president Hugo Chávez touched down in Anchorage, Alaska, for a quick stop on the way to China. The president was not alone. He had flown in with such a large group of people that they booked forty-three hotel rooms just to eat and take showers.[48] Chávez was there for one reason, to hold a breakfast chat with the officials who ran the Alaska Permanent Fund that invests part of the money the state pockets from oil. The Alaska fund became famous for mailing annual checks to state residents with a cut of its returns. In the world of oil, the Alaska fund is a rare, successful example of how to safeguard cash from the hands of politicians with a weakness for spending, a tool that helps the government handle its finances prudently.

Alaska's governor, Jay Hammond, a bearded, Santa-Claus-looking bear of a man, created the fund in 1976, fearful that politicians could end up wasting the state's oil windfall. Hammond knew about Venezuela's oil troubles and didn't want Alaska to make the same mistakes.[49] He had spent years trying to persuade skeptical Alaskans to create a transparent fund, run by out-of-state financial experts who would invest oil money and send an annual dividend from the fund's returns to residents. When Hammond became governor in 1974, Alaskans were finally ready. They had seen how politicians blew through the US$900 million Alaska got from leasing the Prudhoe Bay oil field, the largest in the United States. Hammond persuaded lawmakers to create the fund and save as much as a quarter of oil revenues. He had three goals in mind: saving oil money for future Alaskans, forcing politicians to do more while spending less, and turning check-happy Alaskans into rabid defenders of the fund and its dividend. Hammond reasoned that once you give someone a check, you cannot take it away. And any politician who tried to do so would be dead politically. Hammond once put it this way: "I wanted to pit collective greed against selective greed."[50]

The Chávez visit was odd in many ways. Here was the leader of the broken oil nation that partly served as inspiration for the Alaska fund in the first place. He had just flown in with an embarrassingly large entourage that attracted media attention, and, ironically, he wanted to learn about a fund designed to make it harder for people like him to practice his brand of state largesse.

Alaska's revenue commissioner at the time, Wilson Condon, explained to Chávez how the fund worked and the safeguards taken to assign yearly checks. The annual check that year amounted to US$1,800 per resident, an especially big help for cash-poor Alaskans. Chávez seemed interested in how the money benefited low-income families and said he was looking for ways to improve the lot of Venezuela's majority poor. Just months before his Alaska trip, the president had said he would save oil revenue in a fund meant to help pay Venezuela's debts.[51] After breakfast, the president took off for Shanghai.

Chávez never came close to following in Alaska's footsteps. He did what Hammond tried desperately to prevent in Alaska. Once Venezuela had saved enough money, Chávez began to spend it all even at a time when he arguably didn't need to, because oil prices were rising.[52] Soon Chávez stopped saving altogether. The concept of saving money is anathema to Venezuelan politicians of all stripes. In 2006 Manuel Rosales, an opposition presidential candidate, ran on a platform to give Venezuelans credit cards so they could spend a portion of oil money without politicians getting in the way. But his plan made no mention of a fund to save money for the future. At the time, however, Chávez was too popular and too powerful to be beaten. He managed to ridicule his opponent's ideas and won reelection.

Other leaders around the world have been known to make fake promises of giving oil wealth directly to the people to stay in power longer. In 2008 Libya's Muammar Gaddafi announced he would dismiss nearly all his ministers and hand over oil revenues directly to the people for them to spend.[53] His people, Gaddafi said, didn't need corrupt bureaucrats. The plan was to funnel money to organized community groups beholden to Gaddafi. At some point someone must have explained to the dictator that he would just be replacing one corrupt bureaucracy for another, because he chose to do nothing. It turns out Libya's people didn't need Gaddafi either.

While Venezuela has been unable to save a portion of its petrodollars, smart oil nations have gone beyond that. Norway and the United Arab Emirates, for example, have created investment funds—known as sovereign wealth funds—that save and carefully invest billions of dollars to generate even more money. In March 2016 Norway's oil fund was worth U S $853 billion,[54] twice the value of Norway's estimated gross domestic product in 2015. Abu Dhabi's fund, considered the second largest in the world after Norway's, invests in prime assets such as luxury hotels, Michelin-starred restaurants, and real estate the world over, seeking the best returns for its money. Eventually, a sovereign fund can churn out more in annual returns for a nation than the amount of money the country obtains from oil, but that requires discipline, savvy investing, and patience. In 2012 even Nigeria, a country with a far more complex ethnic and religious makeup than Venezuela, set aside US $1 billion in seed money in an attempt to set up a sovereign wealth fund that is divided into three parts, one to stabilize government spending in bad times, another to finance infrastructure, and a third to save money for future generations.

A group of academics at IESA—Venezuela's top business school—led a series of focus groups with low-income Venezuelans in 2011 to test the viability of directly distributing money to citizens. To their surprise, participants embraced the idea of receiving funds directly in their bank accounts in lieu of government spending, but they preferred receiving vouchers to pay for education and health.[55] Most respondents also agreed with the idea of saving money to sustain government spending in times of low oil prices. And they favored money be given to all Venezuelans, to avoid the corruption that could come from politicians deciding who is poor enough to get cash.

The results suggest people are open to a scheme that could force politicians to be less wasteful while giving Venezuelans more ownership over their oil. After all, a 2010 survey by Venezuelan pollster Consultores 21 showed that nearly seven of every ten Venezuelans believed they had not benefited from the nation's oil income during Chávez's mandate.[56] The findings suggest that Venezuelan leaders would find support for a mechanism to give people part of the country's oil revenue in the form of vouchers, while saving enough in a rainy day fund that could sustain government spending in times when oil revenues decline.

Encouraged by these findings, Venezuelan oil economist Francisco Monaldi and two colleagues explored how to give Venezuelans an oil dividend. Monaldi's research showed that every Venezuelan would have received US $2,097 in 2011 if that year's oil income had been wholly distributed equally among all.[57] And if the country's oil income, together with gasoline subsidies and the money the country failed to earn from selling oil on credit to neighbors, had all been bundled up into a dividend in 2008—at the height of the oil boom—each Venezuelan would have gotten almost US $3,000 in cash.[58] Of course giving the country's entire oil income away via checks is not realistic or desirable. Monaldi favors carefully calibrating the portion of oil riches given to Venezuelans directly to prevent the money from stifling their incentive to work, while at the same time leaving enough money for politicians to provide basic public services as well.

Monaldi estimates that the US$44 billion Chavez funneled to his favorite spending fund FONDEN over a period of nine years through 2011 would have been enough to send nearly US$480 a year to every Venezuelan.[59] That may not seem like much for those living outside Venezuela. But it would have amounted to three months of work for a minimum-wage earner in 2011,[60] which suggests that there is enough oil money to offer people, especially the poorest Venezuelans, a meaningful oil dividend.

There are ways to give Venezuelans an initial taste of what an oil dividend could do for them. Monaldi's study proposes raising the price of Venezuela's gasoline to half the level of international prices. That would help cover the cost of producing it, and whatever is left over could be wired back to Venezuelans' bank accounts. If the government had done that in 2011, Monaldi reckons that every household would have received US$674 that year—the equivalent of more than four minimum-wage salaries. This plan could balance the scales of a gasoline subsidy that for years has benefited wealthy car owners far more than the poor. Indeed, in 2010, the richest 25 percent of Venezuelan households received more than US$3,000 in the form of subsidized gasoline, while the poorest got less than US$500.[61] This is hardly a fair distribution or even an efficient use of a country's oil wealth.

The radical government of Mahmoud Ahmadinejad in Iran, a close ally of Chávez, got rid of gasoline subsidies with a similar scheme. In December 2010 Iran raised the price of its gasoline by twenty times and at the same time gave its citizens bank accounts with half the cash the country saved from scrapping the subsidy.[62] Iran, like Venezuela, had ridiculously low gasoline prices that prompted fuel smuggling across its borders. To sell the Iranians on the idea, the Ahmadinejad government launched a media blitz and recruited academics and civilian leaders to actively promote the change. Government officials also spoke often about the price hike and promised to give people and companies part of the savings in return for giving up subsidies.

Persuading Venezuelans to save money for future generations or simply to spend in lean times would not be easy. It took Hammond years of campaigning to bring Alaskans around to adopting his idea. And Alaskans agreed to do it only because they became angry enough about wasted oil wealth.

Alexandra Gillies, an academic who has studied examples of direct distribution of oil wealth found that to bring about change, it takes either a major historical crisis or a fresh leader eager to leave a legacy.[63] Chavismo is unlikely to adopt such a reform because the leftist rhetoric of its most radical members stands against the principle of saving oil riches, an idea most Chavistas consider impractical, neoliberal, and elitist. What is now the worst economic crisis in the history of Venezuela may yet force Venezuelans to face their addiction to the misspending of oil riches and prompt them to adopt policies to treat it.

* * *

Venezuela still has a problem with S U S I, the central bank money press that prints far too many bolivars. By March 2016 S U S I continued to work at full capacity. By the end of 2015 Venezuela had put nearly three-and-a-half times as many new bills into circulation that year as it did the year before.[64] Most of them were 100 bolivar bills, because lower denominations are practically worthless. By March 28, 2016, a large cup of coffee at Cafe Ole in Caracas cost 350 bolivars. It takes 175 bills of the lowest 2-bolivar denomination to pay for that coffee. A few blocks away, the Casa del Llano sells Reina Pepiada arepas for 990 bolivars. That's almost ten 100-bolivar bills and a ridiculous 485 bills of the 2-bolivar kind. Venezuelans are forced to handle increasingly large wads of cash because prices keep rising. The Casa del Llano hikes up the price for arepas every three months. In February 2016 the government capitulated and announced it would print new 500 and 1,000-bolivar notes to make life easier for people.[65]

Other countries have been down this path before, and it doesn't end well. It usually leads to episodes of hyperinflation such as those in Austria, Germany, and Hungary after World War I, the Philippines under Japanese occupation during World War II, and even China when the Yuan Dynasty printed cash to finance its wars. The most notable hyperinflation episodes in history have occurred in countries trying to recover from a war or attempting to finance a military campaign. Venezuela is a country at peace, and the runaway spending that left the country with triple-digit inflation cannot be explained away by a military conflict.

Zimbabwe under dictator Robert Mugabe cranked up the money press, and by 2008 inflation topped 231 million percent.[66] The president did so to pay for the government's involvement in the Second Congo War, considered the deadliest war the world has seen since World War II. At the height of its inflationary spiral, prices for goods in Zimbabwe doubled in twenty-four hours. People used wheelbarrows to carry cash around. Zimbabwe eventually printed a 100 trillion Zimbabwean dollar bill. The economy naturally collapsed because people can't live like that. It all ended when the country adopted the U.S. dollar as currency in 2009, but Zimbabweans had already discarded the country's funny money and used dollars instead. The only good thing to possibly come out of the mess was that people learned to count high. How often does one hear about quadrillions anyway? The biggest lesson Zimbabweans learned was that their leaders could not be trusted with a money press.

Things don't need to get that bad for people to dump their currency. Oil-rich Ecuador, a member of OPEC, suffered its worst crisis ever in 1999, when inflation topped 60 percent (a fraction of Venezuela's 180.9 percent inflation in 2015), with a severe economic contraction to boot.[67] President Jamil Mahuad, holed up in the presidential palace with regular protests raging outside, chose to adopt the U.S. dollar as the country's official currency and chucked the 115-year-old sucre. In both Zimbabwe and Ecuador, adopting the dollar brought inflation immediately under control and tied the hands of politicians who would otherwise be tempted to print cash to remain popular. Ecuador no longer has a money press, and most Ecuadorians support the decision to dollarize the economy.

Ecuador is now a more economically stable country than Venezuela. And it has arguably done a more sustainable job of reducing poverty too. When Ecuador adopted the dollar in 2000, roughly four of every ten Ecuadorians were living on less than US$2 a day. By 2012 that same metric was 8.4 percent, according to the World Bank.[68] With a dollarized economy, leftist president Rafael Correa, an ally of Chavismo, still managed to invest enough money in infrastructure and social initiatives to continue reducing poverty. Under Chavismo, poverty did come down but the country's new economic crisis has practically erased those gains. Dollarization has offered a more stable platform for Ecuador to address poverty, but the dollar experiment has barely been around for fifteen years. As oil prices decline, it remains to be seen how an oil nation like Ecuador can cope with wild swings in oil prices.

Dollarization is a radical, risky choice. Taking away the money press means a country cannot devalue or use monetary policy to stimulate the economy in bad times, say, when oil prices decline. Plus, the dollar can make an economy less competitive than those of its neighbors, who can devalue their currencies to make their exports cheaper to the world. Dollarizing an economy is like severing one's arm to stop gangrene from spreading to the rest of the body. One does survive, but the body is limited by having one less limb. It's a permanent decision that cannot be reversed. Few human beings or countries want to be in that position.

Saudi Arabia and its neighbors, Qatar and the United Arab Emirates, and other oil-rich members of the GCC have chosen a more flexible path by linking their currency to the dollar,[69] which means they also cannot print their own money freely. This forces politicians to spend only as many dollars as they earn. But in the face of dire crisis, these countries could still resort to their monetary policy to help the economy along.

Unfortunately, Venezuela has rarely used its monetary policy responsibly. Venezuelan politicians spend large amounts of money in good times, when petrodollars are plentiful, and they scrimp when money runs out, the opposite of what they should do. They should save money in times of wealth so they can spend money in tough economic times. The country's burden has always been not knowing when enough spending is enough. The oil-rich nation has become a shopaholic that needs to learn how to handle credit cards.

Those who believe Venezuela will one day run its economy responsibly don't want the country to adopt the dollar as its official currency, and those who think future Venezuelan politicians will continue to ruin the nation push for a dollarized Venezuela. Johns Hopkins University economics professor Steve Hanke, a well-known dollarization proselytizer, who at one point advised Ecuador on adopting the greenback, advocates the idea of allowing Venezuelans to use the dollar side by side with the bolivar. In October 2015 President Maduro publicly dismissed the idea that his government would ever allow products and services to be sold in dollars in Venezuela, but his administration had already allowed Ford to sell some of its cars locally in US dollars.

Ruth de Krivoy, a former Venezuelan central bank president, told me dollarization makes her uneasy because it involves giving up an important economic policy tool. To push Venezuela to more responsibly manage its currency and its spending, possibly by linking the currency to the dollar, saving money, and adopting more strict fiscal rules, she said, would "require an event strong enough to force a change in people's values." Otherwise, Venezuela is unlikely to do it on its own. Krivoy put it this way: "If I happen to be a crazy person that needs to be tied down, it's unlikely that I will readily ask someone to put a straightjacket on me. That just doesn't happen in real life."[70]

A more prudent management of spending and currency could rein in inflation over time. It would teach Venezuelans to once again trust their currency and provide an incentive to save money again instead of buying U.S. dollars and spending their money on large assets, shopping sprees, and going into debt as a way to stay ahead of an increasingly worthless bolivar. In 2015 Venezuelans themselves increasingly began to realize that the bolivar has become a worthless piece of paper that politicians control and force them to use as money. In a world where inflation reaches unsustainable levels, eventually people choose on their own to stop using the local currency. A Venezuela with out-of-control, triple-digit inflation could soon be forced to adopt a more sound currency practice: pegging or linking the bolivar to the dollar or fully adopting the greenback as legal tender.

The first step in managing Venezuela's addiction to spending oil money uncontrollably is admitting the problem. Venezuela's long tradition of trying to spend more oil money than it can safely digest has deformed its economy, its institutions, and its society. Venezuela has become an upside-down world where politicians are not accountable to voters but to themselves, and voters have learned to beg their government for a living. The military is run by entitled generals who have never fought a war but who demand privilege, shiny new planes, and power over civilians. Businesses expect abnormally high profits without being competitive or efficient. Credit-card-happy consumers have no incentive to save any money but go into debt to shop compulsively instead. Poverty and inequality are legitimate concerns in Venezuela, but the country's underlying problem is wealth mismanagement. No amount of money has even been enough for Venezuela to become a stable, well-managed country. No amount of money has helped Venezuela consistently reduce poverty. In fact it often seems as if the more money Venezuela earns, the worse off it becomes. Venezuela has become a country with no future that lives only in the present.

For human beings, managing a life-long addiction requires attending meetings and undergoing some form of therapy. It also involves safeguards: alcoholics empty the liquor cabinet, food addicts lock the fridge, and shopaholics stay away from credit cards until they learn how to use them responsibly. The deepest economic crisis in Venezuela's history may yet force Venezuelans to adopt more sensible spending and currency practices like those of other oil-rich nations to make their economy more stable, less unpredictable, less crazy. Venezuela may yet come to realize that saving money for lean times and the future, while still investing enough money to strengthen human capital and help people overcome poverty, is a sound policy. More important, a deep economic crisis may teach a new generation of Venezuelan politicians that they need to spend more time trying to fix problems instead of causing them, that price controls on goods and arcane exchange rate rules are patchwork solutions that, held for long periods, create corrosive incentives and end up making the country less well off. Venezuela has relied on such practices as a crutch far too long. Venezuelans may also be prompted to run their oil industry more efficiently, learning from state oil companies such as Saudi Arabia's Aramco that invest to keep their oil businesses strong while still spending enough money to help their populations.

Venezuelans may not be ready yet to embrace monumental changes, but then no meaningful change comes fast and easy. It often takes years and a lot of pain for people to accept their addictions too. Simply hoping Venezuela will see better days is not enough. Mendoza Potellá, the central bank oil expert, is no fan of adopting a mechanism similar to that of Alaska because, he argues, it would leave the government with less money to do its job. Countries with oil wealth can and do manage their financial affairs responsibly, he says. "Look at Norway," he told me, referring to its government. Unlike Venezuela, however, Norway has a long history of strong institutions and prudent financial management, before and after finding oil. In contrast, Venezuelan leaders have never really taken serious steps that span several administrations to manage wealth the way Norway does. Promises of saving oil riches have quickly been discarded, and politicians have then spent any money saved. Venezuela did experience a long stretch during which the bolivar was a stable currency, but that largely happened during a time when oil was a far less volatile commodity than it is today.

It is imperative for us to accept who we are and to come to terms with our actions as human beings, and the same applies to countries. Venezuela never has behaved like Norway; it doesn't behave like Norway and likely never will become Norway. It may be far more realistic for Venezuelans to aspire to become a more responsible nation like copper-rich Chile. But that would require a modern, forward-thinking political class bent on leaving a positive, lasting legacy in Venezuela instead of perpetuating their hold on power. It may also require a more educated population. Giving Venezuelans a compulsory and basic economic education is of paramount importance. The country will continue to make the same mistakes of the past century if people lack the basic understanding of the way money works and the problems that have shaped Venezuela into what it is today. Children must learn early on the source of the problems of their oil-drunk nation.

Understanding how history has shaped Venezuela is a good first step. Venezuelans idolize Simón Bolívar as a mythical, almost religious figure. Bolívar reminds Venezuelans of a more heroic time prior to the discovery of oil, when the region sacrificed blood and sweat to become independent from the rule of the Spanish empire. That was more than two hundred years ago. Venezuela became a different country when it discovered crude. The agricultural nation became a petrostate. Politics no longer revolved around a fight for freedom; it became a roulette of dictators, populists, and coups. Not even the country's constitution is the same as it was then. Since Venezuela became an independent nation in 1811, the country has had twenty-three different constitutions. Venezuelans became accustomed to generous governments and quick riches. People's ideology, their habits, even their tastes changed. Yet images of Bolívar are everywhere, and so are statues of the leader, sword in hand, riding a spirited horse. Plazas and buildings are named after him. Venezuelans' obsession with Bolívar's glorious past clouds their vision of who they are in the present, a nation with a reckless political class that struggles with being too rich.

Few people remember the man largely responsible for making modern Venezuela possible, Juan Pablo Pérez Alfonzo. Many remember him as the founder of OPEC but for little else. Late in life, Pérez Alfonzo became known in Venezuela as a doomsayer. No one wanted to hear his warnings of the calamities that would visit Venezuela from the waste of excess oil money. No one wanted to hear how oil had ruined Venezuelans' work ethic. No one likes a killjoy. He died in Washington DC from liver cancer on September 3, 1979. In his will he asked to be cremated in the United States. His family justified that decision, saying he wanted to spare Venezuelans having to mourn him.[71]

Venezuela may very well continue down the same rocky path it took since it discovered crude, with the resulting backward economy. After several generations many Venezuelans don't know any other way. When I asked Robert Bottome, the octogenarian analyst and publisher of the Venezuelan economic newsletter *VenEconomía*, if he remembered a time when cars did not retain their value in Venezuela, he thought about it and said that had never been the case during his lifetime. Younger generations of Venezuelans have known nothing else either.

Venezuela has much to offer. It has one of the world's largest gold deposits, much iron ore, vast fertile lands, a well-known ocean of oil underground, and one of the world's largest reserves of natural gas. The country's natural beauty is without question. It has breathtaking white sand beaches with crystal clear water, the highest waterfall in the world, and flat-top mountains, created when the continents split—the same that inspired Arthur Conan Doyle to write his novel *The Lost World*—that are a UNESCO world heritage site. Venezuelans enjoy life and easily embrace and welcome others as their own.

Venezuela's people may not readily do what they need to build a less insane economy. But as long as there is a perverse incentive for Venezuela to spend its riches with abandon, every ten or twenty years the country's painful economic debacles may remind everyone that it still has the world's craziest oil economy. During the past century Venezuela became a painful moral lesson for the world. It is time for Venezuela to learn from others.

AFTERWORD

In early December 2015, Venezuelans voted against Chavismo in congressional elections, giving opposition parties control over 112 seats in the National Assembly, a two-thirds supermajority. It was the biggest electoral defeat in Chavismo's seventeen years in power and a clear message from Venezuelans frustrated with an economy in free fall. A photo of a crestfallen Che immediately following the results appeared in several international news outlets. In the following weeks, the outgoing Chavista congress used its last few days in office to stuff the Supreme Court with loyal judges. And a month later, in January 2016, those same Supreme Court judges moved to contest the electoral victory of three lawmakers who were then forced to resign their seats. Unseating these members of congress was a way to strip away the supermajority that gave the opposition enough power to change key laws (including the constitution), dismiss members of the Chavista cabinet, and more easily begin a process to recall President Nicolás Maduro. Venezuela seemed headed for political paralysis in 2016 with a congress dominated by the opposition and all other branches of government still in the hands of Chavismo.

President Maduro did not take defeat well. In a televised appearance soon after the election, Maduro blamed voters for deserting Chavismo and suggested he would no longer continue building homes for the poor because many had abandoned him. "My goal was to build 4 million homes, but now I don't know. I asked for your help and you didn't give it to me," he said.[1] It was a clear show of how Venezuelan politicians have come to expect political support in return for patronage. Opposition lawmakers vowed to pass a law that would eventually give people like Jenny's mother, Rosa Meza, a legal title to their new homes. Maduro said he would never allow such a law because it would essentially privatize the government's housing program. By mid-January, thousands of Venezuelan families living in government-built homes faced a legal limbo. They didn't own the property, and many continued to live in their homes without paying their mortgages. Their ability to keep a roof over their heads depended on the will of a generous president.

Venezuela's economy was in tatters in early 2016. Water and power outages in Caracas had become so bad that the government ordered hotels to limit the water and electricity use of their guests. Hotel rooms had no electricity from 11 a.m. to 3 p.m. as dictated by law to help save power. Restaurant employees sometimes worked extra hours waiting for overworked trucks to deliver water late at night, and laundry services had trouble washing their customers' clothes. The long lines of desperate shoppers and the shortages of food worsened. To address a lack of food production, Maduro asked that Venezuelans keep chickens in their homes and grow their own vegetables in their gardens to survive food shortages. In late 2015 Maduro named a young sociologist, Luis Salas, as the economic czar to address the country's most pressing problems. Salas was known for arguing in his writings that "inflation does not exist in real life."[2] Inflation, Salas argued, is not the result of a government printing too much money but of capitalists raising prices indiscriminately in unison. However, a mere two months after his appointment Maduro replaced Salas with a minister with slightly more business-friendly credentials in an attempt to placate his critics.

In January 2016 Maduro declared an "economic emergency" and asked congress to give him the power to continue printing money and the freedom to seize any company to ensure adequate supply of consumer products. Also in early 2016 the central bank released September 2015 data on economic growth, the first such release in more than a year. According to the central bank, gross domestic product had contracted 4.5 percent in the first nine months of 2015 and inflation for all of 2015 had reached 180.9 percent, the highest the country had ever seen.

The bolivar was increasingly devalued too. By late March 2016, more than a year after my initial three-week stay at the Caracas Renaissance hotel, a U.S. dollar could fetch as much as 1,200 bolivars on the black market, up from 180 bolivars in just twelve months. Venezuela's largest denomination, the 100-bolivar bill, was now worth a mere eight U.S. cents. In February Maduro was forced to devalue the main official exchange rate to 10 bolivars per dollar from the 6.3 rate and eliminated one of the three official exchange rates. That didn't do anything to address the lack of dollars available in the economy.

Declining oil prices promised to bring even more pain to Venezuela in 2016. The price the oil-rich country received for its crude fell to US$25.40 a barrel on average at the end of March, dangerously close to what it cost Venezuela to produce a barrel of oil. And prices showed no sign of rebounding much anytime soon. Venezuela could no longer afford to give its citizens the world's cheapest gasoline, and President Maduro was forced to increase the price of gasoline for the first time in two decades.[3] His increase was meager, however, and it left the multibillion-dollar gasoline subsidy intact. Venezuelans continued to enjoy the cheapest domestic gasoline sold anywhere in the world. Fewer dollars coming in meant that Venezuela would still struggle to import food and medicine and to pay its debts to banks and bondholders. By January, Del Pino, the president of state-owned PDVSA, had announced the company would seek to refinance its debts to push pressing payment obligations further into the future. Venezuela's dire financial situation suggested the country would be forced to cease paying its debts sometime in 2017 if the country didn't find a way to refinance its obligations.

The opposition vowed to use a referendum to unseat Maduro in 2016, but with the Chavistas in control of the Supreme Court and with enough backing from the military, it seemed likely that Chavismo would remain in power a while longer despite the ongoing economic debacle.

While Venezuela suffered the worst economic crisis since the country discovered oil, no politician or public figure made any proposals to embrace policies in the future to reduce spending and save money. It didn't seem the right time politically for politicians of any stripe to bring that up. Venezuelans and their leaders were more than ever focused on their present predicaments. They were once again, as so many times before in their history, left with little more to do but pray that rising oil prices would soon rescue the nation from its own mistakes.

CHRONOLOGY

1908   Vice President Juan Vicente Gómez takes power by force while the president is on a medical trip to Paris.

1914   Venezuela's first commercial oil well, Zumaque, begins production.

1922   Gómez passes Venezuela's first oil law, giving foreign companies free range to explore for and pump oil.

1930–39   Venezuela experiences overvaluation of its currency, the bolivar.

1935   Gómez dies, ending his twenty-seven-year dictatorship.

1940–44   President Isaías Medina Angarita imposes price controls on basic goods, restricts imports.

1943   Venezuela passes new oil law, imposing royalties and income taxes on oil companies. The 50-50 principle, under which the state and companies split oil gains equally, is enshrined.

1945   The military leads coup against President Medina Angarita. Venezuela decrees subsidized gasoline prices.

1947   Oil prices surge on the back of rising demand following the end of World War II.

1948   The military unseats first democratically elected president, Rómulo Gallegos, in "telephone coup" and establishes junta.

1953   General Marcos Pérez Jiménez declares himself president after rigging 1952 election and vows to modernize Venezuela with oil revenue.

1958   Pérez Jiménez abandons the presidency after the military turns on him. Political parties sign democracy pact, "Pacto de Punto Fijo."

1960   Pérez Alfonzo persuades Middle Eastern nations to create Organization of Petroleum Exporting Countries, OPEC.

1973   Arab countries declare embargo of oil shipped to Western nations. Oil prices rise 260 percent in the span of one year.

1973–79 Venezuelans elect Carlos Andrés Pérez, who promises to use oil riches to bring economic development and create the "Gran Venezuela." Venezuela experiences bolivar overvaluation.

1976   Venezuela nationalizes the oil industry.

1980   Global oil glut sends oil prices tumbling.

1983   Venezuela's bolivar sees biggest devaluation ever on "Black Friday," losing decades of currency stability. Recadi exchange control agency created.

1989   Venezuela lifts capital controls, devalues currency, and eliminates rotten Recadi dollar administrator. El Caracazo uprising takes place on back of 100 percent increase in domestic gasoline prices, among other price adjustments for basic consumer goods.

1992   Paratrooper Hugo Chávez leads a failed coup against President Carlos Andrés Pérez and is jailed.

1993   President Carlos Andrés Pérez is impeached after being accused of corruption.

1994–96   Venezuela imposes currency exchange controls again.

1998   Venezuelans elect Chávez as their president.

1999   Chávez wins referendum to reform constitution, enacts new oil law.

2002   Chávez survives an April coup attempt. In December oil workers begin nationwide oil strike.

2003   In February oil workers end a two-month oil industry strike that fails to unseat Chávez. Chávez imposes capital and price controls, fires thousands of PDVSA employees, and begins spending on missions.

2004   Chávez wins referendum on his mandate.

2005   Chávez vows to create Twenty-First-Century Socialism. He seizes first company and begins campaign to nationalize private-sector companies.

2007   Venezuela nationalizes oil ventures run by ExxonMobil and ConocoPhillips.

2008   Oil prices reach record highs, then begin to tumble.

2009   Inflation tops 27 percent on back of price controls and generous government spending.

2013   Chávez dies. Nicolás Maduro elected president. Shortages of food and basic goods like toilet paper become widespread.

2014   Venezuelans launch nationwide protests, and inflation tops 68 percent. Zumaque oil well turns one hundred years old. Oil prices decline as U.S. shale oil production floods the crude market.

2015   Venezuela's inflation reaches 180.9 percent, the highest level in its history and the highest inflationary level in the world at the time. The opposition wins majority control of the National Assembly, and opposition leaders vow to find a way to push Maduro and his party out of office.

2016   Early in the year, Maduro devalues the main currency exchange rate 37 percent and eliminates one of the three official exchange rates. Maduro increases gasoline prices sixty-fold, the first gasoline price hike in almost twenty years. Venezuela suffers from low oil revenues and struggles to pay for imports and to service its debts.

NOTES

1. 1-800-LEO

1. Calculated at the country's main rate of 6.3 bolivars per U.S. dollar.
2. Calculated at the 12-bolivar-per-dollar exchange rate, the Sistema Cambiario Alternativo de Divisas 1, or SICAD 1.
3. Calculated at the going rate of 50 bolivars per dollar, known as the Sistema Cambiario Alternativo de Divisas 2, or SICAD 2.
4. The going black market rate in late January 2015 was 180 bolivars per dollar.
5. Barclays estimated Venezuela's 2014 nominal GDP at 4.15 trillion bolivars.
6. The various Venezuela GDP valuations are calculated accordingly at 6.3, 12, 50, and 180 bolivars per dollar.
7. Calculated at 180 bolivars per dollar.
8. The value of the LG television was estimated at Venezuela's second, 12-bolivar-per-dollar exchange rate, the cheapest at which a Venezuelan could obtain greenbacks, with some luck.
9. At the going annual minimum wage in February 2015 of 5,622.48 bolivars, the cost of the television amounted to slightly more than fourteen months' salary.
10. Roughly thirty-seven months of minimum wages.
11. Andew Rosati, "BRICS and Beyond: Currency Controls Leave Venezuelan Food Sector in Crisis," Just-Food.com, May 12, 2014.
12. Anatoly Kurmanaev, "Venezuelan Prostitutes Earn More Selling Dollars Than Sex," Bloomberg, June 9, 2014, http://www.bloomberg.com/news/articles/2014 -06-09/venezuela-prostitutes-earn-more-selling-dollars-than-sex.
13. The Marshall Plan cost US$13.3 billion at the time. The July 30, 2014, report of the Special Inspector General for Afghanistan Reconstruction, page 5, estimates that a dollar in 1950 had the purchasing power of ten dollars in 2014,

putting the Marshall Plan bill at $103.4 billion. https://www.sigar.mil/pdf/quarterlyreports/2014-07-30qr.pdf.

14. The calculation adds the annual oil sales of PDVSA from 1999 through 2014. Part of that money goes to pay for costs of production and investment in the oil sector, but most goes to government coffers.

15. In early 2015, Barclays calculated the size of Venezuela's GDP using a weighted average exchange rate of 22.9 bolivars per dollar.

16. Antonio María Delgado, "Gobierno de Venezuela Otorgó $125 Millones a Empresas de Maletín," *El Nuevo Herald*, February 15, 2015, http://www.elnuevoherald.com/noticias/mundo/america-latina/venezuela-es/article9369356.html.

17. "Venezuela Politics: The Billion-Dollar Fraud," *Economist*, August 10, 2013.

18. Calculated assuming a population of 30.4 million Venezuelans.

19. "Saddam 'Took $1bn from Bank,'" BBC News, May 6, 2003, http://news.bbc.co.uk/2/hi/middle_east/3004079.stm.

20. "Detienen a un Hombre con 165 Tarjetas de Crédito en Maiquetía," Ultimas Noticias, November 19, 2014, http://www.ultimasnoticias.com.ve/noticias/actualidad/sucesos/detienen-a-un-hombre-con-165-tarjetas-de-credito-e.aspx.

21. The cardholder pays the government 12 bolivars for every dollar spent using the credit card, or 36,000 bolivars for US$3,000. Selling the quota at 150 bolivars per dollar would net someone 414,000 bolivars after covering the price paid to acquire the dollar quota, 11.5 times the price originally paid.

22. Using the minimum wage at the time of 4,889.11 bolivars a month, it amounts to 84.7 months, or 7.05 years.

23. "Fiscal Publicó Lista con 277 Personas Condenadas por Uso Irregular de Divisas," *El Tiempo*, May 12, 2015, http://eltiempo.com.ve/venezuela/medida/fiscal-publico-lista-con-277-personas-condenadas-por-uso-irregular-de-divisas/181467.

24. "Presos Seis Funcionarios del Cencoex for Sabotaje Informático," *Ultimas Noticias*, May 6, 2015, http://www.ultimasnoticias.com.ve/noticias/actualidad/sucesos/presos-seis-funcionarios-del-cencoex-por-sabotaje-.aspx.

25. "Maduro Anuncia Cierre de Dolar Today y La Lechuga Verde," YouTube video, 0:50, posted by "yoyopressvideos," from VTV, November 9, 2013, https://www.youtube.com/watch?v=w69Ij8klAew.

26. Interviews with two sources working in international money printing companies that did business with Venezuela.

27. See note 26.

28. Eventually Chávez spent the US$7.1 billion the fund had saved up.

29. Castor took out a 12 percent fixed-interest-rate loan.

30. The price of the Ford SUV is adjusted to take into account the bolivar's currency redenomination in 2008, which eliminated three zeros from the bolivar's value.

31. In June 2015 banks paid a maximum 14.5 percent interest to those who saved their money in certificates of deposit for any length of time, while inflation was rising far above 70 percent.

32. Economist Intelligence Unit, Consumer Goods and Retail, Venezuela, February 2015.

33. Defined by economists as a 50 percent inflationary increase in one month.

2. INFINITE WANTS

1. Manuel Rueda, "Hoteles Venezolanos Piden a Huespedes Traer Su Propio Papel Higiénico," Univision.com, April 3, 2015, http://goo.gl/KUHB6q.

2. "Jaua Critíca a Capriles y Pregunta ¿Quieren Patria o Papel Toilet?" *El Nacional*, June 22, 2013, video, http://goo.gl/glJxul.

3. "Eljuri: 95% de los Venezolanos Comen Tres y Cuatro Veces al Día," *Ultimas Noticias*, video posted May 22, 2013, https://www.youtube.com/watch?v=YM dpK5veC_A.

4. "Gobierno Importará 50 Millones de Rollos de Papel Higiénico," *El Nacional*, May 14, 2013, http://www.el-nacional.com/economia/Gobierno-importara -millones-rollos-higienico_0_190181237.html.

5. Memoria y Cuenta 2014, Ministerio del Poder Popular para el Comercio, http:// transparencia.org.ve/wp-content/uploads/2012/10/MEMORIA-Y-CUENTA -2014-Definitiva-Despacho.pdf.

6. Euromonitor International, Tissue and Hygiene, 2015 edition, euromonitor.com.

7. According to Euromonitor, Venezuelans used, on average, 4.9 pounds of toilet paper in 2000. In 2008, however, consumption was 7.7 pounds.

8. Zueli Parra, "Empresa de Papel Higiénico Paveca Advierte Riesgo de Paralización en Julio," *El Venezolano*, June 2, 2015, http://elvenezolanonews.com/paveca-advierte -inminente-riesgo-de-paralizacion-en-julio/.

9. Interview with a toilet paper executive who chose to remain anonymous.

10. Economist Intelligence Unit, Country Commerce Report, 2014, http://www .eiu.com.

11. The cheapest roll, with 193 squares, sold for a maximum price of 5.17 bolivars (US$0.82 at the official 6.3-bolivar-per-dollar exchange rate), and the priciest, 500-square rolls went for no more than 13.40 bolivars (or US$2.12) each. The June 6, 2014, price list by the Superintendencia de Precios Justos was still valid in early 2015.

12. "Maduro Anunció Intervención de Empresa la Manpa," *El Universal*, September 27, 2013, http://www.eluniversal.com/economia/130927/maduro-anuncio -intervencion-de-la-empresa-manpa-imp.

13. The official state announcement referred to each toilet roll packet as a *bulto*. A *bulto* is understood to mean twenty-four units of four toilet rolls, or ninety-six toilet rolls.

14. Calculated at the going 300-bolivar-per-dollar exchange rate in the black market.

15. "Mantenerse Es el Norte," *Producto*, January 28, 2015, http://www.producto.com .ve/pro/negocios/mantenerse-norte.

16. Girish Gupta and Corina Pons, "Venezuela Chides Procter & Gamble over Sanitary Pad Prices," Thomson Reuters, June 15, 2015, http://goo.gl/0nWabA.

17. Estimated at the going black market exchange rate in May 2015 of 300 bolivars per U.S. dollar.

18. The minimum wage in Venezuela stood at 6,746.97 bolivars a month in May 2015. The cost of the Splenda box would amount to 2.3 months of minimum-wage earnings.

19. Johangely Bolívar, "Aumentan los Embarazos Adolescentes ante la Escasez de Anticonceptivos," *El Nacional*, July 1, 2015, http://www.el-nacional.com/sociedad /Aumentan-alarmante-embarazos-adolescentes-anticonceptivos_0_656934335 .html.

20. Anatoly Kurmanaev, "The $755 Condom Pack Is the Latest Indignity in Venezuela," Bloomberg, February 2015, http://www.bloomberg.com/news/articles /2015-02-04/the-755-condom-is-the-latest-indignity-in-venezuela.

21. Marlene Castellanos, "Pfizer Esta Recibiendo Menos de la Mitad de las Divisas," *Notitarde*, April 8, 2015, http://www.notitarde.com/Valencia/Pfizer-esta-recibiendo -menos-de-la-mitad-de-las-divisas-2387553/2015/04/08/505396.

22. At 5 bolivars per box, fifty boxes cost 250 bolivars. A Big Mac in Venezuela sold for 270 bolivars.

23. Jorge Rueda and Frank Bajak, "Restricciones en Compra de Productos Básicos Comienza en un Estado de Venezuela," Associated Press, June 4, 2013. https:// www.telemundo.com/noticias/2013/06/04/restricciones-en-compra-en-un -estado-de-venezuela?page=1.

24. Victoria Orozco, "Prohíben el Envío de Medicinas por Correo," *Ultimas Noticias*, April 30, 2014. http://www.ultimasnoticias.com.ve/noticias/actualidad/economia /prohiben-el-envio-de-medicinas-por-correo.aspx.

25. January 2015 interview with a top Farmatodo executive who asked not to be named in this book.

26. "Privan de Libertad a Presidente y Vicepresidente de Farmatodo por Boicot," press release issued by Ministerio Público República Bolivariana de Venezuela, February 4, 2015, http://www.mp.gob.ve/web/guest/pagina-rss/-/journal_content/56/101 36/6971428?refererPlid=10139.

27. January 2015 interview with Luis Vicente León.

28. "Pese a Largas Filas, Ministro de Alimentación de Vzla Afirmó Que Se 'Exagera' Cuando Se Habla de Crisis en el País," January 6, 2015, NTN24, http://www .ntn24.com/video/ministro-de-alimentacion-de-venezuela-hablo-en-exclusiva-con -ntn24-sobre-crisis-en-el-pais-36423.

3. LET THERE BE OIL

1. As quoted in Fernando Coronil, *The Magical State* (Chicago: University of Chicago Press, 1997).
2. Franklin D. Roosevelt, unsigned correspondence, box 96, Harry Hopkins Papers, Franklin D. Roosevelt Presidential Library.
3. Diego Bautista Urbaneja, *La Renta y El Reclamo* (Caracas: Editorial Alfa, 2013).
4. "Sembrar el Petróleo," *Diario Ahora*, July 13, 1936.
5. Bautista Urbaneja, *La Renta y El Reclamo*, 110–11.
6. Daniel Yergin, *The Prize* (New York: Free Press 1992), 435.
7. Yergin, *Prize*, 434.
8. Coronil, *Magical State*.
9. Coronil, *Magical State*, 107.
10. Terry Lynn Karl, *The Paradox of Plenty: Oil Booms and Petro-States* (Berkeley: University of California Press, 1997).
11. "Venezuela: Approval," *Time*, November 12, 1945.
12. Rómulo Betancourt, *Venezuela Política y Petróleo* (Caracas: Academia de Ciencias Políticas y Sociales, 2007), 293.
13. Betancourt, *Venezuela Política y Petróleo*, 294.
14. Coronil, *Magical State*, 139–40.
15. "Venezuela: Skipper of the Dreamboat," *Time*, February 28, 1955.
16. "Venezuela: How to Get a Quorum," *Time*, December 29, 1952.
17. Bautista Urbaneja, *La Renta y El Reclamo*, 163.
18. Karl, *Paradox of Plenty*, Loc 1286.
19. Coronil, *Magical State*, 183.
20. "Venezuela: The Busy Bs," *Time*, September 21, 1953.
21. "Venezuela: Skipper of the Dreamboat."
22. Estimated by using the U.S. consumer-price-index (CPI) inflation calculator of the U.S. Bureau of Labor Statistics: http://www.bls.gov/data/inflation_calculator.htm.
23. "Venezuela: The Busy Bs."
24. "Venezuela: The Busy Bs."
25. "Venezuela: The Busy Bs."
26. Coronil, *Magical State*, 181.
27. "Venezuela: Fiesta of Good Works," *Time*, December 14, 1953.
28. From a historical recounting by Venezuela's *El Universal* newspaper, "Inaugurada Autopista Caracas–La Guaira," *El Universal*, March 12, 2009.
29. "Venezuela: Skipper of the Dreamboat."
30. Karl, *Paradox of Plenty*, Loc 1285. Also see "Venezuela: Skipper of the Dreamboat."
31. Karl, *Paradox of Plenty*, Loc 1285.
32. Coronil, *Magical State*, 212. See also Bautista Urbaneja, *La Renta y El Reclamo*, 183.

33. Coronil, *Magical State*, 212.
34. Coronil, *Magical State*, 216.
35. Karl, *Paradox of Plenty*, Loc 1296.
36. Karl, *Paradox of Plenty*, Loc 1296.
37. Quoted in Karl, *Paradox of Plenty*, preface.
38. Yergin, *Prize*, 518.
39. Oscar A. Echevarría, *La Economía Venezolana, 1944–1994* (Caracas: Editorial Arte, 1995), 27.
40. "Venezuela: Old Driver, New Road," *Time*, February 8, 1960.
41. "Venezuela: Washington Welcomed a Friend," *Time*, March 3, 1963.
42. "Venezuela: With a Velvet Glove," *Time*, March 19, 1965.
43. "Venezuela: Rosier Than Red," *Time*, November 1, 1963.
44. Karl, *Paradox of Plenty*, Loc 1378.
45. Karl, *Paradox of Plenty*, Loc 1377.
46. Karl, *Paradox of Plenty*, Loc 1387.
47. Quoted in Peréz Alfonzo, *Hundiéndonos en el Excremento del Diablo* (Caracas: Editorial Lisbon, 1976).
48. "Venezuela: The Care and Feeding of Generals," *Time*, December 27, 1963.
49. Based on historic oil price data for Venezuelan crude. See Ruth De Krivoy, *Colapso: La Crisis Bancaria Venezolana de 1994* (Caracas: Ediciones IESA, 2002), data appendix.
50. "Venezuela: Pefro/ecrr Society," *Time*, December 16, 1974.
51. Pérez Alfonzo, *Hundiéndonos*, 136.
52. Karl, *Paradox of Plenty*, Loc 1676.
53. "Venezuela: Pefro/ecrr Society."
54. "Venezuela: Pefro/ecrr Society."
55. Historical data for M2 growth and GDP growth shows that on average the growth of M2, the monetary measure that includes cash, checking, savings accounts, and time deposits, was 3.2 times the rate of GDP growth during the period. See De Krivoy, *Colapso*.
56. Prior to August 1981, Venezuela's central bank had the sole authority to set interest rates. Banks could not adjust them.
57. "Venezuela: Pefro/ecrr Society."
58. Concorde's Paris–Caracas flight ad, http://www.ecrater.co.uk/p/16983070/air -france-1976-paris-caracas-by.
59. Karl, *Paradox of Plenty*, Loc 1584.
60. Karl, *Paradox of Plenty*, Loc 1499.
61. Karl, *Paradox of Plenty*, Loc 1758.
62. Karl, *Paradox of Plenty*, Loc 1368.
63. Karl, *Paradox of Plenty*, Loc 1368.

64. De Krivoy, *Colapso*, data appendix.
65. Simón Romero, "Luis Herrera Campíns, Venezuela Leader, Dies at 82," *New York Times*, November 13, 2007.
66. De Krivoy, *Colapso*, data appendix.
67. Kim Fuad, "Caracas Attacks Sheltered Oil Monopoly—Petróleos de Venezuela's Funds Tempt a Cash-Hungry Government," *Financial Times*, December 7, 1982.
68. Hugh O'Shaughnessy, "Venezuela Has to Work Harder for Its Living—a Campaign Is Underway to Change Habits Acquired over Half a Century," *Financial Times*, February 22, 1983.
69. "Venezuela: New President on Problems Facing Venezuelan Economy," BBC Monitoring Service: Latin America, February 14, 1989.
70. Kenneth Gilpin, "In Venezuelan Campaign, the Fervor Is Lacking," *New York Times*, September 25, 1983, http://www.nytimes.com/1983/09/25/world/in -venezuelan-campaign-the-fervor-is-lacking.html.
71. Miriam Kornblith, *La Crisis de la Democracia* (Caracas: Ediciones IESA, 2002).
72. Karl, *Paradox of Plenty*, table 11.
73. De Krivoy, *Colapso*, data appendix.
74. Venezuela's official rate, which stood at 14.5 bolivars per dollar, jumped to 37 bolivars per dollar. See Simon Fisher, "Devaluation, Rising Prices, and 35% Interest Await Venezuelans," *Globe and Mail*, February 22, 1989.
75. Karl, *Paradox of Plenty*, Loc 2374.
76. De Krivoy, *Colapso*.
77. Naciones Unidas, Comisión Económica para América Latina y el Caribe (CEPAL [ECLAC]), "Panorama Social de América Latina 2014," 96, http://www.cepal.org /es/publicaciones/37626-panorama-social-america-latina-2014.
78. Steven Gutkin, "Venezuelan Presidential Candidate Tries to Soothe Investor Fears," Associated Press, October 9, 1998.
79. "Failed Revolutionary Seeks Power through Ballot Box," *Financial Times*, April 22, 1998; Steven Gutkin, "Venezuelan Presidential Candidate Tries to Soothe Investor Fears," Associated Press, October 9, 1998.
80. "Las Famosas y Polémicas Frases de Hugo Chávez," *La Nación*, March 5, 2013, http://www.nacion.com/mundo/famosas-polemicas-frases-Hugo-Chavez_0 _1327467377.html.
81. Bart Jones, "After 40 Years of Democracy, Venezuelans Ask: What Went Wrong?," Associated Press, January 23, 1998. See also "Venezuela's Chávez Seen a Shoo-In on Protest Vote," Reuters, November 24, 1998.
82. Peter Fritsch and Thomas T. Vogel Jr., "Jump Start: Venezuela Expands Oil Industry Rapidly, Irking Others in OPEC—Its Pressure on U.S. Prices Raises Fears in Mexico; Foreign Firms Plunge In—the Lure of the Orinoco Belt," *Wall Street Journal*, August 14, 1997.

83. Bernard Mommer, "Ese Chorro Que Atraviesa El Siglo," Caracas, 2000.

84. Raúl Gallegos, "3rd Update: Venezuela Ctrl Bk Sets Caps on Interest Rates," Dow Jones Newswires, April 28, 2005.

85. María Isabel Capiello, "Air France Aumenta la Frecuencia de Viajes a Venezuela," *El Nacional*, April 18, 2005.

86. Raúl Gallegos, "Cracks Showing in Venezuela's Socialist Business Model," Dow Jones Newswires, January 9, 2009.

87. Mommer, "Ese Chorro Que Atraviesa El Siglo."

88. Sebastián Edwards, *Left Behind: Latin America and the False Promise of Populism* (Chicago: University of Chicago Press, 2010).

89. "Venezuela Spends More on Food, but Shortages Remain—Market Talk," Dow Jones Newswires, April 14, 2015.

90. Asdrúbal Baptista, *Teoria Económica del Capitalismo Rentístico* (Caracas: Banco Central de Venezuela, 2010).

91. The Gini coefficient was reduced from 49.5 in 1998 to 39 in 2011. Central Intelligence Agency, The World Factbook, https://www.cia.gov/library/publications/the-world-factbook/geos/ve.html. See also Kevin Voigt, "Chávez Leaves Venezuelan Economy More Equal, Less Stable," CNN, March 6, 2013, http://edition.cnn.com/2013/03/06/business/venezuela-chavez-oil-economy/.

92. Voigt, "Chávez Leaves Venezuelan Economy More Equal, Less Stable."

93. According to the United Nations Human Development Index, Venezuela's income Gini coefficient in 2013 had risen again to 44.8, still lower than 49.5 back in 1998, the year before Chávez took office, but coming closer: http://hdr.undp.org/en/content/income-gini-coefficient; Andres Oppenheimer, "Oil Rich Venezuela's Miracle: Record Poverty," *Miami Herald*, February 4, 2015. Also see the 2014 poverty study by Andrés Bello Catholic University under Professor Luis Pedro España.

4. EVERYMAN

1. Calculated at 50 bolivars per dollar, the most widely obtainable official exchange rate for regular Venezuelans at the time.

2. Plastic surgeon salary estimate in the United States based on data reported by Salary.com: http://www1.salary.com/Surgeon-Plastic-Reconstructive-salary.html.

3. Estimated at 180 bolivars per dollar, the going black market rate in Venezuela in January 2015.

4. Estimated at the going Venezuelan monthly minimum wage of 4,889.11 bolivars in late January 2015.

5. Estimate puts annual U.S. minimum wage salary at US$15,080 a year in early 2015.

6. Interview with Daniel Slobodianik, January 23, 2015.

7. Each bottle of Grappa Elevata Sassicaia was priced at 72,973 bolivars, with the U.S. dollar cost estimated at the fifty-bolivar-per-dollar rate.

8. "Jorge Rodríguez Inauguró el Restaurante Bistro del Libertador: Funcionará Como una Cafeteria Gourmet," *Noticias 24*, December 18, 2014, http://www. noticias24.com/venezuela/noticia/268127/jorge-rodriguez-inauguro-el -restaurante-bistro-del-libertador-funcionara-como-una-cafeteria-gourmet/. Also see http://www.noticias24.com/fotos/noticia/20033/en-fotos-asi-se-llevo -a-cabo-la-inauguracion-del-restaurante-bistro-del-libertador/.

9. Average real wages in Venezuela contracted 5.77 percent in 2013 and 7.5 percent in 2014, according to data from the Economist Intelligence Unit.

10. The Datanalisis 2015 Consumer Trends Survey shows that middle-income Venezuelans saw their real income decline by as much as 25 percent in the previous year, taking into account the excess prices people ended up paying for food in the black market. Datanalisis estimates that Venezuelan real incomes overall declined nearly 19 percent during the previous year.

11. Estimated with the third legal exchange rate for dollars, known as SIMADI, of 190 bolivars per dollar in May 2015.

12. See note 11.

13. See note 11.

14. "Estiman Salario de Docentes Universitarios entre Bs. 40 Mil y 120 Mil," *El Universal*, February 4, 2015.

15. "Cendas: Costo de la Canasta Básica subió a Bs.35,124 en Marzo," *El Mundo*, April 20, 2015, http://www.elmundo.com.ve/noticias/economia/politicas-publicas/cendas --costo-de-la-canasta-basica-subio-a-bs--35-.aspx.

16. María Yanes, "El Salario Indigno e Injusto del Médico Venezolano," *El Nacional*, July 21, 2015, http://www.el-nacional.com/maria_yanes/salario-indigno-injusto -medico-venezolano_0_668333310.html.

17. Víctor La Cruz, "Dr. Leyba: Se Estan Yendo del País los Médicos Que Salvan Vidas," *El Universal*, July 21, 2014.

18. Carmen María Rodríguez, "Migración Venezolana de Profesionales Amenaza el Desarrollo," *El Universal*, July 21, 2014, http://www.eluniversal.com/nacional-y -politica/140721/migracion-venezolana-de-profesionales-amenaza-el-desarrollo.

19. Víctor Salmerón, "Tarjetas de Crédito en Venezuela: Una Burbuja a Punto de Explotar?" Prodavinci, May 11, 2015, http://prodavinci.com/2015/05/11 /actualidad/tarjetas-de-credito-en-venezuela-una-burbuja-a-punto-de -explotar-por-victor-salmeron/.

20. Sudeban annual data series, banking sector data, http://sudeban.gob.ve.

21. Salmerón, "Tarjetas de Crédito en Venezuela."

22. Axel Capriles, *La Picardía del Venezolano o el Triunfo del Tío Conejo* (Caracas: Editorial Santillana Taurus, 2008).

23. Rafaél Di Tella, Javier Donna, and Robert MacCulloch, "Oil, Macro Volatility and Crime in the Determination of Beliefs in Venezuela," February 16, 2007, http://www.people.hbs.edu/rditella/papers/WPVenFeb16.pdf.

24. Population projections for 2014 by pollster Datanalisis based on data from the National Statistics Institute's 2011 census results. Also from Datanalisis, the average age in 2012 was 29.4 years.

25. José Luis is a composite of a poor consumer created for this book from data provided by Datanalisis surveys.

26. Nearly 80 percent of Venezuelans are classified as belonging to strata D and E, which means they live in modest homes in barrios, most often in cinderblock shacks. Datanalisis 2014 Consumer Trends Survey.

27. Potable water service is unreliable for those classified in stratum E. Datanalisis 2014 Consumer Trends Survey.

28. Datanalisis 2014 Consumer Trends Survey. Most homes in stratum E lack a formal contract with a local electric utility company. Trash collection is spotty and many lack basic sewer systems.

29. Datanalisis 2014 Consumer Trends Survey. The homes of D and E strata members are known to have septic tanks if they are not connected to the sewer system.

30. According to the Datanalisis 2014 Venezuelan Consumer Trends report, 88 percent of people classified in the E stratum own a cellular phone.

31. The Datanalisis 2014 Venezuelan Consumer Trends report indicates that 82 percent of people classified in the E stratum have a television subscription service.

32. Datanalisis 2014 Venezuelan Consumer Trends Survey.

33. Roughly 83 percent of respondents surveyed by Datanalisis for its 2014 Consumer Trends Report reported owning a DVD player, and 80 percent claimed to own a washing machine.

34. Datanalisis notes that 53.2 percent of stratum E survey respondents owned an air conditioner.

35. Datanalisis 2014 Venezuelan Consumer Trends Survey.

36. Datanalisis 2014 Venezuelan Consumer Trends Survey.

37. The top four foods consumed by Venezuelans, according to the Datanalisis 2014 Venezuelan Consumer Trends Survey.

38. Datanalisis Omnibus survey, February 2014. Roughly 9 percent of responses from members of stratum E mentioned fish as one of their frequent foods. A and B strata members mentioned fish in 24 percent of the responses.

39. Datanalisis Omnibus Survey, February 2014. Members of stratum groups D and E prefer to shop in privately owned, modern supermarkets and in small grocery stores close to home. State-owned supermarkets are only a third option.

40. Datanalisis found that 65 percent of people standing in line outside most outlets were in the business of reselling products with price controls.

41. Datanalisis Omnibus Survey, February 2014. Between 2012 and 2015, Venezuelans showed increasing agreement with the idea that shopping causes stress. While 45 percent of respondents in 2012 agreed with the idea that shopping was fun, less than half that percentage thought so in the 2015 Datanalisis survey.

42. Poverty as measured by level of income fell from 45 percent of households in 1999 when Chávez assumed office to 32 percent in 2009. However, the number had risen back to 48 percent in 2014, higher than when Chávez took office. See Luis Pedro España, IIES-UCAB Encuesta Condiciones de Vida Venezuela 2014.

43. Interview with Luis Vicente León from Datanalisis

44. "Acusación de Cubanización en Venezuela Desea Opacar Cooperación Ejemplar," Agence France Presse, October 22, 2010.

45. Exchange rate calculated using Venezuela's third official exchange rate of 50 bolivars per dollar in late January 2015.

5. FUNNY BUSINESS

1. Santa Teresa's overall sales fell because at the time the company was not yet exporting its rum. The company's successful attempt to export its rum bottles began in 1997.

2. José De Córdoba, "As Venezuela Tilts Left, a Rum Mogul Reaches Out to Poor," *Wall Street Journal*, November 10, 2004.

3. Rosa Amelia González and Patricia Márquez, "Ron Santa Teresa's Social Initiatives," case study, *Harvard Business Review*, https://hbr.org/product/ron-santa -teresa-s-social-initiatives/an/SKE059-PDF-ENG?Ntt=ron%2520santa %2520teresa.

4. Based on estimates by Ron Santa Teresa. Venezuela's nationwide sugar cane output data obtained from the Confederación de Asociaciones de Productores Agropecuarios, Fedeagro, a federation of agriculture trade groups. http://www.fedeagro.org /produccion/.

5. Diageo 2015 20-F filing, http://www.diageo.com/en-row/investor/regulatory news/Pages/US-Announcement.aspx.

6. Interview with Miriam Briceño, the executive director of Venezuela's glassmaker trade group Camara de la Industria del Vidrio, Ceramica, Refractarios, e Industrias Afines, July 4, 2015.

7. According to figures from Venezuela's central bank from January through September 2014, construction, commerce, transport, telecommunications, banking, real estate services, and water and electricity services amounted to 48 percent of GDP.

8. According to Venezuela's central bank, the weight of manufacturing in GDP declined from 17.4 percent in 1998, the year before Chávez took office, to 13.4 percent as of the third quarter of 2014. Imports rose from 25.4 percent of GDP in 1998 to 50 percent of GDP by 2012.

9. "Adiós a la Fidelidad," *Producto*, November 2014.

10. "¿A Que Huele?" *Producto*, November 2014.

11. Telefónica's Form 20-F for March 2013. Venezuela's average revenue per user (ARPU) rose from EUR14.3 in 2010 to EUR21.2 in 2012. In Brazil, Telefónica saw

ARPUs go from EUR11 to EUR8.9 in the same period. And in Germany, Telefónica's ARPUs went from EUR14.8 in 2010 to EUR13.8 in 2012.

12. Sara Schaefer Muñoz, "Venezuela Property Boom Gets Fueled by U.S. Companies," *Wall Street Journal*, September 3, 2013, http://www.wsj.com/articles/SB100 01424127887323446404579008740799535778.

13. Calculated at the going black market rate of 1,000 bolivars per dollar in early March 2016.

14. Forbes ranking as of September 9, 2015, http://www.forbes.com/profile/lorenzo -mendoza/.

15. Interview with Manuel Larrazábal, CEO of Alimentos Polar, the food division of Empresas Polar, May 12, 2015.

16. The company estimated in February 2015 annual losses of 683 million bolivars for the Harina P.A.N. line, or US$13.7 million, conservatively calculated at the official 50-bolivar-per-dollar exchange rate.

17. Calculated at the third official exchange rate of 190 bolivars per dollar in May 2015.

18. Polar television spot, https://www.youtube.com/watch?v=TWlKsreju84.

19. Interview with Larrazábal and a look at international prices for corn. Polar paid 7 bolivars per kilo of corn to the government, but the state imported corn from Mexico, paying roughly 2 bolivars per kilo.

20. Memoria y Cuenta 2014, Vicepresidencia de la República Bolivariana de Venezuela, chapter 7, http://transparencia.org.ve/wp-content/uploads/2012/10 /MEMORIA_2014-VICEPRESIDENCIA.pdf.

21. "Cárcel a los Directivos de Farmatodo en Venezuela por Ocasionar Filas," *El Colombiano*, February 5, 2015, http://www.elcolombiano.com/carcel-para-dos -directivos-de-farmatodo-en-venezuela-por-ocasionar-filas-EE1226363.

22. "Director de Supermercado Dia Dia Acusado por Boicot," *El Impulso*, March 24, 2015, http://elimpulso.com/articulo/director-de-supermercado-dia-dia-acusado -por-boicot#.

23. Matt Taibbi, "The Great American Bubble Machine," *Rolling Stone*, April 5, 2010.

24. As measured by total assets, Banesco controlled 15.2 percent of total banking system assets as of June 2015, according to data from Venezuela's banking superintendency SUDEBAN. Banesco's nominal return on average assets stood at 6.21 percent in 2014, compared with Goldman's return on average assets of 0.96 percent that same year, according to data from U.S. credit rating agency Fitch Ratings. Fitch Ratings, Banesco Banco Universal, Full Rating Report, July 6, 2015, and Goldman Sachs Group, Full Rating Report, April 6, 2015.

25. Fitch Ratings, Banesco Banco Universal, Full Rate Report, and Goldman Sachs Group, Full Rating Report. Banesco's return on equity stood at 78.95 percent, compared with Goldman's 10.5 percent.

26. Michael J. Moore, "Lloyd Blankfein Is Now a Billionaire," *Bloomberg*, July 17, 2015, http://www.bloomberg.com/news/articles/2015-07-17/blankfein-becomes -billionaire-riding-goldman-s-shares-to-riches.

27. Forbes list of the world's billionaires, November 11, 2015.

28. Interview with Oscar García Mendoza, September 11, 2015.

29. "Gobierno Anunció Incremento a 20% de Gabeta Hipotecaria," *El Tiempo*, February 13, 2013, http://eltiempo.com.ve/venezuela/economia/gobierno-anuncio -incremento-a-20-de-gaveta-hipotecaria/79838.

30. Based on GDP data from the Venezuelan central bank. See macroeconomic aggregate data on the BCV website, http://www.bcv.org.ve/c2/indicadores.asp.

31. Raúl Gallegos, "Amid Tough Times, Venezuelan Bankers Thrive under Chávez," Dow Jones Newswires, August 12, 2004.

32. "2015 Outlook: Andean Banks," Fitch Ratings, January 13, 2015; interview with Mark Narron at Fitch Ratings, September 9, 2015.

33. As of June 2015, measured by total assets, according to data from banking regulator SUDEBAN.

34. Ludmila Vinogradoff, "Víctor Vargas, un Banquero Chavista con 120 Millones de Euros en Suiza," ABC, March 30, 2015.

35. Venezuelan banking sector 2006 financial results from banking regulator SUDEBAN. In 2006, 40 percent of BOD's income came from investing in securities, and 56 percent from lending activity. At the time the overall banking sector received 31 percent of its income from securities investments.

36. "Boda de Luis Alfonso de Borbón con Maria Margarita Vargas," Hola.com, November 7, 2004, http://www.hola.com/famosos/2004110727248/famosos /bodaluisalfonso/bodaluisalfonso/.

37. "Luis Alfonso de Borbón y Margarita Vargas Disfrutan de un Día en Familia Junto a Sus Padres," Hola.com, August 17, 2012, http://www.hola.com/famosos /2012081760250/margarita-vargas-luis-alfonso-vacaciones/.

38. Michael Smith, "Venezuela Sees Chávez Friends Rich after His Death amid Poverty," Bloomberg, August 12, 2014, http://www.bloomberg.com/news/articles/2014-08-12 /venezuela-sees-chavez-friends-rich-after-his-death-amid-poverty.

39. John Lyons, "Polo-Loving Banker Lives Really Large in Chávez Socialism— Venezuela's Mr. Vargas Has Yachts, and Good Timing; 'I've Been Rich All My Life,'" *Wall Street Journal*, January 29, 2008.

40. Andy Webb-Vidal, "Venezuela Magnate Ruperti Cruises to Fortune," *LatinFinance Magazine*, September 1, 2008.

41. Webb-Vidal, "Venezuela Magnate."

42. Webb-Vidal, "Venezuela Magnate."

43. "Venezolano Adquirió Pistolas de Bolívar," *El Universal*, November 19, 2004, http://www.eluniversal.com/2004/11/19/imp_til_art_19253D.

44. "Video en el Que Chávez Agradece a Ruperti por Dos Pistolas de Bolívar," *El Universal*, September 12, 2013, http://www.eluniversal.com/nacional-y-politica /120913/video-en-el-que-chavez-agradece-a-ruperti-por-dos-pistolas-de -bolivar.

45. José De Córdoba, "Venezuelan High Life: Bulletproof BMW and Vote for Chávez—Oil Tycoon Ruperti Supports Socialist's Re-Election; Gift of Bolivar's Pistols," *Wall Street Journal*, December 1, 2006.

46. De Córdoba, "Venezuelan High Life."

6. OIL FOR THE PEOPLE

1. Venezuela sold gasoline at 0.097 bolivars for a liter of 95-octane, unleaded fuel and 0.07 bolivars for the 91-octane kind. The price of a premium gallon of gas, or 3.79 liters, stood at between 6 U.S. cents—estimated using the official 6.3-bolivar-per-dollar rate—and 0.000925 U.S. cents, a price calculated using the going black-market-dollar rate in May 2015 of 300 bolivars per dollar.

2. Lucas Davis, "The Cost of Global Fuel Subsidies," *Milken Institute Review*, third quarter 2014: 48–57.

3. Mery Mogollón and Chris Kraul, "Venezuela Begins Overnight Closures of Border to Deter Smuggling," *Los Angeles Times*, August 12, 2014, http://www.latimes .com/world/mexico-americas/la-fg-venezuela-closures-border-smuggling-20140 812-story.html.

4. "Fiscalía Acusa a Gladis Parada de Peculado Doloso," *La Verdad*, March 21, 2015, http://www.laverdad.com/economia/71758-fiscalia-acusa-a-gladys-parada-de -peculado-doloso.html.

5. Rómulo Betancourt, *Venezuela Política y Petróleo*, 6th edition (Academia de Ciencias Políticas y Sociales, 2007), 294.

6. Estimates by local analysis firm Ecoanalitica. Asdrúbal Oliveros, "Subsidios en Venezuela, ¿Un Problema o Parte de la Solución para 2015?," *Prodavinci*, December 12, 2014, http://prodavinci.com/2014/12/12/economia-y-negocios/subsidios -en-venezuela-un-problema-o-parte-de-la-solucion-para-2015-por-asdrubal-oliveros -y-gabriel-villamizar/.

7. In fact PDVSA is a partner in the construction of the Refineria del Pacífico in Ecuador with a total cost of US$12 billion. PDVSA has had trouble putting in its share of the cash for that business. See Alexandra Valencia, "Ecuador Says China's CNPC Joins US$12 Billion Refinery Project," Reuters, July 6, 2013, http://www .reuters.com/article/2013/07/06/us-ecuador-refinery-cnpc-idUSBRE9650CN 20130706.

8. Video posted on YouTube by Rocío Angela Pérez, January 23, 2015, https://www .youtube.com/watch?v=48Iwdm3vpR4.

9. Saudi Arabia controlled 266.6 billion barrels of proven crude oil reserves according to OPEC figures as of August 2015, http://www.opec.org/opec_web/en/about

_us/169.htm. The calculation about satisfying U.S. demand is based on the daily oil consumption estimate by the U.S. Energy Information Administration (EIA) of 19.05 million barrels of crude a day and Venezuela's total proved reserves of 299 billion barrels of oil. EIA figures obtained from http://www.eia.gov/tools/faqs /faq.cfm?id=33&t=6.

10. Calculated by using the OPEC estimates of Venezuelan production at 2.68 million barrels a day and proved reserves of 299.95 billion barrels of crude in late July 2015. http://www.opec.org/opec_web/en/about_us/171.htm.

11. Includes calculation by Venezuelan economist Francisco Monaldi and takes into account figures by the U.S. Geological Survey on oil in place in Venezuela's Orinoco Oil Belt. http://pubs.usgs.gov/fs/2009/3028/pdf/FS09-3028.pdf.

12. PDVSA Informe Gestión Anual 2014.

13. PDVSA Informe Gestión Anual 2014.

14. Producing a barrel of oil in Venezuela can cost roughly US$23 on average, but prices for Venezuela's basket of crude stood at US$49 per barrel in July 2015. Prior to October 2014, Venezuelan oil was averaging nearly US$100 per barrel.

15. Alexandra Ulmer and Deisy Buitrago, "Venezuela's PDVSA Says Schlumberger Poised to Extend Credit Line," February 27, 2015, Thomson Reuters, http://www. reuters.com/article/2015/02/27/venezuela-schlumberger-idUSL1N0W1300 20150227.

16. As of the end of 2014, PDVSA's total financial debt amounted to US$46.15 billion, according to the company's 2014 Financial Consolidated Debt Balance report.

17. By March 2015, PDVSA had accrued a debt with the central bank estimated at US$51 billion, roughly half a year of oil sales.

18. The company's annual social spending contributions averaged US$34 billion from 2010 through 2014.

19. Lucas Aristizábal and Xavier Olave, "Special Report: PDVSA—Something's Got to Give," February 10, 2015, Fitch Ratings. Petrodollars from PDVSA feed half the government's annual budget and amount to more than 90 percent of the country's exports.

20. According to 2014 PDVSA financial statements, the company spent US$26.08 billion to fund social programs, but its operating costs and exploration costs amounted to US$24.6 billion combined (Informe de Gestion Anual PDVSA 2014). PDVSA financial statements from 2009 through 2014.

21. PDVSA doesn't make public a breakdown of the finances of each of these businesses and considers spending on these companies as part of PDVSA's social obligations.

22. "Venezuela: Reducing Generosity," Barclays, March 25, 2015.

23. See note 22. Venezuelan shipments to allies in the region were cut in half between 2012 and March 2015.

24. Keith Collister, "Was the Petrocaribe Buyback a Good Deal for Jamaica?," *Jamaica Observer*, July 31, 2015.

25. César Arias, "Petrocaribe Deal Benefits Dominican Republic Finances," Fitch-Wire, February 3, 2015. In January 2015 the Dominican Republic paid PDVSA US$1.93 billion to cover its US$4 billion outstanding bill for oil shipments.

26. "Venezuela y Cuba Logran un Acuerdo para Refinanciar la Deuda Petrolífera," AméricaEconomía, April 21, 2003, http://www.americaeconomica.com/numeros4 /209/noticias/ravenezuelaycubama.htm; Antonio María Delgado, "Chávez Condonó Secretamente Millonaria Deuda Nicaragüense," El Nuevo Herald, May 10, 2015.

27. Lucas Aristizábal and Xavier Olave, "Special Report: PDVSA—Something's Got to Give," February 10, 2015, Fitch Ratings.

28. Sebastian Boyd and Katia Prozsecanski, "These 30-Cent Bonds Are Barclays's Top Pick in Venezuela Default," Bloomberg, August 26, 2015, http://www.bloomberg .com/news/articles/2015-08-27/these-30-cent-bonds-are-barclays-s-top-pick-in -venezuela-default.

29. "Alberta's Royalty System—Jurisdictional Comparison," Price Waterhouse Coopers, June 2009, http://www.energy.alberta.ca/org/pdfs/royalty_jurisdiction.pdf; Osmel Manzano and José Sebastián Scrofina, "Resource Revenue Management in Venezuela: A Consumption-Based Poverty Reduction Strategy," http://www .resourcegovernance.org/sites/default/files/Venezuela_Final.pdf.

30. The figure includes the oil produced by PDVSA partners in Venezuela. OPEC's Monthly Oil Market Report, March 14, 2016, http://www.opec.org/opec_web /static_files_project/media/downloads/publications/MOMR%20March%20 2016.pdf.

31. PDVSA 2014 Balance de la Gestión Social y Ambiental, the company's annual report, shows that oil-industry employees totaled 116,806 people, while workers in non-oil-related units run by PDVSA totaled 30,320 workers, for an overall total of 147,126 employees on the company's payroll.

32. ExxonMobil produced 3.97 million barrels of oil equivalent in 2014. ExxonMobil 2014 Financial and Operating Review.

33. Saudi Aramco's workforce totaled 61,907 employees, Saudi Aramco 2014 Facts and Figures; Wael Mahdi, "Saudi Aramco's 2014 Oil, Gas Output Reaches Near-Record High," Bloomberg, May 11, 2015, http://www.bloomberg.com/news /articles/2015-05-11/more-saudi-aramco-shipped-2-5b-bbl-of-oil-in-14-annual -report.

34. Data obtained from Balance de la Gestión Social y Ambiental 2014.

35. Maru Morales and Hernán Lugo-Galicia, "Viajes Familiares de Directivos de PDVSA y de Citgo Costaron a la Nación $418,801 en 2009," El Nacional, December 7, 2014.

36. Morales and Lugo-Galicia, "Viajes Familiares." Also see Marianna Párraga, Oro Rojo (Caracas: Ediciones Punto Cero, 2010).

37. "Venezuela Sells Planes to Fund Social Programs," Reuters, September 14, 1999.

38. José De Córdoba and Joel Millman, "Venezuelan Businessman Details Corruption—Durán Offers Glimpse into Chávez's Rule in Interview with FBI," *Wall Street Journal*, March 12, 2008.

39. David G. Victor, David R. Hults, Mark Thurber, *Oil and Governance: State-Owned Enterprises and the World Energy Supply* (Cambridge: Cambridge University Press, 2012).

40. Alexei Barrionuevo, "Management Revolt: How Technicians at Oil Giant Turned Revolutionaries—State Petroleum Firm Holds Out in Venezuela's Strike; Business Won't Be Usual—the Engineer Who Roared," *Wall Street Journal*, February 10, 2003.

41. Barrionuevo, "Management Revolt."

42. "High Oil Prices to Bankroll PDVSA US$56bn Investment Plan," Business News Americas, August 31, 2005.

43. Alexandra Ullmer and Marianna Párraga, "Its Red Shirts Fading, Venezuela's Oil Giant Embraces Pragmatism," Reuters, March 13, 2015.

44. *Revista Informativa de Sísmica BieloVenezolana*, edición 3.

45. Under Chávez Venezuela offered to pay foreign players book value for their assets, even though market value was much higher given the higher cost at the time of replacing those installations and the future revenues to be derived from those operations.

46. In October 2014 an arbitration panel at the World Bank's International Center for Settlement of Investment Disputes awarded ExxonMobil US$1.6 billion in its dispute with PDVSA, a fraction of the US$16.6 billion the company had sought in compensation for its assets in the Cerro Negro oil upgrader. Kejal Vyas, "Exxon Mobil Awarded $1.6 Billion in Venezuela Case," *Wall Street Journal*, October 9, 2014, http://www.wsj.com/articles/exxon-mobil-awarded-1-4-billion-in -venezuela-case-1412879396.

47. Based on conversations conducted with PDVSA and foreign oil company executives that conducted and responded to the Bell Pottinger survey.

48. Ley del Plan de la Pátria, Segundo Plan Socialista de Desarrollo Económico y Social de la Nación, 2013–2019.

49. By May 2015 PDVSA had agreed to allow oil foreign companies that invested new money through the trust fund mechanism to exchange capital expenditures using Venezuela's third legal rate, known as SIMADI, which stood at 190 bolivars per dollar. However, PDVSA was still evaluating whether to allow foreign companies to convert dollars at the 6.3-bolivar-per-dollar rate to pay the local salaries and other operating costs of oil ventures.

50. Based on AVHI estimates, assuming a barrel of oil remains at US$50 and a project is fully financed with foreign capital, the net present value of some projects is negative. PDVSA officials were not available to discuss the potential profitability assumptions of new investments in mixed companies. Under best-case scenarios analyzed by AVHI, Venezuelan oil projects offer 15 or even 10 percent returns. Assuming US$70 per barrel, some ventures offer a 15 percent return but

only if PDVSA allows all CAPEX and OPEX to be converted at Venezuela's third exchange rate, known as SIMADI.

51. Some of those terms included royalties as low as 1 percent for many years, while companies recouped their investments.

52. Under Chávez foreign companies had a maximum 40 percent stake in mixed companies, with PDVSA owning the rest. Venezuela's oil legislation calls on the government to control more than 50 percent of a project, which gives the government leeway to give foreigners slightly larger stakes than 40 percent.

53. Petrocabimas estimates its costs per barrel at US$24 assuming it is forced to exchange dollars at the 6.3-bolivar rate. PDVSA's partners have been asking the government to allow oil companies to convert the bolivars they need to pay for operating costs at the US$12-bolivar-per-dollar rate.

54. I had access to reading the confidential report, titled "Informe Técnico de Toma Física de Campo Tía Juana Tierra."

7. MANGO MANAGEMENT

1. Flora Drury, "Woman Is Given a New Home after Hitting Venezuelan President on the Head with a Mango," *Daily Mail*, April 29, 2015, http://www.dailymail.co .uk/news/article-3054656/Woman-hit-Venezuela-leader-mango-rewarded-new -home.html.

2. "Datanalisis: Oposición Mantiene Ventaja de 20% de Cara a las Parlamentarias," *El Universal*, April 21, 2015, http://www.eluniversal.com/nacional-y-politica /150421/datanalisis-oposicion-mantiene-ventaja-de-20-de-cara-a-las-parlamentar.

3. "Woman Who Hit Venezuelan Leader with Mango Rewarded with New Home," *Telegraph*, April 25, 2015, http://www.telegraph.co.uk/news/worldnews /southamerica/venezuela/11562934/Woman-who-hit-Venezuela-leader-with -mango-rewarded-with-new-home.html.

4. "Venezuelan President's Bout with Thrown Mango Inspires Game," *Daily Mail*, May 6, 2015, http://www.dailymail.co.uk/wires/ap/article-3069656/Venezuelan -presidents-bout-thrown-mango-inspires-game.html.

5. Mac Margolis, "Venezuela Sues the Messenger," Bloomberg, May 21, 2015, http:// www.bloombergview.com/articles/2015-05-21/venezuela-sues-the-messenger.

6. "La Mujer a la Que Venezuela Le Prometió una Vivienda Tras Lanzar un Mango a Maduro," BBC Mundo, April 26, 2015, http://www.bbc.com/mundo/noticias /2015/04/150425_venezuela_mujer_lanzo_mango_maduro_lv.

7. Omar Lugo, "Chávez, 'el Santo de los Milagros' de Empobrecidos Venezolanos," Reuters, July 24, 1999.

8. Lugo, "Chávez, 'el Santo de los Milagros.'"

9. Quoted in Pedro L. Rodríguez, José R. Morales, and Francisco J. Monaldi, "Direct Distribution of Oil Revenues in Venezuela: A Viable Alternative?," Center for Global Development, September 13, 2012, www.cgdev.org.

10. Rodríguez, Morales, and Monaldi, "Direct Distribution."

11. "Taller de Alto Nivel: 'El Nuevo Mapa Estratégico,'" November 12 and 13, 2004. http://www.minci.gob.ve/wp-content/uploads/downloads/2013/01/nuevo mapaestrategico.pdf.

12. Diego Ore, "Venezuela to Crush Cars, Bikes to Build Houses," Reuters, April 29, 2014.

13. Luis Pedro España, "Pobreza y Programas Sociales," Encuesta sobre Condiciones de Vida Venezuela, 2014.

14. España, "Pobreza y Programas Sociales."

15. In 2011 Venezuela was number 12 on the list according to data from *The CIA World Factbook*.

16. Kejal Vyas, "Venezuela's Latest Woe: Water Shortages," *Wall Street Journal*, July 8, 2014, http://www.wsj.com/articles/venezuelas-latest-woe-water-shortages -1404849526.

17. Vyas, "Venezuela's Latest Woe"; Andrew Rosati, "Caracas Poor Go Thirsty amid Political Strife and Poor Planning," *Miami Herald*, July 5, 2014, http://www .miamiherald.com/news/nation-world/world/americas/venezuela/article 1974102.html. The government now expects the waterway system to be ready in 2017, after more than a decade of construction delays: "Sistema Tuy IV, Entrará en Servicio en Octubre de 2017," *El Universal*, June 11, 2015, http://www.eluniversal .com/caracas/150611/sistema-tuy-iv-entrara-en-servicio-en-octubre-de-2017.

18. "Sistema Tuy IV."

19. Venezuela Energy Industry Report, Economist Intelligence Unit, June 2014, eiu. com. Also see "45% de las Plantas Eléctricas de Caracas No Funcionan," *El Nacional*, August 21, 2015.

20. Electric power consumption data, The World Bank, http://data.worldbank.org /indicator/EG.USE.ELEC.KH.PC/countries?order=wbapi_data_value_2012 %20wbapi_data_value%20wbapi_data_value-last&sort=desc&display=default.

21. "Venezuela Cuts Working Hours to Tackle Energy Crisis," BBC, April 29, 2015, http://www.bbc.com/news/world-latin-america-32506572.

22. Raúl Gallegos, "Venezuela's Sidor Workers Rally, Call for Nationalization," Dow Jones Newswires, May 8, 2007; Darcy Crowe and Raúl Gallegos, "Venezuela Ternium Seen Reaching Agreement in 15 Days—Sanz," Dow Jones. January 13, 2008.

23. Memoria y Cuenta 2014 Ministerio del Poder Popular para Industrias, 602, https://drive.google.com/file/d/0B65M4qe0vsR1TmlhLWp0am5ra28/view.

24. Ahiana Figueroa and Blanca Vera Azaf, "La Mayoría Rechaza el Trueque y Cree Que Habrá Devaluación," *El Nacional*, January 5, 2007.

25. Raúl Gallegos, "Chávez's Agenda Takes Shape—'Co-Management' Helps to Advance Socialism in Venezuela," *Wall Street Journal*, December 27, 2005.

26. "Misión Eficiencia o Nada Destituye a Funcionarios por Incumplimiento de Sus Funciones," Venezolana de Televisión, September 30, 2013, http://www.vtv.gob

.ve/articulos/2013/09/30/mision-eficiencia-o-nada-destituye-a-funcionarios-por
-incumplimiento-de-sus-funciones-8009.html.

27. "Venezuela Viewpoint," *The Red Book: 4Q2015 edition*, Bank of America Merrill
Lynch, February 12, 2016.

28. "Venezuela Viewpoint."

29. "Venezuela Carries Out $1 Bln Gold Swap with Citibank-Media," Reuters, April
24, 2015, http://www.reuters.com/article/2015/04/24/venezuela-cenbank-id
USL1N0XL0TY20150424.

30. Kejal Vyas, "Venezuela Says China to Give $5 Billion Oil Loan," *Wall Street Journal*, September 1, 2015, http://www.wsj.com/articles/venezuela-says-china-to
-give-5-billion-oil-loan-1441159070.

31. "Gremio Funerario Alerta sobre Disminución en Producción de Ataudes," *El
Tiempo*, December 10, 2014, http://eltiempo.com.ve/venezuela/gremio/gremio
-funerario-alerta-sobre-disminucion-en-produccion-de-ataudes/164443.

32. Ibis León, "Trabajadores de Minalba Exigen Eliminar Control de Precios en Agua
Embotellada," Efecto Cocuyo, June 23, 2015, http://www.efectococuyo.com
/efecto-cocuyo/la-cartera/trabajadores-de-minalba-exigen-eliminar-control-de
-precios-en-agua-embotellada.

33. María E. Moreno, "96 Familias en Riesgo Habitan en la OPPPE 36 de Playa
Grande," *Diaro de Vargas La Verdad*, August 5, 2014, http://laverdaddevargas.com
/24/96-familias-en-riesgo-habitan-en-la-opppe-36-de-playa-grande/.

34. Ewald Scharfenberg, "Maduro Sugiere Que Los Que Reciben Viviendas del
Estado Paguen por Ellas," *El Pais*, May 17, 2103.

35. Scharfenberg, "Maduro Sugiere."

36. Mayela Armas, "Cuatro Años Después del Inicio de la Misión Vivienda, Gobierno
Regulariza la Propiedad," *Crónica Uno*, August 15, 2015, http://cronica.uno
/cuatro-anos-despues-del-inicio-de-la-mision-vivienda-gobierno-regulariza-la
-propiedad/.

37. Venezuela's minimum wage in March 2014 stood at 3,270.3 bolivars, or US$54, a
month, estimated at the going black market dollar rate of 60 bolivars per dollar.

38. Estimated using the going black market dollar in late October 2013 of 60 bolivars
per dollar.

39. World Economic Forum, *The Global Competitiveness Report, 2015–2016*, 1.08,
"Wastefulness of Government Spending," http://reports.weforum.org/global
-competitiveness-report-2015-2016/competitiveness-rankings/.

40. World Economic Forum, *Global Competitiveness Report*, 2, "Ethics and
Corruption."

41. Kerry Dolan, "Daddy's Girl: How An African 'Princess' Banked $3 Billion in a
Country Living on $2 a Day," *Forbes*, August 14, 2013, http://www.forbes.com
/sites/kerryadolan/2013/08/14/how-isabel-dos-santos-took-the-short-route-to
-become-africas-richest-woman/.

42. World Economic Forum, *The Global Competitiveness Report, 2014–2015*, "3rd Pillar: Macroeconomic Environment," http://reports.weforum.org/global-competitiveness-report-2014-2015/rankings/.

43. As quoted in "Unhappy Nordic Boom," *Time*, December 23, 1974.

44. For more on Chile's fiscal approach see "Saudi Arabia: Tackling Emerging Economic Challenges to Sustain Growth," International Monetary Fund, 2015, www.imf.org/external/pubs/ft/dp/2015/1501mcd.pdf.

45. World Economic Forum, *Global Competitiveness Report, 2015–2016*.

46. "Saudi Arabia: Tackling Emerging Economic Challenges to Sustain Growth," International Monetary Fund, 2015.

47. World Economic Forum, *Global Competitiveness Report, 2014–2015*.

48. "Venezuelan Leader Discusses Permanent Fund," Associated Press, October 10, 1999.

49. Jay Hammond, *The Governor's Solution: How Alaska's Oil Dividend Could Work in Iraq and Other Oil-Rich Countries* (Washington DC: Center for Global Development, 2012).

50. Hammond, *Governor's Solution*, 19, http://www.cgdev.org/sites/default/files/Moss-Governors-Solution_0.pdf.

51. "Venezuela Aprueba Fondo Especial para Pagar Deudas," Reuters, July 31, 1996.

52. The fund had US$6 billion in 2001; Pedro L. Rodríguez, José R. Morales, and Francisco J. Monaldi, "Direct Distribution of Oil Revenues in Venezuela: A Viable Alternative?," Center for Global Development, September 2012, www.cgdev.org.

53. Roula Khalaf and Andrew England, "The Colonel's Risky Foray," *Financial Times*, September 17, 2008, http://www.ft.com/intl/cms/s/0/be623624-8462-11dd-adc7-0000779fd18c.html#axzz3mlAKLU9I.

54. Norway Oil Fund figures, March 2016, http://www.nbim.no/en/the-fund/market-value/key-figures/.

55. Rodríguez, Morales, and Monaldi, "Direct Distribution of Oil Revenues in Venezuela."

56. Rodríguez, Morales, and Monaldi, "Direct Distribution of Oil Revenues in Venezuela."

57. Rodríguez, Morales, and Monaldi, "Direct Distribution of Oil Revenues in Venezuela."

58. Rodríguez, Morales, and Monaldi, "Direct Distribution of Oil Revenues in Venezuela."

59. Rodríguez, Morales, and Monaldi, "Direct Distribution of Oil Revenues in Venezuela."

60. Estimated using 1,500 bolivars as minimum wage and a black market rate of 9.17 bolivars per dollar.

61. Rodríguez, Morales, and Monaldi, "Direct Distribution of Oil Revenues in Venezuela."

62. Dominique Guillaume, Roman Zytek, and Mohammad Reza Farzin, "Iran—the Chronicles of the Subsidy Reform," IMF Working Paper, July 2011, https://www.imf.org/external/pubs/ft/wp/2011/wp11167.pdf.
63. Alexandra Gillies, "Giving Money Away? The Politics of Direct Distribution in Resource-Rich States," Center for Global Development, November 2010, www.cgdev.org.
64. Banco Central de Venezuela data on new bills placed in circulation as of Feburary 2016.
65. Fabiola Sánchez, "Banco Central de Venezuela Emitiría Este Año Nuevos Billetes," Associated Press, Feburary 29, 2016, http://www.bloomberg.com/news/articles/2015-08-26/venezuela-said-to-ready-larger-bank-notes-as-inflation-soars.
66. Review and Outlook editorial, "How Zimbabwe and the Dollar Beat Inflation," *Wall Street Journal*, March 29, 2011, http://www.wsj.com/articles/SB10001424052748704050204576218690273479676.
67. "Ecuador Accepts Dollar as Its New Currency," ABC News, September 9, 2000, http://abcnews.go.com/International/story?id=82666.
68. "Poverty Headcount Ratio at $2 a day (PPP) (% of population)," The World Bank website, http://data.worldbank.org/indicator/SI.POV.2DAY?page=2.
69. "Saudi Arabia: Tackling Emerging Economic Challenges to Sustain Growth," International Monetary Fund, March 18, 2015, www.imf.org.
70. Phone interview with Ruth de Krivoy, September 30, 2015.
71. "Juan Pérez Alfonzo, Venezuelan, Regarded as Founder of OPEC," *New York Times*, September 4, 1979.

AFTERWORD

1. Tal Cual, "Maduro Reprocha Que Regaló Viviendas, Taxis y Tabletas y No Recibió el Apoyo Esperado," December 8, 2015, http://www.talcualdigital.com/Nota/121213/maduro-reprocha-que-regalo-viviendas-taxis-y-tabletas-y-no-recibio-el-apoyo-esperado.
2. Luis Salas Rodríguez, "22 Claves para Entender y Combatir la Guerra Económica," Fundación Editorial El Perro y la Rana, Caracas, 2015, http://www.elperroylarana.gob.ve/catalogo/colecciones/fuera-coleccion/474-22-claves-para-entender-la-guerra-economica.html.
3. "Tras Veinte Años, Maduro Aumenta Precio de la Gasolina en Venezuela," *El Nuevo Herald*, February 17, 2016, http://www.elnuevoherald.com/noticias/mundo/america-latina/venezuela-es/article60913632.html.

SELECTED BIBLIOGRAPHY

ARCHIVAL MATERIAL

Roosevelt, Franklin. Unsigned correspondence. Box 96. Harry Hopkins Papers. Franklin D. Roosevelt Presidential Library.

PUBLISHED WORKS

Baptista, Asdrúbal. *Teoría Económica del Capitalismo Rentístico*. Caracas: Banco Central de Venezuela, 2010.

Baptista, Asdrúbal, and Bernard Mommer. *El Petróleo en el Pensamiento Económico Venezolano: Un Ensayo*. Caracas: Ediciones IESA, 1987.

Bautista Urbaneja, Diego. *La Renta y El Reclamo: Ensayo Sobre Petróleo y Economía Política en Venezuela*. Caracas: Alfa, 2013.

Betancourt, Rómulo. *Venezuela, Política y Petróleo*. Caracas: Academia de Ciencias Políticas y Sociales, 2007.

Capriles, Axel. *La Pircardía del Venezolano o el Triunfo de Tío Conejo*. Caracas: Editorial Santillana, 2008.

Coronil, Fernando. *The Magical State: Nature, Money, and Modernity in Venezuela*. Chicago: University of Chicago Press, 1997.

De Krivoy, Ruth. *Colapso: La Crisis Bancaria Venezolana de 1994*. Caracas: Ediciones IESA, 2002.

De La Plaza, Salvador. *El Petróleo en la Vida Venezolana*. Caracas: Universidad Central de Venezuela, 1974.

Edwards, Sebastián. *Left Behind: Latin America and the False Promise of Populism*. Chicago: University of Chicago Press, 2010.

Gillies, Alexandra. "Giving Money Away? The Politics of Direct Distribution in Resource-Rich States." Working Paper 231. Center for Global Development, 2010. http://www.cgdev.org/.

González, Félix. *Finanzas Personales en Tiempos de Revolución*. Caracas: Alfa, 2014.

Karl, Terry Lynn. *The Paradox of Plenty: Oil Booms and Petro-States*. Berkeley: University of California Press, 1997.

Kornblith, Miriam. *Venezuela en los noventa: La Crisis de la Democracia*. Caracas: Ediciones IESA, 1997.

Mommer, Bernard. Petróleo Global y Estado Nacional. Caracas: Comala.com, 2003.

Moss, Todd, ed., *The Governor's Solution: How Alaska's Oil Dividend Could Work in Iraq and Other Oil-Rich Countries*. Washington DC: Center for Global Development, 2012.

Pérez Alfonzo, Juan Pablo. *Hundiéndonos en el Excremento del Diablo*. Caracas: Editorial Lisbona, 1976.

Rodríguez, Pedro L., José R. Morales, and Francisco Monaldi. "Direct Distribution of Oil Revenues in Venezuela: A Viable Alternative?" Working Paper 306. Center for Global Development, 2012. http://www.cgdev.org/.

Yergin, Daniel. *The Prize: The Epic Quest for Oil, Money, and Power*. New York: Free Press, 1991.

INDEX